THE CONSTITUTION
GOES TO COLLEGE

THE CONSTITUTION
GOES TO COLLEGE

*Five Constitutional Ideas That Have
Shaped the American University*

Rodney A. Smolla

NEW YORK UNIVERSITY PRESS
New York and London

NEW YORK UNIVERSITY PRESS
New York and London
www.nyupress.org

References to Internet websites (URLs) were accurate at the time of writing.
Neither the author nor New York University Press is responsible for URLs
that may have expired or changed since the manuscript was prepared.

Library of Congress Cataloging-in-Publication Data
Smolla, Rodney A.
The constitution goes to college : five constitutional ideas that
have shaped the American university / Rodney A. Smolla.
p. cm.
Includes bibliographical references and index.
ISBN 978-0-8147-4103-0 (cl : alk. paper) —
ISBN 978-0-8147-8378-8 (e-book)
1. Universities and colleges—Law and legislation—United States.
2. Civil rights—United States. 3. Equality before the law—United States.
I. Title.
KF4225.S636   2011
344.73'074—dc22   2010041975

New York University Press books are printed on acid-free paper,
and their binding materials are chosen for strength and durability.
We strive to use environmentally responsible suppliers and materials
to the greatest extent possible in publishing our books.

Manufactured in the United States of America
10 9 8 7 6 5 4 3 2 1

CONTENTS

PREFACE

Reflecting on my life as a parent, my role as an educator, and my work as a lawyer, scholar, and advocate on issues of constitutional law, I have come to realize that in each setting my world is converging. In all three facets of my life, I face variations on the same themes. As an educator, I want for my students very much the same things that, as a parent, I want for my children. What are these things that I want, as both educator and parent? I want students, including my own children, to prosper academically, reaping the intellectual benefits of a liberal education. I also want students to grow in their character and moral sensibilities, to develop lives of consequence and meaning. In turn, as a constitutional lawyer and scholar, I sense the American "constitutional unconscious" at work, as the challenges, tensions, and tradeoffs that dominate our national life seem increasingly to infiltrate and influence my two closer worlds, at home and on the university campus.

This book is a meditation on these connections. My hypothesis is that five large themes of the American constitutional experience—the debate over whether we have a "living Constitution," the division between the "public" and "private" spheres of society, the distinction between "rights" and "privileges," our seemingly contradictory commitment to "ordered liberty," and our competing conceptions of "equality"—have exerted a profound influence on identity of American colleges and universities. I intend for this argument to be taken seriously, but not literally. To speak as lawyers speak, the influence of the American Constitution on the American campus is not so much *controlling authority* in shaping universities, but *persuasive precedent*.

In writing this book, however, I speak not only as a lawyer, but also as a parent and educator. In those roles, seeking for my children, students, and colleagues "the good life," the learned wisdom of time teaches us to strive for balance. I recently had the honor of being appointed the eleventh president of Furman University. In addressing the Furman students for the first time, I conveyed this same message. There is a sense, I told the students, in which everything that surrounds them "is all about you." The building and constant renovation of a beautiful campus; the devoted faculty who work hard as teacher-scholars, as mentors and counselors; the dedicated staff who labor conscientiously to provide all the myriad services that support the students in their education and well-being; the alumni, trustees, and other friends of the University who donate their money, time, and energy to its service—all of this is done to create an extraordinary experience for the students in their bright college years. And so it may well seem, I told the students, that "it's all about you." Yet the secret to the good life, the core value that is at the center of the University's mission, I told them, "is to help you realize, deep in your hearts, that it is *not* all about you. This experience is all about you realizing that it's not all about you."

I then stated my case: "The most important lesson you can learn while you are here, is that for your life to have authentic meaning, fulfillment, and consequence, you must learn the importance of connection: to larger causes, and to the greater community." This central insight to human existence resonates through history, and indeed through the history of liberal education. It is evidenced in the wisdom of Aristotle, who wrote in *The Politics* that human beings are by nature "political" or "civic" animals; he taught that we are not fully human, not fully realized, except through community, through which all that elevates humanity from the animals is made possible: justice, expression, science, art, invention. It is witnessed in the words of St. Paul, when he wrote to the Romans: "We have different gifts, according to the grace given us. If a man's gift is prophesying, let him use it in proportion to his faith. If it is serving, let him serve; if it is teaching, let him teach; if it is encouraging, let him encourage; if it is contributing to the needs of others, let him give generously; if it is leadership, let him govern diligently; if it is showing mercy, let him do it cheerfully." It is captured in the lyrics of the group U2, who say in their song "Mysterious Ways," "If you want to kiss the sky, better learn how to kneel."

I believe this insight is indelibly etched in the American spirit. One of the most resonant themes of American history begins with the sermon of the Puritan John Winthrop, who preached to the congregation of the Massachusetts Bay Colony "that we shall be as a city upon a hill." Winthrop's image was brought before the American people in modern times in President Ronald Reagan's farewell speech to the nation, in which he urged us to be "a shining city upon a hill." As a child, it was captured for me as I listened to President John F. Kennedy challenge a generation of Americans, "Ask not what your country can do for you, but what you can do for your country." It is the same spirit from which Martin Luther King drew his dream, that all of us would someday be judged solely by the content of our character.

For universities, the creative tension that emerges from this spirit is the same creative tension that emerges from our constitutional tradition. Our American constitutional experience is largely about balance. Our constitutional history is the story of centuries of struggle to strike the *right balance* among such competing values as liberty, morality, and order, as captured in the Supreme Court's repeated refrain that our constitutional tradition is grounded in the ideal of "ordered liberty." This same creative tension guides those of us who live and work in the wonderful environment of the modern American campus, in which we are at once participants in a robust marketplace and citizens of a principled moral space.

Five Constitutional Ideas That Have Influenced the Identity of American Universities

The essentiality of freedom in the community of American universities is almost self-evident. No one should underestimate the vital role in a democracy that is played by those who guide and train our youth. To impose any straitjacket upon the intellectual leaders in our colleges and universities would imperil the future of our nation. No field of education is so thoroughly comprehended by man that new discoveries cannot yet be made. Particularly is that true in the social sciences, where few, if any, principles are accepted as absolutes. Scholarship cannot flourish in an atmosphere of suspicion and distrust. Teachers and students must always remain free to inquire, to study and to evaluate, to gain new maturity and understanding; otherwise our civilization will stagnate and die.

> —Chief Justice Earl Warren in
> *Sweezy v. New Hampshire* (1957)

This, I think, is what happens when a censor looks over a teacher's shoulder. This system of spying and surveilance with its accompanying reports and trials cannot go hand in hand with academic freedom. It produces standardized thought, not the pursuit of truth. Yet it was the pursuit of truth which the First Amendment was designed to protect. A system which directly or inevitably has that effect is alien to our system and should be struck down. Its survival is a real threat to our way of life. We need be bold and adventuresome in our thinking to survive. A school system producing students

trained as robots threatens to rob a generation of the versatil-
ity that has been perhaps our greatest distinction. The Framers
knew the danger of dogmatism; they also knew the strength
that comes when the mind is free, when ideas may be pursued
wherever they lead.

—Justice William O. Douglas, dissenting in
Adler v. Board of Education of the City of New York (1952)

De Tocqueville with a Twist

Alexis de Tocqueville, in his classic nineteenth-century study of the
United States, *Democracy in America*, observed that "scarcely any political
question arises in the United States that is not resolved, sooner or later,
into a judicial question."[1] What de Tocqueville aptly observed arose from
the special role of law and lawyers in American society, particularly the
special role of constitutional law and constitutional lawyers. This book is
an update on de Tocqueville, with a twist. The argument advanced here is
that there is scarcely any constitutional question that arises in the United
States that does not devolve, sooner or later, into a campus question.

The issues and conflicts that arise on our college and university campuses constantly present themselves in a *constitutional* dimension. Constitutional law, constitutional values, and constitutional traditions appear
to either directly control or indirectly influence the ebb and flow of many
campus decisions and events. The reverse is also true. Our constitutional
law is constantly being shaped and forged by the hydraulic pressure
exerted by our national culture. The nation's colleges and universities in
turn exert a powerful influence on our culture, creating a feedback loop
in which constitutional values influence the nature of universities, which
then influence the nature of our constitutional values.

There is nothing novel about the observation that issues of American
constitutional law often surface on the modern American college campus. Modern campuses are visibly and notoriously awash in conflicts
implicating such constitutional themes as freedom of speech, separation
of church and state, race and gender discrimination, or privacy. But there
is more to it than just that.

The American university is not simply a *location* where constitutional conflicts may arise. The American university is also *a collection of ideas*—a collection that parallels, in striking ways, the collection of ideas that have influenced and shaped the American political, legal, and cultural identity for over two centuries, ideas that emanate from the unique role that the American Constitution plays in the forging of our national identity. The "idea of the American university" is not just the "idea of *a* university," but the idea of an *American* university. A large part of this conception of the American university is influenced by the central ideas that define American society, which are expressed in the Constitution of the United States.

My claim is that a handful of large "American constitutional ideas" have heavily shaped the "idea of the American university." In arguing that American constitutional ideas have "shaped" the idea of the American university I mean both *more* and *less* than a claim that "constitutional law" has often been brought to bear, in a formal and legal sense, on American colleges and universities. Lawyers and judges know that some precedents are "controlling" and some merely "influential." I will talk about both, but the heart of this book is less about control than influence. My thesis is that the American Constitution and the American college campus are in a very deep and fundamental sense *connected*, and that we may learn a great deal by exploring that connection.

Lessons from Einstein

In the critical formative years of the modern American university, the great centers of higher education in the United States sought to emulate the great centers of learning in Europe. Albert Einstein was a professor at one such center, the University of Berlin, when in 1918 student revolutionaries seized control of the University, jailing the University rector and deans. In an act of extraordinary individual courage, Einstein sought to secure the release of his imprisoned colleagues by personally addressing the agitated mob of students. He mounted the stage and stated, boldly and defiantly, "I have always thought that the German university's most valuable institution is academic freedom."[2] The students, perhaps embarrassed by Einstein's invocation, took a middling position, voting that they lacked the legal authority to release the jailed academics. And so Einstein set out to visit the new German Chancellor, who was apparently overwhelmed with the surge of events. The Chancellor scribbled a written order releasing the rector and deans.

Buoyed by his newfound success as a legal advocate, Einstein the next day returned to the maelstrom, addressing yet another restless mass meeting, at which he described himself as "an old-time believer in democracy." He then lectured the new self-important revolutionaries: "All true democrats," Einstein warned, "must stand guard lest the old class tyranny of the Right be replaced by a new class tyranny of the Left."[3]

Academic freedom is a value cherished by scholars and institutions of higher learning throughout the world. In the United States, however, the traditions of academic freedom of which Einstein spoke blended with our constitutional traditions to create a uniquely powerful combination. Higher education in the United States absorbed what D. H. Lawrence, describing American literature, once called the "spirit of place."[4]

The idea of the university that was imported from Europe married with the idea of robust protection of civil liberties that is at the soul of the American constitutional unconscious, to place the ideal of academic freedom at the center of the value system and the sense of identity that would become the modern American university. The European ideals of *Lernfreiheit*, or "freedom to learn," and *Lehrfreiheit*, or "freedom to teach," merged with the American Constitution, including the Bill of Rights.[5]

Poetic Tensions

Justice Oliver Wendell Holmes once observed that "general propositions do not decide concrete cases."[6] Our constitutional law is replete with "general propositions," as captured in phrases such as "freedom of speech," the "equal protection of the laws," or the "system of checks and balances." In our broader public discourse, these phrases may become a kind of partisan verbal confetti, strewn into debates by zealous advocates who often presume, wrongly, that all within earshot agree with the meaning they have assigned to these phrases.

As the Holmes aphorism suggests, few Americans are likely to be against "freedom of speech," "equal protection," or "checks and balances" as broad abstractions. On these points, there's a general consensus of sorts: that we are a nation conceived in dedication to certain ideals about freedom and equality and checked power, and that we continue to feel so strongly about those ideals that they have become "national brands" resonant with symbolic meaning.

Beyond these broad ideals, however, notions of liberty, equality, and checked and balanced power are highly contentious and controversial, shaped and stressed by historical events, cultural forces, political pressures, and judicial interpretation. Our Constitution is *not* just a symbol, stored behind glass in the National Archives, with facsimile copies sold as souvenirs in gift shops in Philadelphia or Colonial Williamsburg. Our Constitution is a working stiff, a laborer in the arenas of national law, politics, and culture. As an active, dynamic, *working* document, the Constitution is filled with tension and conflict. Just as Newton's third law of motion poses that for every action there is an equal and opposite reaction, in American constitutional experience, for every value there is a counter-value, for every argument a counter-argument. The story of our constitutional experience has been an ongoing story of resolution of competing constitutional values.

This is not necessarily a negative thing. Not all tensions are bad. There are certain "poetic tensions" in the life of the mind and the life of society that bring out the best of human potential, spurring our creativity and enterprise. My view of the brilliance of the American Constitution, and my view of the brilliance of American higher education, is grounded in a positive and optimistic belief in the good that can come from the creative and thoughtful resolution of poetic tensions.

Five fundamental tensions within our constitutional tradition have exerted a particularly significant influence on the shape and definition of American universities: (1) the debate over whether we have a "living Constitution"; (2) the division between the public and private sphere; (3) the distinction between "rights" and "privileges"; (4) the notion of "ordered liberty"; and (5) competing conceptions of equality.

Do We Have a "Living" Constitution?

If you had to pick just *one* issue of American constitutional law, an issue that most centrally defines the character of the American constitutional experience, what would it be? Perhaps you would nominate the question of the proper scope of the War Powers, and whether the authority to make society's ultimate decisions over war and peace should reside with the President or the Congress. Or perhaps you would choose the meaning of the phrase "equal protection of the laws," and the consequences of that meaning for matters relating to race, gender, or affirmative action. Or you might claim that what matters most is the meaning of "life, liberty, or property," and the question of whether decisions relating to reproduction, sexuality, or death with dignity are encompassed by that phrase. Or maybe you would argue that the most important constitutional issues we face involve the meaning of phrases such as the "freedom of speech," or the "free exercise of religion," or "cruel and unusual punishment."

All of these would be worthy candidates, but not my nominee. My suggestion is that *the* most important constitutional issue, rising above all others, and cutting across all of the Constitution's famous clauses, is an issue of interpretation: do we have a "living" Constitution? This is, in a sense, the mother of all American constitutional debates, an issue that transcends all questions of constitutional law.

At the threshold, before we begin ciphering through solutions, we must come to some understanding of the nature of our algebra. At the threshold, we must grapple with the issue of constitutional meaning itself, the question of how we are to read, interpret, and apply the Constitution as a functioning legal document and working charter of government. Should our approach to constitutional interpretation be static or dynamic? Static answers treat the Constitution as a set piece, and look for its meaning in the literal words of the text, the intent of those who wrote the text, or the original understanding of those words within society at the time the words were adopted into law. Dynamic answers treat the Constitution as a moveable feast. Dynamic approaches look for the meaning of the Constitution "in between the lines" of the text, are willing to credit the intent of those who must currently live with the text over the intent of those who wrote it, and care more for the contemporary understanding of those words than the understanding at the time the words were originally adopted. The dichotomy posed here goes by many different names in our cultural lexicon, which have positive or negative casts depending on one's point of view. One person's original understanding is another's reactionary slavishness to a dead past. One person's "living Constitution" is another person's unprincipled subjective relativism.

If the mother of all constitutional issues is this question of interpreta-
tive methodology in determining the Constitution's proper meaning, the
mother of all matters relating to the character of the university is wrapped
up in the pliable phrase "academic freedom," and the struggle to supply
that concept's proper meaning. As discussed in chapter 2, academic freedom is inexorably pulled into the maelstrom of the "living Constitution"
debate, because the words "academic freedom" do not appear anywhere
in the text of the Constitution.

Our thinking about academic freedom permeates all elements of university life. Virtually all issues central to the identity of the American university
gather sustenance from this font. Traditions of shared governance, intellectual rigor, justifications for tenure, requirements of due process, arguments
for diversity and affirmative action—essentially all the central organizing values of the American university partake in one way or another in assumptions
about a larger transcendent value that permeates the very idea of the American university, an idea large enough and profound enough to mean many different things to many different people: the idea of academic freedom.

If academic freedom is to exist as an American value of *constitutional
dimension*, it must therefore be an implied right, not a literal right. The
principal values encompassed by academic freedom in the ways we now
typically employ the phrase were not within the forefront of the minds
of those who adopted the Constitution, if they were even within their
minds at all. If academic freedom is to be recognized as an implied right,
it must thus be one implied by *contemporary understandings* of the meaning of the constitutional text rather than historical understandings.

The Public and the Private Sphere

A second powerful assumption of American constitutional law is that
society is divided between a public and a private sphere, between that
which is governmental and that which is not. Throughout the history
of the republic we have, as a nation, debated how much of our society
should be swept within the superintendence of the state, and how much
left to individual choice and private enterprise. When suddenly confronted by the precipitous collapse of credit markets and financial institutions in the autumn of 2008, our entire national conversation turned to

bailouts, the use of "TARP money," billion-dollar government shares in banks and auto companies, and the larger questions of political and economic organization that bear on what should or should not be treated as an appropriate government enterprise.

Parallel to issues of ownership and control are issues of conduct and accountability. The Constitution directly constrains the conduct of government, imposing on government restraints such as the obligation to respect freedom of speech, to not respect any establishment of religion, or to extend to all citizens the equal protection of the laws. Private individuals and private organizations, from corporations to nonprofits, are not bound by such constitutional norms. Yet as a nation, we have often chosen to extend constitutional norms outside the public sphere and into the private sector. The Civil Rights Act of 1964 imposed sweeping rules of equality on virtually all segments of private commerce, for example, effectively extending the sweep of the guarantee of "equal protection of the laws" outside the public sphere and across most of the private sphere.[7]

These extensions of public norms to the private sphere have always come at cost. They extend the jurisdiction of the state and simultaneously reduce the autonomy of individuals and private associations. In economic terms, this replaces government decision-makers for the private decision-makers of the marketplace. In political and social terms, this replaces public values with private values, and consequently diminishes our freedom. This is not always bad. The Civil Rights Act diminished the freedom of hotels and restaurants to discriminate against blacks. But it is always a cost, and we must always be aware of the trade-offs.

The United States' robust dual system of public and private universities invites constant engagement with the distinction between the public and private sphere. As discussed in chapter 3, private universities are not legally bound by the First Amendment's guarantee of freedom of speech, nor its prohibition on the establishment of religion; neither are they bound by the Fourteenth Amendment's Equal Protection Clause. Even so, we may, by either public law or private custom, import these constitutional norms, in whole or in part, to the sphere of private universities. Laws such as Title IX thus extend constitutional conceptions of equality and nondiscrimination on the basis of gender to any private university that wants to receive federal money.[8] Even without law, many private universities embrace rules regarding freedom of speech essentially identical to those that bind public universities. Once again, however, extensions of public norms into the private sphere always come at cost. In the world of higher education, this cost may be the sacrifice of a private university's unique history, culture, or identity.

Rights and Privileges

As a matter of common sense, most of us understand the difference between a "right" and a "privilege." A right is an entitlement, a privilege is not. A privilege is more like a gift, something optional, something that may come with certain strings attached, certain provisos, caveats, and quid pro quos.

In the United States, rights are *birthrights*. Our foundational national documents, from the Declaration of Independence to the Constitution of the United States, buttress the conception of rights as entitlements *that we are born with*, independent of government. Americans think of themselves as holding rights from the moment of birth, by virtue of our humanity. We may differ some in our philosophical or theological vocabulary as to where exactly these rights come from, but we tend not to differ much in our devotion to the idea that they are real and must be respected. To some, the rights are entitlements of "natural law," to others, endowments from the "Creator," to others still, simply liberties enjoyed by men and women in their natural condition, as essential defining elements of humanity. The framers of the Constitution, following the social contract theories of philosophers such as John Locke,[9] saw government as a voluntary compact entered into by individuals to provide security for rights such as "life, liberty, and property." To the framers these human rights were not creatures of the state; rather, the state was the creature of humans, invented to secure human rights.[10] In the words of Thomas Jefferson's Declaration of Independence, "To secure these rights governments are instituted among men, deriving their just powers from the consent of the governed."[11]

This notion of "rights as birthright" is reinforced in several places in the text of the Constitution. The Ninth Amendment, for example, declares, "The enumeration in the Constitution, of certain rights, shall not be construed to disparage others retained by the people." On its face, the phrasing of this Amendment appears to contemplate that people *retain* certain rights other than those explicitly listed in the constitutional text. If they retain these rights, they presumably possessed them before the Ninth Amendment was written.

In contrast to rights, "privileges" are usually understood as interests bestowed by some privilege-creator on some privilege-consumer. The privilege may come from an almost infinite array of sources—from a parent (as in the privilege to drive the family car or stay up past bedtime) a credit card company, a country club, a government, a university. Privileges may take virtually any form. Privileges created by government, for example, may include public jobs, welfare benefits, permits to operate a business, licenses to operate a television or radio station, allowances to release pollutants into the atmosphere, or offers of admission to a state university.

For a long time, American constitutional law recognized this distinction between rights and privileges, and treated the distinction as critical to whether the interest at stake received constitutional protection.[12] "Rights" were protected by the Constitution, "privileges" were not. The rationale for this on-off switch was straightforward and had a simple commonsense appeal. A privilege seemed to be either a gift or something obtained through a barter or contract of some kind. Either way, the privilege could come with strings attached. If the privilege is a gift, the donor may specify certain restrictions as conditions attached to the receipt of the gift. The homespun wisdom is that "beggars can't be choosers" and "you don't look a gift horse in the mouth." Similarly, if the privilege comes about as a result of a contract, the contracting parties may prescribe the terms of the exchange. If you don't like the terms of the contract, don't sign it.

The distinction between rights and privileges in early constitutional law was intuitively appealing, in part because the types of government benefits normally thought of as "privileges" were usually conceived of as economic transactions, rather than regulations impinging on civil liberties. When the government dispenses privileges, it was thought, the government simply was operating as the proprietor of public business, not as the regulator of private conduct. The rights enshrined in the Constitution, such as those listed in the Bill of Rights, appeared to apply only when the government passed laws restricting the life, liberty, or property of citizens in a direct sense, such as laws that abridged the freedom of speech, subjected citizens to unreasonable searches and seizures, took away property without due process of law, or inflicted cruel and unusual punishment.

Such laws seemed different in kind from government actions dealing with privileges, such as decisions on whether to hire an employee, enter into a contract, grant a license, dispense a welfare check, or grant a student a seat at a university. Private corporations make these sorts of decisions daily, and typically these entities are thought to be exercising business judgment. It's quite easy to accept that nobody has a "right" to a job working for Microsoft or McDonald's. It's just as easy to accept that nobody has a "right" to work for the United States government, the state of Massachusetts, or the city of Boston. When the government is engaging in such economic transactions, we might thus think of taxpayers as akin to the shareholders in a massive state corporation. Government officials, as caretakers of the public treasury, should therefore strike hard bargains on behalf of those taxpayer-shareholders.

The force of the right-privilege distinction in modern American constitutional law has been diminished, however, by a counter-doctrine, a principle known as the doctrine of "unconstitutional conditions."[13] This doctrine has evolved as an antidote to the tough-minded right-privilege distinction. It evolved from the recognition that in light of the enormous leverage that modern governments possess over the various forms of public benefits that we historically would have regarded as "privileges," we must devise constitutional principles that deter the government from using that leverage in a manner that effectively squelches constitutional rights.

For decades, the right-privilege distinction and the doctrine of unconstitutional conditions have lived side by side in uneasy juxtaposition in American constitutional law.[14] The two doctrines coexist in leery constitutional détente, neither one able to obliterate the other. The two doctrines continue to survive because the two doctrines each partake of certain sound values. In favor of the right-privilege distinction is the fundamental notion that in virtually all aspects of our lives we accept that one must often pay some price in return for the receipt of some benefit, including enrollment in some program or organization. In favor of the doctrine of unconstitutional conditions is the counter-notion, equally fundamental, that there must be outer limits to the price government may exact from its citizens as a condition of such enrollment.

Cast in these terms, it is easy to see why the right-privilege distinction and its nemesis, the doctrine of unconstitutional conditions, have played such a profound role in our thinking about the character of the university. As discussed in chapter 4, the right-privilege distinction continues to exert a strong intuitive appeal on the world of higher education. When a professor, student, or administrator accepts a position at a university, they are voluntarily agreeing to participate in a voluntary association, and ought very well be expected to abide by that association's community norms and rules. As an easy example, it seems clear that however much a distinguished educator enjoys complete freedom of speech as a private citizen, a university's board of trustees could impose restraints on the exercise of that freedom if the educator seeks to become the university's president. Determining precisely what freedom should be surrendered—and what freedom retained—when one voluntarily joins a university community is a matter that poses difficult questions of policy and law, and is of central importance to the character of the modern university.

Ordered Liberty

The American constitutional tradition is steeped in respect for "ordered liberty," a deliberate fusion of two concepts. The American constitutional experience is an ongoing struggle to strike the best balance among competing social interests in freedom, morality, and order. We are, on the one hand, a nation of free and robust "marketplaces." We are deeply committed to open economic markets and entrepreneurial enterprise. And more than any other society in the world, the United States has demonstrated an abiding national faith in free creative and intellectual markets—the "marketplace of ideas." Yet at the same time, we are also a nation constantly struggling to preserve the rule of law, and to develop a cohesive sense of national identity as a moral community.

A central defining challenge of our constitutional tradition is our ongoing effort to strike an appropriate balance among the values of liberty, morality, and order. Life is a constant tug and pull among these opposing instincts—the impulse of the free spirit, the intuitions of morality, and the yearning for stability and structure. Our free spirit beckons us to creativity, invention, enterprise, and movement. Our moral intuitions temper the free spirit with understandings of right and wrong. Our yearning for order pushes us to seek predictability, solidity, and security. Striking the right balance is a key to the good life for individuals, institutions, and societies.

The most successful societies are those that have managed to achieve a healthy balance between freedom and order in the three great marketplaces of human endeavor: the political marketplace, the economic marketplace, and the marketplace of ideas. Our efforts to find this healthy balance are best guided by one overarching goal: to achieve the maximum freedom possible, consistent with our basic needs for stability and security.

American constitutionalism is built on the premise that the rule of law is not in irreconcilable tension with liberty. Quite the opposite, we have always understood the social compact from which we derive the rule of law as designed to secure the blessings of liberty. Yet too much concern for stability and order tempts us to overregulate, smothering the creative spirit with too much law. Overregulation of economic markets acts as a drag on investment and entrepreneurial enterprise; overregulation of political systems interferes with democracy and discourages civic participation; overregulation of the marketplace of ideas stifles creativity and discovery in the arts and sciences. Societies that are able to approach an optimal balance in all three marketplaces will fare better, in the long haul of history, than societies that achieve such balance in only two, one, or none.

Finding the optimal balance, however, is never easy. External and internal forces constantly conspire to threaten our physical security and safety, and it is only natural that we respond to these threats by diminishing rights and freedoms. Abraham Lincoln put the problem as directly as any American ever has when, in defending his suspension of the writ of habeas corpus in his message to Congress on July 4, 1861, he asked, "To state the question more directly, are all the laws, but one, to go unexecuted, and the government itself go to pieces, lest that one be violated?"[15]

As discussed in chapter 5, these same tensions play out on modern campuses with heightened intensity. The real world of the university is what A. Bartlett Giamatti, former President of Yale (and then commissioner of Major League Baseball), described as "a free and ordered space."[16] Tragedies such as the Virginia Tech and Northern Illinois University shootings sadly remind us that this is not an abstract discussion, but a concrete and pressing problem that requires us to balance our campus traditions of open access, spontaneity, and respect for individual privacy with the imperative that we act reasonably and responsibly to ensure the physical safety of our students, faculty, and staff.

This core tension between liberty and order extends far beyond "order" in the physical sense. The modern university is sometimes conceived of as a cauldron of fierce competition—for admission, for tenure and promotion, for athletic championships, for giant endowments—and as a "super marketplace of ideas," a place where anything goes, nothing is censored, and only the strongest and fittest survive. Yet simultaneously, the modern campus is often conceived of as an orderly and moral space—a community of scholars and students organized around such values as respect for human dignity, cultural and religious pluralism, collegial civility, and rational discourse.

Competing Conceptions of Equality

The Constitution begins with the wonderful phrase, "We the People." Our nation was born with the ideal that "all men are created equal," and that the Constitution guarantees the "equal protection of the laws." Yet a large part of our constitutional history has consisted of contention over "who counts" as part of the "We" in "We the People." Indians, African slaves, and women were among those who initially did not count.

Fortunately, we have now vastly expanded the scope of those to whom the promise of "equal protection of the laws" extends. The *meaning* of "equality," however, is intensely disputed. For "process equality" thinkers, the equal protection of the laws simply means that everyone is entitled to play by the same rules. If the process is equal for all, the law is equal for all. For "outcome equality" thinkers, the conception of equality is also tied to outcomes, so a just society contemplates a shared society, in which representation in our most important public and private institutions roughly reflects the diversity of our populace.[17] Mark Yudof, the former University of Texas System Chancellor who is now President of the University of California system, once described this strain of thought as the "universalist ethic,"[18] which takes as a fundamental premise the idea that "a stable, just society, without violence, alienation, and social discord, must be an integrated society," and that our collective goal should be "a shared culture in which all segments of the population participate."[19]

There is no arena in American society in which the debate between these competing notions of equality is more acutely contested than education. As discussed in chapter 6, it was in the arena of education that the pernicious doctrine of "separate but equal"—emanating from *Plessy v. Ferguson*[20]—was first attacked, and ultimately overturned. The assault on *Plessy* began with cases involving law schools and graduate schools, such as *Missouri ex rel. Gaines v. Canada*,[21] *Sweatt v. Painter*,[22] and *McLaurin v. Oklahoma State Regents for Higher Education*.[23] The *Plessy* doctrine would ultimately be overruled in *Brown v. Board of Education*.[24] The meaning of *Brown* for the world of higher education has been vigorously contested. In *United States v. Fordice*,[25] for example, the Supreme Court struggled with how the mandate of *Brown* to dismantle a system of racially segregated schools should be translated, decades later, to the entire system of Mississippi's public colleges and universities. Yet no American debate over the meaning of "equality" has been more intensely contested than the debate over affirmative action, and no aspect of that debate has more sharply divided the body politic than the role of affirmative action and "diversity" in admissions to the nation's colleges and universities. As the discussion in chapter 6 explains, in such famous higher education affirmative action cases as *Regents of the University of California v. Bakke*,[26] *Grutter v. Bollinger*,[27] and *Gratz v. Bollinger*,[28] fundamental questions about the American identity and the identity of the American university have been fused. The Supreme Court remains sharply divided on this issue, and so are the nation's legislatures, university boards, faculties, student bodies, and alumni.

Tracing the Constitution's Impact on the Identity of the University

The following chapters explore seriatim these constitutional ideas in greater detail, examining their impact on the identity of the American university. As with the American constitutional experience itself, the "story" of how these ideas have been absorbed and processed to shape the contours of our public and private universities is not entirely linear or logical. Above all else, it remains an unfinished business, a perpetual work in progress, a dissertation forever in revision.

2

Academic Freedom and the Living Constitution

Academic freedom, though not a specifically enumerated constitutional right, long has been viewed as a special concern of the First Amendment. The freedom of a university to make its own judgments as to education includes the selection of its student body.

—Justice Lewis F. Powell, Jr., in *Regents of the University of California v. Bakke* (1978), invoking academic freedom principles to support a university's pursuit of a diverse student body

That the burden of which the University complains is neither content-based nor direct does not necessarily mean that petitioner has no valid First Amendment claim. Rather, it means only that petitioner's claim does not fit neatly within any right of academic freedom that could be derived from the cases on which petitioner relies. In essence, petitioner asks us to recognize an expanded right of academic freedom to protect confidential peer review materials from disclosure. Although we are sensitive to the effects that content-neutral government action may have on speech, . . . and believe that burdens that are less than direct may sometimes pose First Amendment concerns, . . . we think the First Amendment cannot be extended to embrace petitioner's claim.

—Justice Harry O. Blackmun, writing for a unanimous Court in *University of Pennsylvania v. Equal Employment Opportunity Commission* (1990), rejecting an academic freedom claim

Implied Rights

In interpreting the Constitution, a natural (but sometimes overlooked) starting place *is* the Constitution. If "academic freedom" is to be understood as a constitutional right, then it is a right that most plausibly fits within the meaning of the First Amendment. Indeed, Justice Lewis Powell's statement in *Regents of the University of California v. Bakke* might be read as an oblique endorsement of the notion that "academic freedom" should be treated as such an "implied" First Amendment right. To dissect this argument, let us look to the actual text of the First Amendment, inserting numbers to keep track of the different clauses: "Congress shall make no law [1] respecting an establishment of religion, [2] or prohibiting the free exercise thereof; [3] or abridging the freedom of speech, [4] or of the press; [5] or the right of the people peaceably to assemble, [6] and to petition the government for a redress of grievances." Here is how we would have to understand the text if we treat academic freedom as a distinct and severable constitutional right: "Congress shall make no law [1] respecting an establishment of religion, [2] or prohibiting the free exercise thereof; [3] or abridging the freedom of speech, [4] or of the press; [5] or the right of the people peaceably to assemble, [6] and to petition the government for a redress of grievances, [7] or abridging the right of academic freedom."

The Ninth Amendment arguably provides a rule of construction that could be invoked to justify recognition of a right of academic freedom, declaring, "The enumeration in the Constitution, of certain rights, shall not be construed to deny or disparage others retained by the people." The Supreme Court has held that a constitutional right to privacy exists, though no right of privacy is specifically mentioned in the Bill of Rights. And even within the confines of the First Amendment, the Supreme Court has held that the Amendment includes a right—freedom of association—that is not named, in so many words, within the text. If privacy and freedom of association have been recognized as implied rights, why not academic freedom?

Any candid answer to this question requires honest engagement with a broader "living Constitution" question that hovers over all American debate about how to approach interpretation of the Constitution. The legitimacy of the entire project of recognizing implied rights, whether under the auspices of the Ninth Amendment or any other "dynamic" theory of the Constitution as a "living" document, is one of the most fiercely contested issues of constitutional interpretation. Liberals are generally more open to construing the Constitution as a living document that may evolve in its meaning over time. Conservatives are more apt to be restrictive in their approach to constitutional rights, vigorously criticizing judicial activism (which to conservatives usually means liberal activism), and severely critiquing any notion of rights not enumerated in the text, arguing instead that all constitutional rights must be firmly tethered in the text of the Constitution, with the words of the text construed in a manner faithful to the original understanding of those words at the time the text was adopted.

The intensity of this debate is fueled largely by the fact that the right that has been most notoriously implied in modern constitutional law is that of privacy. The right to privacy in American constitutional law first surfaced in a relatively noncontroversial setting. In *Griswold v. Connecticut* (1965),[1] the Supreme Court held that a married couple had a constitutional right to use contraceptives as a form of birth control. Connecticut, a heavily Roman Catholic state that seemed to prefer the rhythm method, made the use of contraceptives illegal, even for married couples, in the absence of a doctor's prescription written for medical purposes. The various Justices composing the majority in *Griswold* invoked a variety of legal theories to explain why the Connecticut law was unconstitutional, even though the Constitution does not explicitly mention a "right to privacy." Justice William O. Douglas, who wrote the opinion of the Court, argued that a right to privacy may be implied from the emanations of other rights explicitly articulated in the Bill of Rights, stating that "that specific guarantees in the Bill of Rights have penumbras, formed by emanations from those guarantees that help give them life and substance."[2] Justice Arthur Goldberg, in what may have been the most famous and controversial opinion of his relatively short career on the Court, invoked the Ninth Amendment itself as his justification for recognizing the existence of the right of privacy. Justice Goldberg's opinion was joined by Chief Justice Warren and Justice Brennan. Justice Goldberg's reliance on the Ninth Amendment, however, was somewhat confusing. He stated that he did

not "mean to state that the Ninth Amendment constitutes an independent source of rights protected from infringement by either the States or
the Federal Government."[3] Thus the Ninth Amendment, in Justice Goldberg's view, was not the "source" of a right to privacy. "Rather," Justice
Goldberg wrote, "the Ninth Amendment shows a belief of the Constitution's authors that fundamental rights exist that are not expressly enumerated in the first eight amendments and an intent that the list of rights
included there not be deemed exhaustive."[4] Justice John Marshall Harlan
concurred with the result in the case, but refused to accept the reasoning of either Justice Douglas, with his "emanations" and "penumbras," or
Justice Goldberg, with his invocation of the Ninth Amendment. Justice
Harlan turned instead to legal tradition, as reflected in what he described
as "basic values 'implicit in the concept of ordered liberty.'"[5]

The cases that followed *Griswold*, however, were far more controversial. *Eisenstadt v. Baird* (1972)[6] held that *unmarried* persons also had a
constitutional right to use contraceptives. The theory of *Eisenstadt* was
that constitutional rights are possessed by individuals, not couples. The
right to privacy would ultimately lead to the decision in *Lawrence v. Texas*
(2003),[7] in which the Supreme Court held that the Constitution granted
gay and lesbian couples the right to choose their own sexual partners, and
that states could no longer make homosexual conduct a crime. *Lawrence*
would fuel yet another debate, over whether the right to privacy, com-
bined with the Equal Protection Clause, gives same-sex couples a right to
marry. The most controversial application of the implied right of privacy,
of course, is the decision in *Roe v. Wade* (1973),[8] holding that a woman's
right to privacy extended to a right to abortion on demand in roughly the
first two trimesters of pregnancy, prior to the viability of the fetus.

To be sure, the notion of an implied right to academic freedom does
not carry the same cultural, spiritual, and ideological intensity as the
notion of an implied right of privacy, and its associations with same-sex
marriage or abortion. If the Supreme Court were to recognize an implied
right of academic freedom, we would not witness yearly protest marches
from the Washington Monument to the Supreme Court building, which
is now a ritual on the anniversary of the *Roe v. Wade* decision.

Nonetheless, implied rights, even when pressed to the service of a
worthy cause such as academic freedom, are never able to command

the same level of legal and political legitimacy as explicitly enumerated rights. And why would we expect anything different? From the earliest days of American constitutional law, we have enshrined the Constitution on its special pedestal as the "supreme law of the land" in part because it is written. It was this very quality of "being in writing" that Chief Justice John Marshall emphasized in *Marbury v. Madison*,[9] the decision that forged the supremacy of the Constitution, and the role of the Supreme Court as its ultimate arbiter. "Certainly all those who have framed written constitutions contemplate them as forming the fundamental and paramount law of the nation," Chief Justice Marshall stated in *Marbury*, "and consequently the theory of every such government must be, that an act of the legislature, repugnant to the constitution, is void."[10]

It is, in short, perilous business to stake a constitutional claim on the existence of a right that does not appear in the text. A powerful lesson in these perils is provided by the ill-fated effort to establish a special First Amendment right for journalists, a so-called reporter's privilege that provides to journalists a special constitutional right protecting the identity of the their sources. In *Branzburg v. Hayes* (1972), the Supreme Court rejected, by a 5–4 vote, the existence of a "reporter's privilege."[11] The opinion of the Court was brusque and unequivocal, making it plain that no privilege exists, because journalists, like everyone else in society, are bound by the rule of law. The opinion of the Court in *Branzburg* was replete with language expressing stern rejection of the privilege, with scores of sentences pointing out, in different ways, the Court's unwillingness to read such a privilege into the First Amendment. The Court thus declared, "Of course, the press has the right to abide by its agreement not to publish all the information it has, but the right to withhold news is not equivalent to a First Amendment exemption from the ordinary duty of all other citizens to furnish relevant information to a grand jury performing an important public function."[12] The Court rejected the view advanced by journalists that the sky would fall on hard-hitting investigative reporting in the absence of such a constitutional privilege.

The effort to convince the Supreme Court to recognize a reporter's privilege failed, even though there was at least a colorable textural claim to special constitutional protection for "the press," distinct from the First Amendment's protection of freedom of speech. The First Amendment does in fact contain a "Press Clause," in addition to a "Speech Clause." Even so, the claim for unique protection for reporters lost. The claim for special protection for academics, who do not even have the benefit of their own clause, must surely be weaker.

This weakness was revealed in *University of Pennsylvania v. Equal Employment Opportunity Commission* (1990),[13] in which the Supreme Court addressed an action brought by the EEOC to enforce a subpoena that the organization had issued to the University of Pennsylvania, seeking the release of confidential peer review materials relating to the tenure review process of Associate Professor Rosalie Tung, who had been denied tenure by Penn's Wharton School of Business. Professor Tung sued Penn under Title VII of the Civil Rights Act of 1964, claiming she had been discriminated against on the basis of race and sex. To support her claim Professor Tung and the EEOC wanted to view the confidential tenure files.

Penn took the position that it had a First Amendment academic freedom right that protected the confidentiality of the peer review tenure files. In its brief for the Supreme Court, Penn argued that it exercises its constitutional right to determine "on academic grounds who may teach" through the tenure process. A tenure system, Penn claimed, determines what the university will look like over time, arguing that "in making tenure decisions, therefore, a university is doing nothing less than shaping its own identity." Confidential peer reviews of scholarship from scholars both inside and outside the university, Penn asserted, are critical to obtaining candid and detailed written evaluations of a candidate's scholarship.

For the EEOC to pierce the veil of confidentiality surrounding peer reviews of scholarship, Penn claimed, would undercut the school's institutional right of academic freedom, by exerting a "chilling effect" on candid evaluations and discussions of candidates. This would debase the currency of peer review evaluations, Penn maintained. "This will work to the detriment of universities, as less qualified persons achieve tenure causing the quality of instruction and scholarship to decline," Penn argued in its brief, and "also will result in divisiveness and tension, placing strain on faculty relations and impairing the free interchange of ideas that is a hallmark of academic freedom."[14]

The Supreme Court rejected the argument. In a unanimous decision written by Justice Blackmun, the Court roundly repudiated Penn's First Amendment academic freedom claim for a special privilege to avoid disclosure of documents in a civil rights suit alleging race and sex discrimination, refusing to place universities on a different legal footing than other employers. In its tenor, the opinion of Justice Blackmun was almost mockingly hostile to Penn's argument. Justice Blackmun thus rejected Penn's reliance on what he described as the "the so-called academic-freedom cases." *So called.*[15]

Justice Blackmun observed that there was no need to define "the precise contours of any academic-freedom right against governmental attempts to influence the content of academic speech," because no one had argued that the EEOC subpoenas were "intended to or will in fact direct the content of university discourse toward or away from particular subjects or points of view." Having held that Penn could not plausibly rely on traditional free speech principles protecting academic freedom to support its argument, Justice Blackmun turned to an alternative approach: the notion that the First Amendment might require recognition of a custom-built "academic freedom privilege." This argument for a special academic freedom privilege was also rejected.[16] Tellingly, Justice Blackmun's opinion for the Court drew an explicit comparison between the effort to establish an implied right protecting journalists and an implied right protecting academics, rejecting both:

> The case we decide today in many respects is similar to *Branzburg v. Hayes*. In *Branzburg*, the Court rejected the notion that under the First Amendment a reporter could not be required to appear or to testify as to information obtained in confidence without a special showing that the reporter's testimony was necessary. Petitioners there, like petitioner here, claimed that requiring disclosure of information collected in confidence would inhibit the free flow of information in contravention of First Amendment principles. In the course of rejecting the First Amendment argument, this Court noted that "the First Amendment does not invalidate every incidental burdening of the press that may result from the enforcement of civil or criminal statutes of general applicability." We also indicated a reluctance to recognize a constitutional privilege where it was "unclear how often and to

what extent informers are actually deterred from furnishing information when newsmen are forced to testify before a grand jury." We were unwilling then, as we are today, "to embark the judiciary on a long and difficult journey to . . . an uncertain destination."

The decision in *University of Pennsylvania* seemed to shut the door on the recognition of academic freedom as a distinct implied right. This shutting of the door may be unpopular within the world of higher education, but it should not be. In the long run, an interpretation of the Constitution that does not attempt to establish academic freedom as a freestanding implied right is sound as constitutional law, and will actually encourage a healthy balance of competing interests in the shared governance of American colleges and universities. The case against academic freedom as an implied constitutional right is buttressed by three principle arguments.

(1) The text and structure of the Constitution, as demonstrated above, do not support it. To imply a freestanding right of academic freedom requires loading on the baggage that attaches to recognition of an implied constitutional right, injecting a divisive quality to the debate and placing academic freedom on unnecessarily strained and fragile intellectual grounds. The case for academic freedom is far more solid, ideologically neutral, and bipartisan if it is grounded in explicit First Amendment rights such as freedom of speech.

(2) Precedent does not support it. The opinions of the Supreme Court of the United States that discuss academic freedom, as explored in detail below, do not support the proposition that it is a distinct right. At the same time, however, Supreme Court decisions regarding the application of constitutional conflicts on American campuses demonstrate thoughtful and generous solicitude for the traditions of freedom of inquiry and expression in universities. Supreme Court Justices have frequently written, eloquently and forcefully, of the Constitution's protection of academic freedom. These statements are powerful, well-grounded in our constitutional tradition, and sound as constitutional policy and principle. The frequency and force of these judicial expressions of the importance of academic freedom might well lead one to reify them into hard constitutional doctrine, elevating academic freedom as a freestanding constitutional right. A more careful examination of the language of these pro-

nouncements and the theories that undergird them, however, yields a subtler conclusion. It would be too much to dismiss academic freedom as a merely architectural facade, contributing nothing to the load-bearing walls. It would be wrong, however, to treat academic freedom as load-bearing in itself. Academic freedom values may add strength and solidity to the load-bearing walls of constitutional doctrines such as freedom of speech when applied to the world of higher education, but academic freedom does not form that wall by itself.

(3) The recognition of a special constitutional right of academic freedom tends to strike most of those who are not in the world of colleges and universities as elitist. To put either academic institutions or academic individuals on a constitutional pedestal runs counter to the egalitarian impulses that inform traditional constitutional doctrines. Just as the Supreme Court has been unwilling to bestow heightened First Amendment protection on the mainstream media or individual journalists by invoking the Press Clause as a constitutional provision with distinct meaning, we should expect the Supreme Court to be skeptical of a similar claim to bestow heightened protection for universities or university professors under an implied "Academic Freedom Clause." Recognition of such a special right will smack of superiority and privilege, further distancing higher education from the mainstream United States, and undermining the political currency and perceived legitimacy of academic freedom as a value worthy of thoughtful and principled protection.

Supreme Court Precedent on Academic Freedom

The first mention of the phrase "academic freedom" in an opinion of a U.S. Supreme Court Justice came in a losing cause. In *Adler v. Board of Education of the City of New York* (1952),[17] the Supreme Court upheld New York's "Feinberg Law," which prohibited New York public schools and universities from employing anyone who "willfully and deliberately advocates, advises or teaches the doctrine that the government of the United States or of any state or of any political subdivision thereof should be overthrown or overturned by force."[18] *Adler* was a 6–3 decision and may be dismissed as prehistoric. Virtually none of the vibrant legal protections that have now come to be deeply ingrained in contemporary

First Amendment law had yet emerged in 1952. *Adler* is notable, however, for three dissenting opinions, written by Justices Hugo Black, William O. Douglas, and Felix Frankfurter. The opinion of Justice Douglas was the first opinion written by an American Supreme Court Justice to use the phrase "academic freedom." In haunting prose, Justice Douglas, in an opinion joined by Justice Black, linked academic freedom to the core values of the First Amendment:

> What happens under this law is typical of what happens in a police state. Teachers are under constant surveillance; their pasts are combed for signs of disloyalty; their utterances are watched for clues to dangerous thoughts. A pall is cast over the classrooms. There can be no real academic freedom in that environment. Where suspicion fills the air and holds scholars in line for fear of their jobs, there can be no exercise of the free intellect. Supineness and dogmatism take the place of inquiry. A "party line"—as dangerous as the "party line" of the Communists—lays hold. It is the "party line" of the orthodox view, of the conventional thought, of the accepted approach. A problem can no longer be pursued with impunity to its edges. Fear stalks the classroom. The teacher is no longer a stimulant to adventurous thinking; she becomes instead a pipe line for safe and sound information. A deadening dogma takes the place of free inquiry. Instruction tends to become sterile; pursuit of knowledge is discouraged; discussion often leaves off where it should begin.[19]

Justice Frankfurter dissented in *Adler* on technical grounds, arguing that the Court should not have taken the case because it was not yet clear how New York's Feinberg Law would be applied in actual operation. Yet Justice Frankfurter did hint that he shared some of the deep concerns of Black and Douglas, writing that "as the case comes to us we can have no guide other than our own notions—however uncritically extra-judicial—of the real bearing of the New York arrangement on the freedom of thought and activity, and especially on the feeling of such freedom, which are, as I suppose no one would deny, part of the necessary professional equipment of teachers in a free society."

Constitutional protection for academic freedom is often described in judicial opinions and scholarly commentary as having begun with *Sweezy v. New Hampshire* (1957).[20] The Attorney General of New Hampshire, Louis Wyman, set out to investigate Paul Sweezy, a Marxist economist, on suspicion that Sweezy was a communist subversive. As part of the investigation, the New Hampshire Attorney General issued a subpoena to determine the content of a lecture Sweezy had delivered as a guest lecturer at the University of New Hampshire, titled "Socialism." The incident was vintage 1950s red-baiting. Attorney General Wyman's inquisition included the following series of questions, all of which Paul Sweezy refused to answer:

> "What was the subject of your lecture?"
> "Didn't you tell the class at the University of New Hampshire on Monday, March 22, 1954, that Socialism was inevitable in this country?
> "Did you advocate Marxism at that time?"
> "Did you express the opinion, or did you make the statement at that time that Socialism was inevitable in America?"
> "Did you in this last lecture on March 22 or in any of the former lectures espouse the theory of dialectical materialism?"
> "I have in the file here a statement from a person who attended your class, and I will read it in part because I don't want you to think I am just fishing. 'His talk this time was on the inevitability of the Socialist program. It was a glossed-over interpretation of the materialist dialectic.' Now, again I ask you the original question."[21]

Sweezy would not answer these specific questions, but he did offer an umbrella response to the entire investigation: "I would like to say one thing in this connection, Mr. Wyman. I stated under oath at my last appearance that, and I now repeat it, that I do not advocate or in any way further the aim of overthrowing constitutional government by force and violence. I did not so advocate in the lecture I gave at the University of New Hampshire. In fact I have never at any time so advocated in a lecture anywhere. Aside from that I have nothing I want to say about the lecture in question."[22]

Sweezy was convicted of contempt for his refusal to answer Wyman's questions. That conviction was overturned in the United States Supreme Court. The decision in *Sweezy* was rich in eloquent statements lauding the value of freedom at American colleges and universities, but poor in any precise articulation of the specific legal grounds for reversing *Sweezy's* contempt citation. A four-Justice plurality of the Court, in an opinion written by Chief Justice Earl Warren and joined by Justices Hugo Black, William O. Douglas, and William Brennan, was particularly muddled. Warren's opinion was the only one in *Sweezy* to use the phrase "academic freedom." Warren's opinion thus stated, "We believe that there unquestionably was an invasion of petitioner's liberties in the areas of academic freedom and political expression—areas in which government should be extremely reticent to tread."[23] In the very next passage of the opinion, Warren spoke powerfully of "the essentiality of freedom in the community of American universities." Yet the formal legal ground on which the Warren opinion rested did not seem to be the First Amendment, nor academic freedom, but rather the theory that New Hampshire had violated due process of law when the Legislature empowered the state's Attorney General to conduct his broad subversive-hunting investigation, seeming to merge legislative and executive functions. Much of Warren's opinion thus echoed the same constitutional disquiet that drove the decision in yet another Communist Party investigation case it decided the same day, *Watkins v. United States* (1957).[24] In *Watkins*, the Court held that the House Un-American Activities Committee violated due process of law when it held John Watkins in contempt of Congress for refusing to answer questions regarding alleged subversive propaganda. The *Watkins* decision, also written by Warren, had separation-of-powers overtones. A solid majority of the Court was clearly troubled in *Watkins* by the unseemly merging of the legislative and prosecutorial functions undertaken by the Un-American Activities Committee, and used the Due Process Clause to rein in the congressional body.

In *Sweezy*, by contrast, the Court was more divided. Justice Whittaker did not participate in the case, leaving only eight Justices. Four of the Justices (Frankfurter, Harlan, Burton, and Clark) appeared unwilling to impose such separation-of-powers concepts on the state of New Hampshire, and chastised the four Justices who composed the plurality opinion (Warren, Black, Douglas, and Brennan) for doing so. Seemingly bothered by this critique, Earl Warren sought to disclaim any such imposition of federal separation-of-powers concepts on the sovereign state of New Hampshire, stating at the end of his opinion that the "conclusion that we

[28]

have reached in this case is not grounded upon the doctrine of separation of powers," he acknowledged that "this Court has held that the concept of separation of powers embodied in the United States Constitution is not mandatory in state governments."[25] In a final sentence that bordered on doublespeak, however, the Chief Justice almost stubbornly insisted, "Our conclusion does rest upon a separation of the power of a state legislature to conduct investigations from the responsibility to direct the use of that power insofar as that separation causes a deprivation of the constitutional rights of individuals and a denial of due process of law."[26]

Justice Felix Frankfurter, a former Harvard Law School professor, wrote a concurring opinion in *Sweezy*, joined by Justice John Marshall Harlan. Justice Frankfurter's opinion did not use the phrase "academic freedom," nor did it rest explicitly on the First Amendment. Indeed, Justice Frankfurter's only formal and specific reference to any provision of the constitutional text as the basis for his ruling was the Due Process Clause. Yet the two dissenting Justices in *Sweezy* (Clark and Burton), and most jurists and scholars who would later interpret *Sweezy*, would treat the Frankfurter opinion as the first great exposition of a First Amendment academic freedom right. This might have been due, in part, to the fact that Frankfurter, in the early part of his opinion, deliberately rebuffed the notion that the Supreme Court had any power to review how New Hampshire might organize its internal system of government. Frankfurter thus rejected any attempt to meld the analysis in *Sweezy* with the analysis in *Watkins*, calling *Sweezy* "a very different case."[27] Yet the mythology that would come to envelop the Frankfurter opinion in *Sweezy* undoubtedly grew not from the technical holding of his opinion (which remained, not unlike the Warren opinion, a somewhat obscure invocation of the Due Process Clause), but rather from Frankfurter's soaring defense of freedom in the context of universities.

Justice Frankfurter's opinion well deserves its place as one of the great towering constitutional defenses of academic freedom. Too often, however, citation to the Frankfurter opinion is limited to one snippet, an excerpt from a long quotation in his opinion from a plea for freedom at universities in South Africa, in which Frankfurter cited language articulating the "four essential freedoms" of the university: the freedom "to determine for itself on academic grounds who may teach, what may be taught, how it shall be taught, and who may be admitted to study,"[28] which emphasize only the university's *institutional* autonomy and freedom. Justice Frankfurter's opinion was actually far richer.

Frankfurter's opinion, taken as a whole, braided respect for Sweezy's individual freedom with that of the larger university community. "When weighed against the grave harm resulting from governmental intrusion into the intellectual life of a university," he thus wrote—particularly "where the witness has sworn that neither in the lecture nor at any other time did he ever advocate overthrowing the Government by force and violence"[29]—stronger justifications for the state's intrusion must exist than those proffered by New Hampshire. In his own words, Justice Frankfurter then described the society's powerful need for freedom of inquiry within its universities:

> Progress in the natural sciences is not remotely confined to findings made in the laboratory. Insights into the mysteries of nature are born of hypothesis and speculation. The more so is this true in the pursuit of understanding in the groping endeavors of what are called the social sciences, the concern of which is man and society. The problems that are the respective preoccupations of anthropology, economics, law, psychology, sociology and related areas of scholarship are merely departmentalized dealing, by way of manageable division of analysis, with interpenetrating aspects of holistic perplexities. For society's good—if understanding be an essential need of society—inquiries into these problems, speculations about them, stimulation in others of reflection upon them, must be left as unfettered as possible. Political power must abstain from intrusion into this activity of freedom, pursued in the interest of wise government and the people's well-being, except for reasons that are exigent and obviously compelling.[30]

This passage does not sharply differentiate between the rights of individual scholars and the rights of the university itself, but rather conflates the two as part of the "intellectual life of the university." The important divide for Justice Frankfurter was not between university scholars and administration, but between the world of the university and the world of government intruders. Bear in mind that this was the University of New Hampshire, a public, *state* institution. Even so, Frankfurter lauded "the dependence of a free society on free universities."[31] For Frankfurter this meant "the exclusion of governmental intervention in the intellectual life of a university."[32] After citing the address of T. H. Huxley at the opening of Johns Hopkins University, the Annual Reports of President A. Lawrence Lowell of Harvard, and the Reports of the University Grants Committee in Great Britain, Justice Frankfurter quoted at length from a manifesto from a conference of senior scholars from the University of Cape Town and the University of the Witwatersrand, which included the two Chancellors of those universities:

> In a university knowledge is its own end, not merely a means to an end. A university ceases to be true to its own nature if it becomes the tool of Church or State or any sectional interest. A university is characterized by the spirit of free inquiry, its ideal being the ideal of Socrates—"to follow the argument where it leads." This implies the right to examine, question, modify or reject traditional ideas and beliefs. Dogma and hypothesis are incompatible, and the concept of an immutable doctrine is repugnant to the spirit of a university. The concern of its scholars is not merely to add and revise facts in relation to an accepted framework, but to be ever examining and modifying the framework itself.
>
> Freedom to reason and freedom for disputation on the basis of observation and experiment are the necessary conditions for the advancement of scientific knowledge. A sense of freedom is also necessary for creative work in the arts which, equally with scientific research, is the concern of the university.
>
> . . . It is the business of a university to provide that atmosphere which is most conducive to speculation, experiment and creation. It is an atmosphere in which there prevail "the four essential freedoms" of a university—to determine for itself on academic grounds who may teach, what may be taught, how it shall be taught, and who may be admitted to study.[33]

While this wonderful quotation ends with an endorsement of the freedom of the university, the statement, like the Frankfurter opinion as a whole, treats the values of the university as in alignment with the values of the individual scholar, and both are inextricably intertwined with classic free speech values, where dogma and hypothesis are incompatible.

This detailed look at *Sweezy* offers multiple insights. First, *Sweezy* cannot plausibly be interpreted as establishing "academic freedom" as a distinct constitutional right. Neither the Warren nor the Frankfurter opinions purported to formally rest their holdings on academic freedom grounds, or even on the First Amendment. Second, whatever ambiguity might exist as to the constitutional doctrine or doctrines on which Warren and Frankfurter were each relying, it is clear that *both* opinions saw the college and university setting as a highly important element of context in applying their analysis. Both Justices purported to be applying ordinary constitutional law, and both Justices saw the special place of universities in our culture and the extraordinary characteristics of great universities as powerful influencing factors in their analysis. Third, for all its importance as a statement of values, *Sweezy* yields little in the way of helpful concrete legal doctrine. This is not surprising, however, for the year was 1957 and very little of First Amendment law as we now know it had yet developed.

The next important milestone came a decade later, with the Supreme Court's decision in *Keyishian v. Board of Regents of the University of New York* (1967).[34] Members of the faculty of the University of Buffalo suddenly became members of the faculty of the public State University of New York system when the state acquired the formerly private university to create what is now SUNY-Buffalo. New York had a law in place to prevent the employment "subversive persons" by the state. Members of the faculty were required to sign statements that they were not and had never been communists.

The Supreme Court, in an opinion by Justice Brennan, struck down the New York law, finding that it was unconstitutionally vague and overbroad, and applied evolving First Amendment principles to make its case. Among other things, the Court noted, the law essentially made membership in the Communist Party alone a presumptive basis for disqualification from employment, violating a First Amendment norm that distinguishes between mere membership in a group that espouses illegal activity, and specific intent by an individual to further the illegal aims of the group. In the course of his discussion, Justice Brennan spoke of the "transcendent value" of academic freedom: "Our Nation is deeply committed to safeguarding academic freedom, which is of transcendent value to all of us and not merely to the teachers concerned. That freedom is therefore a special concern of the First Amendment, which does not tolerate laws that cast a pall of orthodoxy over the classroom."[35] Justice Brennan's opinion in *Keyishian* did not treat academic freedom as a distinct and severable First Amendment right, but rather as a derivative of larger First Amendment values, arguing that the "Nation's future depends upon leaders trained through wide exposure to that robust exchange of ideas which discovers truth out of a multitude of tongues, rather than through any kind of authoritative selection." These words from *Keyishian* thus merged the importance of one of the most solemn missions of universities, the education of "leaders trained through wide exposure to that robust exchange of ideas which discovers truth," with the wider principles of free speech law, which are also centrally grounded in the faith that it is in our national interest to protect freedom in the marketplace of ideas.

The pattern established in *Sweezy* and *Keyishian* has remained steady over time. In the ensuing years the Supreme Court has often decided cases requiring the application of constitutional principles and other principles of federal law, such as employment or labor laws, in the context of colleges and universities. The Court often acknowledges academic freedom as a *value*, or a *factor*, in its analysis, but it *always* holds short of explicitly enshrining academic freedom as an independent, freestanding constitutional right. Such cases include decisions involving the placing of conditions on the receipt of federal money, such as *Rumsfeld v. Forum for Academic and Institutional Rights Inc.* (2006),[36] and *Grove City College v. Bell* (1984);[37] involving race discrimination and affirmative action, such as *Regents of the University of California Regents v. Bakke* (1978),[38] *Gratz v. Bollinger* (2003),[39] and *Grutter v. Bollinger* (2003);[40] involving labor and employment disputes in the context of universities, including policies implicating shared university governance, such as *Central State University v. American Association of University Professors, Central State University Chapter* (1999),[41] *Minnesota State Board for Community Colleges v. Knight* (1984),[42] and *National Labor Relations Board v. Yeshiva University* (1980);[43] and involving the free speech rights of professors, such as *Garcetti v. Ceballos* (2006).[44]

The pattern established by these cases reinforces a central thesis of this book, which is that constitutional values have operated in an informal, value-laden sense to shape and influence the identity of American colleges and universities. This influence has tended to exert itself not through formal legal doctrines that single out colleges and universities for specialized treatment, but through the application of broader constitutional themes as adapted to the values and settings of academic life.

Each of these cases is discussed in this book in subsequent chapters dealing with other constitutional ideas that have influenced the shape of the American university. When, in the course of those discussions, this issue of academic freedom as an implied right again surfaces, the reprise will be noted. In all cases, the refrain remains the same: the Supreme Court of the United States has been stubbornly unreceptive to the formal recognition of academic freedom as an implied constitutional right. As previously suggested, this reluctance to define specialized constitutional doctrines uniquely applicable to higher education derives in part from the doctrinal and textural awkwardness of engrafting such rights onto a constitutional text that does not contain them. It also derives, however, from a broader concern with the perils of elitism that would attend such a formal recognition of specialized rights for academics and academic institutions.

The Perils of Elitism

The unwillingness of the Supreme Court to formally recognize academic freedom as a distinct right springs in part from an egalitarian, anti-elitist impulse in American constitutional law, which is generally hostile to the creation of specially elevated First Amendment protection for any particular *class* of citizens, such as university faculty or students. This anti-elitist impulse is among the reasons the Supreme Court has been unwilling to engraft a special privilege for journalists under the First Amendment. The argument against such a special privilege has intensified with the rise of the Internet, making it increasingly difficult to describe who is a "journalist" in a world heavily populated with blogs, tweets, and other forms of citizen-journalism. Much the same anti-elitist bias works against the recognition of special constitutional rights for academics and academic institutions. Is a book on Hillary Clinton written by a political science professor to have different constitutional status than a book on Hillary

Clinton written by journalist for the *Wall Street Journal*? And what are we to do about the various books on the Duke lacrosse team rape case, such as that written by Stuart Taylor, Jr., a well-known journalist, and K. C. Johnson, a law professor?[45]

These anti-elitist objections figured significantly in a decision by the United States Court of Appeals for the D.C. Circuit in *Emergency Coalition to Defend Educational Travel v. United States Department of the Treasury* (2008).[46] The case was brought by a coalition of college professors, students, and higher education professionals who sought to teach and attend courses at universities in Cuba. The coalition challenged Treasury Department regulations tightening educational programs offered by American academic institutions in Cuba. The court rejected the challenge to the Cuba regulations. In an interesting side debate, two judges on the court, Judge Harry Edwards and Judge Laurence Silberman, debated whether academic freedom exists as a freestanding right. Judge Edwards, himself a former academic, did not purport to decide the matter, but he did note what he regarded as one of the many unresolved questions surrounding the notion of academic freedom as a constitutional right.[47] Judge Silberman was not so ambivalent. He forcefully rejected the notion that academic freedom exists as a constitutional right distinct from other constitutional rights. "The very notion of academic freedom—as a concept distinct from the actual textual provisions of the First Amendment—is elusive,"[48] Judge Silberman began. After canvasing the principal Supreme Court cases describing academic freedom, Judge Silberman noted that he had little doubt that a university has the right to control, to at least some degree, the content of a professor's classroom presentations. Drawing on the Supreme Court's decision in *University of Pennsylvania v. Equal Employment Opportunity Commission*,[49] Judge Silberman stated that "a state university may well have a right—perhaps even an obligation—to regulate the substance of professors' classroom lectures."[50] As an example, Judge Silberman posited that "were a professor of history to adopt in his lectures bizarre theories of Holocaust denial or a professor of sociology to claim the inferiority of certain races or ethnic groups, surely a university would not be powerless to prevent such pedagogical perversions. After all, the state can be said to 'speak' through its employees."[51] At best, Judge Silberman stated, academic freedom as a distinct right would protect universities, not individual professors.[52] Judge Silberman was also skeptical that academic freedom could be plausibly understood as a vehicle for protecting the internal governance processes of faculty at academic institutions, finding it impossible to distinguish colleges and universities from other organizations, noting that "I do not perceive any principled reason why the First Amendment should be thought to protect internal governance of certain academic institutions (are 'think tanks' included?) but not other eleemosynary bodies or, for that matter, trade unions or corporations."[53]

There are, admittedly, good counter-arguments to the position I am advancing here. One of the country's best scholars on the history of the First Amendment and the history and law of academic freedom, Professor David Rabban, who holds a chair at the University of Texas Law School and was General Counsel of the American Association of University Professors, has forcefully argued that universities and university professors should be understood to possess a distinct constitutional right of academic freedom, based on their functional identity.[54] University professors have a functional role as independent scholars obligated to seek and speak the truth as they see it, a role that may justify treating their First Amendment rights of independence from the control of their university employers as different in kind from the rights of other employees. Following this logic, Professor Rabban concludes that "individual academic freedom should cover expression within a professor's scholarly expertise and intramural speech on matters of educational policy."[55]

Yet I am not persuaded that this is either sound law or good practical politics. It *is* certainly true that professors have a functional societal role that can be pressed to the service of justifying protection for academic freedom, including the transmitting of knowledge to students; developing in students a sense of intellectual curiosity, appreciation for the human quest for life's meaning, and civic engagement; and advancing the frontiers of knowledge and discourse. As a matter of ideal and aspiration, universities and university professors may think of themselves as pursuing these functions with especially dedicated intellectual elevation, intellectual honesty, objectivity, and rigor. But as the Supreme Court's cases persistently insist, there is a difference between the recognition of these functions as justifications for our societal policies, and the recognition of these functions as justifications for the creation of a distinct constitutional right.

Academics should be content with this picture. To borrow from the Rolling Stones, you can't always get what you want, but if you try sometimes, you just might find, *you get what you need*. As discussed in the chapters that follow, in most—not all, admittedly, but *most*—disputes that arise on campuses and are litigated in court, the outcome of the decision *will be the same*, regardless of whether the formal legal doctrine being applied is a "right of academic freedom" or some other recognized right, such as freedom of speech, applied to the context of the academic environment. In short, to say that judicial decisions employing the phrase "academic freedom" are actually applications of other already-recognized constitutional rights is *not* to say that the academic setting *does not count in the balance* when those constitutional rights are interpreted and applied to the world of colleges and universities. While academic freedom may not be, in a strictly legal sense, a distinct constitutional right, this does not mean that the academic setting does not strongly influence the interpretation and application of other recognized constitutional rights when they are placed in contest on a college campus.

As a matter of practical politics, higher education will benefit much more from a well-reasoned application of standard constitutional principles than from a perceived elitist quest for the award of new ones. It is a bit like deciding to work within the system, and not outside it. More significant, to treat academic freedom as a value that is influenced by constitutional norms, and that in turn may exert influence on those norms, creates a beneficial play in the joints, a resistance to osteoporosis, freeing higher education to experiment and innovate. Constitutional doctrines can at times be stultifying, tending to act as both floors and ceilings, diminishing autonomy and diversity. It is not a good idea to try to constitutionalize everything. When constitutional law appropriates too many of our important societal decisions, the currency of the Constitution as a fundamental law is devalued. When everything is constitutionalized, nothing is constitutionalized. And when too much is constitutionalized, too little is left to private choice. It is to that great divide between the public and private sphere, itself one of the core themes in the American constitutional experience, that we next turn.

3

The Public and the Private Sphere

In this connection it is proper to state that civil rights, such as are guarantied by the Constitution against state aggression, cannot be impaired by the wrongful acts of individuals, unsupported by state authority in the shape of laws, customs, or judicial or executive proceedings. . . . Hence, in all those cases where the Constitution seeks to protect the rights of the citizen against discriminative and unjust laws of the state by prohibiting such laws, it is not individual offenses, but abrogation and denial of rights, which it denounces.

—Justice Joseph P. Bradley, writing for the Court in the *Civil Rights Cases* (1883), establishing the "state action" doctrine

Vital First Amendment speech principles are at stake here. The first danger to liberty lies in granting the State the power to examine publications to determine whether or not they are based on some ultimate idea and, if so, for the State to classify them. The second, and corollary, danger is to speech from the chilling of individual thought and expression. That danger is especially real in the University setting, where the State acts against a background and tradition of thought and experiment that is at the center of our intellectual and philosophic tradition. . . . In ancient Athens, and, as Europe entered into a new period of intellectual awakening, in places like Bologna, Oxford, and Paris, universities began as voluntary and spontaneous assemblages or concourses for students to speak and to write and to learn. . . . The quality and creative power of student intellectual life to this day remains a vital measure of a school's influence and attainment. For the University, by regulation, to cast disapproval on particular viewpoints of its students risks the suppression of free speech and creative inquiry in one of the vital centers for the nation's intellectual life, its college and university campuses.

—Justice Anthony Kennedy, writing for the Court in *Rosenberger v. Rector and Visitors of the University of Virginia* (1995)

Dartmouth and Daniel Webster

Daniel Webster, arguing before the Supreme Court of the United States in *Trustees of Dartmouth College v. Woodward* (1819)[1] on behalf of his beloved alma mater, Dartmouth, brought tears to the eyes of Chief Justice John Marshall as he proclaimed that Dartmouth was "a small college, but there are some who love it."

The Supreme Court's decision in what is popularly known as the *Dartmouth College Case* is usually studied by American lawyers as an early nineteenth-century iteration on contracts and corporate law. But looking back at the Court's 1819 decision through the prism of almost two centuries of development of American constitutional law, and American higher education, it is possible to discern deeper forces in play. The decision in *Dartmouth College* is an early example of the influence of the Supreme Court and constitutional law on the character and identity of American higher education. While the Court's judgment would be articulated in the sedate vocabulary of contracts and corporations, it was clear from the arguments of Daniel Webster and the response of Chief Justice Marshall that *Dartmouth College* was a passionate defense of academic freedom and the importance of independence and autonomy for society's colleges and universities. While the phrase "academic freedom" may not yet have been in use, and while the case was litigated not under the First Amendment rights of freedom of speech, but under the comparatively mundane language of the Constitution's "Contract Clause," the soul of the case was the cause of academic autonomy.

The litigation arose when the legislature of New Hampshire sought to modify the charter of Dartmouth College, in order to reinstate the College's ousted president, effectively turning the college from a private to a public university. This academic coup d'état put the College in the political crosshairs, as New Hampshire's newly elected Republican Governor, William Plumer, sought to wrest control of the Dartmouth Board of Trustees from the Federalists who dominated it.

While today such a power grab by a state government against a private university would be thought of as more than just a simple "impairment of contract"—it would be a matter of grave concern to First Amendment values of academic freedom of speech and association—in 1819 the First Amendment, and indeed the entire Bill of Rights, did not bind state governments. It was not until the twentieth century that the fundamental rights guaranteed in the first ten amendments would come to be treated as "incorporated" against the states, through the force of the Fourteenth Amendment.[2] In 1819, the First Amendment bound only the federal government, as suggested literally by its text, which reads, "*Congress* shall make no law . . . "

Yet even before ratification of the Bill of Rights, the Constitution itself contained a limited list of restraints directly binding on the states, including the Contract Clause of Article I, Section 10, Clause 1, which states that "no State . . . shall pass any . . . Law impairing the obligation of contracts." Dartmouth's legal claim was that its corporate charter, which predated the American Revolution, was such a "contract," that it was a private "eleemosynary corporation," and that the state of New Hampshire violated the Constitution in purporting to "impair" that contractual charter.

Daniel Webster's argument was cast as an argument for all colleges in the United States. "*This, sir, is my case!*" his stirring speech began.[3] "It is the case not merely of that humble institution; it is the case of every college in our Land!"[4] Webster argued for "every eleemosynary institution throughout our country," asserting that if the government could extinguish the light of Dartmouth College, it could "extinguish, one after another, all those great lights of science which for more than a century have thrown their radiance over our land!"[5]

Webster's argument moved the Justices and carried his cause to victory. The opinions of the Justices were cast in the language of corporate charters and contracts. To this day economists and legal scholars debate the extent to which government should be permitted to abrogate contractual agreements or retroactively modify corporate charters, and the strict view taken by the Justices in *Dartmouth College*, a view that gave government very little power to alter settled contractual arrangements, has since been modified. Indeed, Chief Justice Marshall's principal opinion for the Court in *Dartmouth College* captured one of the central conundrums of corporate law that persist to this day, noting that a "corporation is an artificial being, invisible, intangible, and existing only in contemplation of law."[6] Elaborating, Marshall observed, "Being the mere creature of law, it possesses only those properties which the charter of its creation confers upon it either expressly or as incidental to its very existence."[7] Yet it was plain that even though the corporation known as "Dartmouth College" was a "mere creature of the law," this did not make an instrument of *government*. The "law" both brought the corporation into existence and endowed it with certain enforceable rights.

But what of the possibility that Dartmouth, as an *educational corporation*, ought to be treated differently? Perhaps the keen interest of society and society's government in the object of education reserved to the government of New Hampshire an ongoing prerogative to exercise oversight of Dartmouth's mission. Might not *all universities*, in a sense, be "public universities," given the importance of their mission to society? Might not all universities be required to operate "in the public interest"? Here is how Chief Justice Marshall put these questions: "Do its objects stamp on it a different character? Are the Trustees and professors public officers, invested with any portion of political power, partaking in any degree in the administration of civil government, and performing duties which flow from the sovereign authority?"[8]

Chief Justice Marshall answered these questions with a resounding no! In doing so, he drew distinctions between the powers of the national government or the states to *form their own universities*, as the national government and all American states would come to do, and the "separation of university and state," if you will, that attaches to private universities and colleges.

"That education is an object of national concern, and a proper subject of legislation, all admit," Marshall conceded. Moreover, that "there may be an institution, founded by government and placed entirely under its immediate control, the officers of which would be public officers, amenable exclusively to government, none will deny." But Dartmouth College was not a public university, and as such was not, as Marshall phrased it, "in the hands of government." Marshall queried, rhetorically, "Does every teacher of youth become a public officer, and do donations for the purpose of education necessarily become public property so far that the will of the legislature, not the will of the donor, becomes the law of the donation?"[9] The answer to these questions, Marshall noted, "are of serious moment to society, and deserve to be well considered." In considering them well, and in deciding that New Hampshire had no inherent authority to act as an officious intermeddler in the affairs of Dartmouth College, Chief Justice Marshall and the Supreme Court delivered a decisive victory for the independence of private colleges and universities, and set the precedent for a series of rulings by the Court over the next two centuries that would bring American constitutional law to bear strongly on the shaping of American higher education.

State Action

In wrestling with the legal and cultural differences and similarities between public and private universities, a key constitutional principle is the "state action doctrine." This is the nickname for a principle of constitutional law holding that only *governmental entities and governmental officers* are legally bound by the restrictions that give legal meaning to the cherished liberties guaranteed in the Constitution of the United States. Thus the Commissioner of the Internal Revenue is bound by the Bill of Rights, but the Commissioner of Major League Baseball is not. The doctrine, which dates back to a decision of the Supreme Court from 1883 titled the *Civil Rights Cases*,[10] follows quite literally the language of the Constitution itself. In the *Civil Rights Cases*, the Supreme Court held that the guarantee of equal protection of the laws contained in the Fourteenth Amendment only prohibited state governments from denying equal protection, not private businesses or individuals. And indeed, this is precisely how the Fourteenth Amendment literally reads—the sentence prohibiting denial of equal protection begins with the words "No *state* shall . . . " This reading of the Fourteenth Amendment was also consistent with the language in the various provisions of the Bill of Rights. As noted above, the First Amendment, for example, begins with the words "*Congress* shall make no law . . . "

Today we treat the fundamental rights contained in the Bill of Rights and the various constitutional amendments passed since the Civil War as binding on all levels of government, including federal, state, and local governments and governmental agencies, as well as government officials, who are said to act "under color of law." (The one exceptional constitutional prohibition that restrains private individuals and businesses directly is the ban on slavery and involuntary servitude, contained in the Thirteenth Amendment. Private individuals owned slaves, so the abolition of slavery operated directly on them.)

Distinctions Between Public and Private Universities

The state action doctrine provides the first level of resolution to this basic question: Does the Constitution of the United States apply only at public universities, or does its influence extend to private universities as well?

When a public, state university regulates the behavior of faculty and students, it is not simply the university acting, but the state itself. Virginia Tech or the University of Virginia are not simply universities *in* Virginia but also *of* Virginia, and those who establish and implement their policies act under color of law. This means that a state college or university's governing board (its Board of Trustees, Regents, Rectors, or Visitors—whatever it may be called) and the state college or university's administrative officers (its presidents, provosts, deans, and police chiefs), are bound by the Constitution of the United States, including the Bill of Rights and the First Amendment.

Correspondingly, those on whom these state university officials act—students or faculty, for example—are holders of constitutional rights that may be legally enforced against those officials. To the extent that at least some of the core content of academic freedom must include elemental constitutional rights such as freedom of speech, it follows that academic freedom is, on a state university campus, real law, as courts know law.

What of private universities? When a governmental agency—federal, state, or local—seeks to regulate the activity of a private university, those agencies also act under color of law. When the United States government, the state of North Carolina, or the city of Durham regulate the affairs of Duke University, those government entities and their officers are bound by the Constitution, the Bill of Rights, and the First Amendment. This means that Yale, Duke, Stanford, Harvard, Tulane, and Notre Dame, as corporate entities, are possessors of free speech rights, just as Dartmouth was held in the *Dartmouth College* case to be the possessor of a constitutionally protected contract right. If a federal, state, or local law were to ban the teaching of evolution, or Einstein's theory of special relativity, that ban would be an affront to First Amendment academic freedom, one that Furman or Vanderbilt or NYU could successfully challenge in a court of law.

There is a curious asymmetrical symmetry to these two examples. In the case of the state university, legally enforceable constitutional rights are limited to individuals who populate the university, such as students and faculty. This does not mean, however, that a state university or college would *itself* possess legally enforceable federal constitutional rights against the government that created it. The University of Texas and Texas Tech are part of the state of Texas, and the University of Colorado and Colorado State are part of the state of Colorado. If the University of Michigan and Michigan State University are both agencies of the state of Michigan—if they *are*, in a legal sense, part of Michigan, as the hand is part of the body—then it is seemingly incoherent to claim that those universities could sue the state that created them for violation of their First Amendment rights. The creature cannot sue the creator.

Conversely, in conceptualizing legally enforceable academic freedom principles in the realm of the private university, private universities and colleges clearly possess legally enforceable constitutional rights as *institutions* in resisting encroachments on their institutional freedom by government agencies. Courts and legal scholars often describe this as the "institutional autonomy" branch of academic freedom. Again, however, this does *not* mean that students and faculty at Northwestern or Furman have legally enforceable constitutional rights against their universities, which are private institutions, not arms of the government, and thus not bound by the Constitution, the Bill of Rights, or the First Amendment.

The litigation in *Princeton University and New Jersey v. Schmid* (1982)[11] illustrates well the conflicting constitutional crosscurrents to be navigated when separating the public and private domain in the context of higher education. The case involved a Labor Party activist named Chris

Schmid, who was passing out material about the Labor Party and an election for the Mayor of Newark, the New Jersey metropolis forty miles north of Princeton. Schmid was not connected to Princeton in any way, a fact that ran afoul of a university regulation that barred persons with no connection to Princeton and not sponsored by any Princeton group from entering the campus for such leafleting and speech-making purposes. (Princeton would later relax its rules to allow such activity by outsiders.) It happens that under a peculiar feature of the free speech guarantee of the New Jersey state constitution, even private entities, such as Princeton, must respect free speech rights. (New Jersey, as a state, thus does not have the equivalent of the federal "state action doctrine" when it comes to free speech claims brought under state constitutional law.) The Supreme Court of New Jersey, while acknowledging that Princeton, as a university, was entitled to some measure of academic freedom, nevertheless held that Schmid's free speech rights would be violated if Princeton were to kick him off campus for trespass, on the grounds that Princeton's rules lacked any reasonable relationships to its academic mission.

Princeton appealed the New Jersey Supreme Court ruling to the United States Supreme Court. In its appeal, Princeton took a bold position with regard to its institutional academic freedom. The University argued that the state of New Jersey had to *leave it entirely alone* in deciding whom it would allow or not allow to speak on its campus, and that "the state cannot use its police powers to control in any way the intellectual activities of the university." Princeton's aggressive and sweeping invocation of institutional academic freedom caused a rebellion by many Princeton faculty members, who accurately saw the University's expansive claim of *institutional* academic freedom as a potential threat to their own *individual* academic freedom. Following the lead of the Princeton faculty critics, the American Association of University Professors filed a brief in the Supreme Court opposing Princeton's sweeping claims of institutional academic freedom, arguing that only individual professors truly possessed "academic freedom," which the AAUP described as "a scholar's right to be free of institutional (or governmental) control in professional utterance."

The *Schmid* case thus showed the potential for tension with regard to three different academic freedom claimants—the university itself, the university faculty, and an outside speaker entering the campus. The case ended with a whimper, not a bang, when the United States Supreme Court declared the controversy moot, in light of the fact that Princeton had subsequently rescinded its restrictive regulations.

The Shadow Constitution

The asymmetrical symmetry described above is not a fully satisfying or complete account of things. Surely, the students and faculty at Stanford enjoy at least some form of "rights" akin to the "constitutional rights" enjoyed by their public university counterparts across the Bay at the University of California–Berkeley. And surely, the University of North Carolina as a great higher education institution enjoys at least some measure of *institutional* academic freedom akin to that of its private school rivals down Tobacco Road at Wake Forest or Duke.

Yet what are the sources of this supplemental coverage if not the Constitution? The sources are multiple, a blend of federal, state, and local statutory law, agreements in the nature of contract, and voluntary fidelity to custom. These are the vehicles through which the "constitutional unconscious," the values and habits of thought that emanate from formal constitutional law, are absorbed into the larger societal bloodstream. In combination, they often mirror the protection for rights that derive directly from the Constitution, providing legal or customary protections that largely reflect constitutional principles and doctrines. This is the "shadow constitution."

Civil rights laws applicable to the private sector are among the most powerful elements of the shadow constitution. Civil rights laws provide a societal antidote to the state action limitation, bestowing on individuals rights enforceable against private entities that mirror the constitutional rights that individuals may enforce against governmental entities. The Fourteenth Amendment prohibits states from denying to citizens the "equal protection of the laws," thereby prohibiting governmental race or gender discrimination. Because of the state action doctrine, however, the guarantee of equal protection does not prohibit race discrimination by private entities like McDonald's, General Motors, or Georgetown University. Various civil rights laws, however, supplement the Fourteenth

Amendment, extending principles of nondiscrimination to the private sector. As employers, McDonald's, General Motors, and Georgetown are all bound by Title VII of the Civil Rights Act of 1964,[12] which prohibits discrimination in employment. Similarly, the Fair Housing Act of 1968[13] operates directly on those private sector entities that sell and rent housing, prohibiting various forms of housing discrimination.

The distinction between rights and privileges, discussed in chapter 4, also extends the shadow constitution to the world of higher education. Title VI of the Civil Rights Act, for example, requires that "no person in the United States shall, on the ground of race, color, or national origin, be excluded from participation in, be denied the benefits of, or be subjected to discrimination under any program or activity receiving Federal financial assistance."[14] This provision has a strong impact on both public and private universities, many of which benefit from federal financial assistance, and it also has the practical legal effect of extending the equal protection principles of the Fourteenth Amendment, which apply only to public universities, to private universities as well. Even more famously, the prohibitions on gender discrimination that flow from another federal law, Title IX, have broadly extended prohibition of gender discrimination in collegiate sports at both public and private universities.[15]

Private universities such as Duke or Wake Forest are thus bound by a matrix of civil rights laws that impose on them obligations largely equivalent to those that bind the University of North Carolina under the Constitution. Indeed, the prohibitions against discrimination in civil rights laws are often more expansive and more stringent than those imposed by the Constitution.

The Constitutional Unconscious

The influence of American constitutional values on the shape and identity of American universities is in one literal sense direct and immediate. Decisions of the Supreme Court of the United States, augmented by many hundreds of decisions from lower state and federal courts that apply Supreme Court precedent, have generated a substantial body of law dealing with freedom of speech, freedom of association, the rights of students, faculty, and administrators, discrimination based on race, gender, sexual orientation, or religion, separation of church and state, and processes of university governance, elaborating on the legal rules that constrain and shape modern universities.

American constitutional law also exerts an influence on American universities that is indirect yet still profoundly important. Our constitutional *values* have a way of permeating our larger American political and social culture, thus shaping our thinking and our resolution of political and social conflicts. Reflecting the unity suggested by Einstein's thought, our society is figuratively shaded by a kind of "constitutional unconscious," a collection of values, principles, struggles, and conflicts in American life that derive from those aspects of our political and social identity embedded in the Constitution of the United States. The figurative phrase "constitutional unconscious" is invoked to suggest that the influence of constitutional values and principles on our social and political life extends beyond the strict confines of formal "constitutional law," in the sense that Presidents, Congresses, and Supreme Courts know law, infiltrating our political and social traditions, patterns of thought, and habits of behavior.

This "constitutional unconscious" shapes the identity of American higher education at both public and private universities. While public universities may at first seem to be the only entities literally and formally bound by "constitutional law," there is a sense in which constitutional law extends to elements of both public and private universities in the United States. And beyond that extension, for both public and private universities a matrix of legal statutes, contractual arrangements, and customs create a kind of shadow constitution that acts in parallel to the actual Constitution as a defining force on American campuses.

If civil rights laws compose a major part of the shadow constitution covering matters relating to equality, such laws generally do not address other constitutional norms, such as the free speech or free association rights traditionally regarded as the core of what we mean by academic freedom. The supplemental coverage extending these academic freedom rights to professors and students at private universities largely emanates from law created through voluntary contractual agreements, or softer still, from the persuasive force of custom.

A student or faculty member at Furman or Duke or Yale or Stanford may not have true free speech rights enforceable under the Constitution or any civil rights laws against those private universities. Yet by academic custom, Furman, Duke, Yale, or Stanford may choose to pretend as if they do. A private university may wish to ensure that its faculty members and students have, for example, the same free speech rights as students and faculty occupying the campuses of their public university neighbors. At some private universities, these academic freedom rights are observed as a matter of custom, but may not, at least in the view of the university, be actual law. At other private universities, however, this custom may be codified. Through university corporate charters, bylaws, regulations, and contracts with faculty and students, for example, a private university may agree to be bound by the free speech principles of the First Amendment, just as if it were a state university.

The same phenomenon is possible for institutional academic freedom. It may at first seem difficult to conceptualize the state university *itself* as the possessor of academic freedom rights against the state that created it, just as values that appear on both sides of an algebraic equation cancel each other out. If the state university *is* the state, it is difficult to conceive any sense in which the university has rights enforceable against the state.

Yet the state of Georgia or Florida or Illinois may decide that for its universities to flourish, they require a measure of independence within the hierarchy of state government, insulating their universities from the pressures of political influence. This may be reflected simply in custom. States may use restraint and forbearance in attempting to micromanage the academic judgments of state universities. Beyond custom, however, a state may choose, through laws and regulations, to create a measure of agency independence for its universities, just as the federal government may chose to create independence for the Federal Reserve Board or the National Endowment for the Humanities or the Corporation for Public Broadcasting. It is possible, in short, for a state government to decide that its public universities should be granted at least some measure of the academic autonomy that private universities enjoy.

When dealing with our constitutional unconscious and our shadow constitution, how should universities decide which elements of formal constitutional law doctrine to adopt and incorporate, and which elements to reject? This is a question frequently confronted by private universities. When a particular private university asks, for example, whether it should choose to adopt a view of freedom of speech equivalent to that which would bind a public university, or should instead strike out on its own, to either expand or contract freedom of speech on the private campus, how should it best organize its thinking on the matter? Should the options be treated as a "fixed menu" or "a la carte"? May the private university adopt "standard" First Amendment free speech norms for some matters, but dilute free speech norms for others and expand free speech norms for others still? Might the private university, for example, decide that it will grant professors the same academic freedom rights to speak out on controversial issues as its public university counterpart, but adopt codes for students that restrict hate speech more severely than a public university would be permitted to do, and grant to its student newspaper free speech rights more expansive than those that the student newspaper would enjoy on a state campus?

It will aid decision making if the private university thoughtfully considers its own values, identity, and mission in relation to the formal constitutional norms that bind the public university. The constitutional unconscious is now brought into the open to be used as a foil, a constitutional conscience. The private university enjoys the constitutional freedom to deviate from the constitutional norm. A private university with a conservative Christian charter, for example, may reach very different judgments on how to balance constitutional freedom of speech, freedom of religion, or equality principles against its other values than a public university would be allowed to reach. When a private university with no defined religious or ideological mission faces these issues, however, resolution of the question of when it is sound to deviate from constitutional norms may be more subtle. We do not typically think of Yale or Duke or Stanford as having an "identity" that sets them apart in distinctive ideologically or politically partisan terms. Yet these universities might well decide to reject a constitutional norm that would bind a public university neighbor, contracting or expanding constitutional norms below or above what the formal law requires on the public campus.

Thoughtful deliberation at such institutions is enhanced by engaging in a process that first determines what the constitutional rule would be if it *were* binding. The private university may then reflectively consider and articulate those elements of its mission or values that justify the decision to deviate from that norm, up or down, at that particular institution. This "justification process" will presumably include an assessment of the pluses or minuses of ordering "a la carte" instead of "fixed menu" from the constitutional plate, such as a weighing of the dangers of inconsistency or hypocrisy against the benefits of flexibility. It is critical to note here the relationship of the "law bending" problem to the "use of the constitutional unconscious as a foil" exercise.

In making *any* comparison it is helpful to begin with a baseline, a fixed target. If constitutional law frequently "bends" when it hits the campus, so that it is difficult to describe the baseline or fix the target, the comparison process becomes increasingly complex. There will be times when it is all but impossible to ascertain what the constitutional rule as applied to a campus setting actually is, because lawyers, legal scholars, and judges have different views of the matter, and no definitive judicial decision (such as a clear resolution from the Supreme Court) has yet to resolve the debate. In such cases, one person's perceived deviation from a constitutional norm would be another person's perceived constitutional conformity.

The "identity" issues posed here have focused on private universities. Is any parallel exercise permissible or appropriate for public universities? On certain levels it is obvious that public universities and private universities are not on equal footing when it comes to their relative freedom to shape their identities. Religion and race provide two examples. The Establishment Clause of the First Amendment clearly prevents any public university from defining itself in overtly religious terms. The University of Utah could not describe itself as dedicated to the principles of the Mormon faith; New York could not divide its many state universities by religion, offering different campuses for Catholics, Muslims, Protestants, or Jews.

Similarly, state universities may not define themselves in terms of race. In the aftermath of *Brown v. Board of Education* (1954)[16] we no longer allow state universities to offer programs for whites only. Similarly, two Supreme Court decisions make it highly unlikely that public universities today could successfully defend decisions to limit admission entirely to students of one gender. In *Mississippi University for Women v. Hogan* (1982),[17] the Court held that the females-only admissions policy at the

Mississippi University for Women violated the Equal Protection Clause, in a case in which an otherwise qualified male applicant to the nursing school was denied admission simply because he was a man. In *United States v. Virginia* (1996),[18] it was held that the males-only admissions policy of the Virginia Military Institute violated the Equal Protection Clause. The Court rejected the alternative proffered by Virginia: the opening of a parallel program at a small women's college about forty miles from VMI, Mary Baldwin College.

Yet private institutions remain free to be single-sex or even single-race. As illustrated by *Bob Jones University v. United States* (1983),[19] a private university may retain a constitutional right to refuse admission to black students, though it might be forced to forfeit its tax-exempt status (a form of government subsidy) as the price for doing so. The reverse would also be true: a historically black private university could choose to not admit whites, though it too might forfeit any eligibility for government benefits.

Setting aside religion, race, and probably gender, the principles that govern the constitutional prerogatives of public universities to fashion unique identities are not as well formed. Public universities certainly do come in many shapes and sizes, with many distinct missions, serving many different constituencies. There is no dispute that state and local governments have essentially unfettered freedom to allocate resources among different kinds of public higher education institutions, deciding for themselves the appropriate missions and resources for everything from their largest research institutions to their local community colleges. Nor is there any dispute over the prerogative of governments and their public institutions of higher education to establish institutional identities in traditional academic or programmatic terms—such as greater or lesser emphasis on research or teaching, or special excellence in science or the arts, or the education of teachers, or dominance in sports. The unsettled territory, however, involves more edgy movements toward a distinctive identity. Should a public university, either on its own or as a result of a mandate from a state legislature, adopt a political or ideological agenda, one that is identifiably conservative or liberal, Republican or Democratic? Or does the infiltration of political and ideological direction offend some combination of hard constitutional doctrine, softer constitutional values, and traditions of academic integrity? The resolutions of these questions are part of an ongoing conversation among those within the world of higher education and the many government officials, legislators, judges, and citizens who are also intensely invested in the shape of that world.

Religious Liberty

There is no aspect of the dichotomy between the public and private sphere that affects the world of higher education more intensely than the intersection of the public and private domains with religion. Public universities feel the force of the First Amendment's Establishment Clause in resisting any overtly religious identity as part of the official public persona of the university. Yet public universities feel the simultaneous force of the Free Exercise Clause of the First Amendment, requiring them to avoid discriminating against the personal free exercise of religion by members of the university community.

Private universities are not bound by either the Establishment Clause or the Free Exercise Clause in their relation to members of their own communities. Private universities, nevertheless, *are* affected by these clauses to the extent that those First Amendment freedoms constrain what the government may do to advance or hinder their mission.

American political and legal debates over the role of religion in public life might be divided into three strains of thought, representing three different positions on the "separation spectrum," three different judgments as to *how much* separation of church and state should be required under our constitutional system. The different strains of thought may be labeled "high separationists," "middle separationists," and "low separationists." These labels are intended to be nonjudgmental. They describe three distinct, intellectually and historically plausible interpretations of the extent to which religion should be kept out of our public rituals and symbols, and should not be provided government support for religious enterprises. Each of these positions has adherents among scholars, civic and religious leaders, and members of the United States Supreme Court. As with most other conflicts in our constitutional unconscious, each view also has its adherents on American campuses.

It is helpful to start with the common ground. "Religious freedom" is a widely shared American value.[20] Once issues of law and policy move past broad generalities to the resolution of specific, concrete controversies, however, society is often deeply conflicted over what religious freedom means. There is a relatively broad American consensus that individuals cannot be coerced to profess a religious belief or participate in a religious ritual against their will. Beyond general acceptance of this principle, however, the positions diverge dramatically.

High separationists will countenance no use of religious language or symbols by the government acting in its "governmental voice." Thus "In God We Trust" on currency should not be permitted, nor should the words "under God" be a part of the Pledge of Allegiance. To the high separationist, it does not matter if the practice has a historic pedigree. Prayers to begin legislative sessions are wrong even though they date back to the beginning of the republic. High separationists are likely to look askance at publicly financed Christmas trees, Easter egg hunts, and other holiday rituals connected to religious holidays.

Theoretically, an extreme high separationist might not permit religious displays, symbols, or language in any governmental enterprise. Such an individual might wish to banish religious art from public museums, prohibit the study of religions at universities, and ban publicly supported symphonies or choral groups from performing religious music.

But such extreme separationism is rarely, if ever, seriously advanced, and most high separationists will acknowledge that government may permit the study or performance of religious phenomena for academic, artistic, or musical purposes. The academic study of religions at state universities (such as in religious studies departments), the display of religious art in government museums, or the performance of religious music by government symphonies are thus accepted as undertaken for a secular academic or artistic purpose. A state university symphony and choir performing Handel's *Messiah* is sharing the music for its musical value, not as an expression of worship.[21]

High separationists are likely to be entirely opposed to the academic study of religion, the playing of religious music, and the display of religious art in the lower public school grades (and for very high separationists, not at any grade level below college), because of the danger that some children will interpret this as an endorsement of religion, or the risk that some teachers will take advantage of these exercises to proselytize.

Middle separationists will tolerate relatively modest invocations of general religious sentiments by government that are not sharply denominational. The middle separationist will not be offended by "In God We Trust" on currency, the inclusion of the phrase "under God" in the Pledge of Allegiance, or the opening of public events and ceremonies with a "nondenominational prayer." Middle separationists are particularly apt to support governmental religious language, symbols, or rituals if the practice has a long historic pedigree. Prayers to begin legislative sessions fall within this category.

Middle separationists are likely to have a number of nuanced positions. Invocations of religion are generally more permissible when directed at the general population than when directed at children or done within the public school setting. It will matter a great deal to middle separationists whether the practice is perceived as an endorsement of religion, particularly of one religion. Most middle separationists will deem such endorsements impermissible, and as jurists they will align with the high separationists to strike such measures down. Similarly, it will matter a great deal to middle separationists whether there is a coercive quality to the expression, and whether there is a "captive audience" that is forced to listen to it, particularly when those captive audience members are children.[22]

Low separationists are likely to find no constitutional fault in government displays of religious language or symbols, or government participation in religious rituals.[23] Short of an official recognition of one established church, or government coercion of professions of faith or belief, low separationists tend to treat such government displays as permissible.

The Supreme Court of the United States in *Rosenberger v. Rector and Visitors of the University of Virginia* (1995)[24] provides a powerful example of the competing tensions. The case involved the university founded by Thomas Jefferson, the University of Virginia. In *Rosenberger* the Court held that the University violated the First Amendment guarantee of freedom of speech when it denied funding to a Christian evangelical student group for the publication of its Christian magazine, *Wide Awake*. Each issue of *Wide Awake* sought to make good on the evangelical mission of the student group. A typical passage read as follows: "When you get to the final gate, the Lord will be handing out boarding passes, and He will examine your ticket. If in your lifetime, you did not request a seat on His Friendly Skies

Flyer by trusting Him and asking Him to be your pilot, then you will not be on His list of reserved seats (and the Lord will know you not)."[25]

Despite the overtly religious content of *Wide Awake*, and the plain fact that this content was being financed by money collected from all students at the University of Virginia under a mandatory fee system, the Supreme Court held that it did not unconstitutionally "establish religion" to fund the magazine, because nobody would believe that the message of the student group and *Wide Awake* was endorsed by the University. The Court held that to disqualify *Wide Awake* was to discriminate against it on the basis of its religious viewpoint.[26]

The presence of religious symbols on a public university campus poses another acutely difficult problem. Gene Nichol, the President of the College of William and Mary, another public university in Virginia, caused a huge uproar when he ordered the removal of an Anglican cross from permanent display on the altar of William and Mary's Wren Chapel, on the ground that removal of the cross would send a signal of greater inclusiveness toward non-Christian students, faculty, and staff.[27] The decision ignited a firestorm of protest, including a "save the cross" Internet campaign, the cancellation of a twelve-million-dollar pledge from a donor, and demands for Nichol's ouster. Shortly after Nichol made a second highly controversial decision, to permit "The Sex Workers Art Show" to be performed on the campus, he was informed by the William and Mary Board that his contract would not be renewed. Nichol resigned, effective immediately, with he and the Board disputing whether the ending of his presidency was caused by ideological or management issues.

The uncertainty of Establishment Clause cases in the context of religious symbols is most famously illustrated by the split decisions of two Supreme Court cases from 2005 dealing with displays of the Ten Commandments. In *McCreary County v. ACLU of Kentucky*,[28] and *Van Orden v. Perry*,[29] the Supreme Court reached different results in the two cases, holding that one Ten Commandments display violated the Establishment Clause and one did not, with Justice Stephen Breyer providing the critical swing vote in each case.

In the *McCreary County* case, two Kentucky county courthouses posted large, readily visible copies of the Ten Commandments. After the American Civil Liberties Union filed lawsuits to enjoin the displays, the two counties adopted resolutions calling for more extensive exhibits to accompany the Ten Commandments. The asserted purpose was to educate the public on the precedents that informed the creation of the legal codes of Kentucky. The ensuing displays included other historical documents containing religious references, such as the Declaration of Independence and the lyrics of "The Star-Spangled Banner," accompanied by statements about their historical and legal significance.

Justice Souter wrote the majority opinion in the *McCreary* case, holding that the Ten Commandments display violated the First Amendment. Justice Souter's opinion for the Court focused heavily on the purpose underlying the displays, finding the purpose religious, not secular. Invoking *Lemon v. Kurtzman* (1971),[30] the Court held that the government's *stated reasons* for undertaking a practice must be genuine, and not merely secondary to a religious objective.

The Court noted that it had previously held, in *Stone v. Graham* (1980),[31] that the Ten Commandments are an instrument of religion, and that the display of the Ten Commandments may be presumptively understood as meant to advance religion. *Stone*, however, dealt with the display of the Ten Commandments in public school classrooms as an isolated exhibition. The Ten Commandments, the Court noted, are "a central point of reference in the religious and moral history of Jews and Christians."[32] The Ten Commandments proclaim the existence of a monotheistic god and no other god, regulate details of religion (e.g., banning graven images, breaking the Sabbath, and taking the name of God in vain), and unmistakably rest such universally accepted prohibitions as murder and stealing on God's laws. The Court pointedly noted that displaying the *actual text* of the Ten Commandments is thus different from artistic or symbolic representations of stone tablets with ten roman numerals, which could be seen as alluding to a general notion of law, not a sectarian conception of faith. Where the text is set out, the Court held, the insistence of the religious message is hard to avoid. The majority opinion of Justice Souter in *McCreary* was joined by Justices Stevens, O'Connor, Ginsburg, and Breyer, with Chief Justice Rehnquist, and Justices Scalia, Thomas, and Kennedy dissenting.

The tables were then turned, however, in *Van Orden v. Perry*. Justice Breyer migrated to the other side, and now a five-justice majority comprising Chief Justice Rehnquist, and Justices Scalia, Thomas, Kennedy, and Breyer upheld the display of the Ten Commandments. *Van Orden* involved a Ten Commandments monument displayed on the grounds of the Texas State Capitol in Austin. There were twenty-one historical markers and seventeen monuments surrounding the building, including a six-foot-high monolith inscribed with the Ten Commandments, a gift to the state of Texas from the Fraternal Order of Eagles, a national social, civic, and patriotic organization.

Coming at the case from a "low separationist" perspective, the opinion of Chief Justice Rehnquist in *Van Orden* began by recognizing the strong role played by religion and religious traditions throughout the nation's history.[33] The Court maintained that its analysis should be driven by both the monument's nature and the nation's history. According to the Court, from at least 1789 there has been an unbroken history of official acknowledgment by all three branches of government of religion's role in American life. The display of the Ten Commandments by Texas was typical of such "acknowledgments," the Court reasoned, indistinguishable from representations of the Ten Commandments that appear in the United States Supreme Court building itself, as well as at the United States Capitol.

While conceding that the Ten Commandments are religious, the Court insisted that they have an undeniable historical meaning. Simply having religious content or promoting a message consistent with a religious doctrine, the Court observed, does not run afoul of the Establishment Clause. Distinguishing *Stone v. Graham*, the Court held that neither *Stone* itself nor subsequent opinions have indicated that the holding would extend beyond the context of public schools to a legislative chamber or capitol grounds. The placement of the Commandments monument on the Texas capitol grounds, the Court reasoned, is a far more passive use of those texts than was the case in *Stone*, where the text confronted elementary school students every day. Indeed, the Court noted somewhat slyly, the very person who challenged the constitutionality of the Texas monument apparently walked by the monument for years before bringing his suit. In this sense, the Court noted, the Texas display was unlike the graduation ceremony at issue in *Lee v. Weisman* (1992),[34] in which the Court struck down religious invocations at a high school graduation ceremony, largely out of captive audience concerns. Texas, the Court concluded, had treated its capitol grounds monuments as representing several strands in the state's political and legal history. The inclusion of the Ten Commandments monument in this group had a dual significance, the Court ruled, partaking of both religion and government, and the inclusion thus did not violate the Establishment Clause.

Justice Breyer, the key swing vote, held that this was a "difficult borderline case." No doctrinal test, he claimed, could operate as a substitute for the exercise of legal judgment. "That judgment is not a personal judgment," Justice Breyer insisted. Rather, Justice Breyer argued, as in all constitutional cases, it must reflect and remain faithful to the underlying purposes of the First Amendment's Religion Clauses. Despite the Ten Commandments' religious message, Justice Breyer reasoned, an inquiry into the context in which the text of the Ten Commandments is used demonstrates that the Commandments also convey a secular moral message about proper standards of social conduct and a message about the historic relation between those standards and the law. In the case before the Court, he stated, the circumstances surrounding the monument's placement on the Texas capitol grounds and its physical setting provided a strong, but not conclusive, indication that the Ten Commandments' use conveyed a predominantly secular message. The determinative factor for Justice Breyer, however, was that forty years had passed in which the monument's presence had not been challenged as illegal. Those forty years suggested to Justice Breyer that few individuals, whatever their belief systems, were likely to have understood the monument as a government effort to establish religion. Rather, he argued, the public visiting the Texas capitol grounds were more likely to have considered the religious aspect of the Ten Commandments' message as part of a broader moral and historical message reflective of a cultural heritage.

The Curious Right Not to Associate

The division between the public sphere and the private sphere is also illuminated by the curious constitutional right *not* to associate. This is a vector at which the values of equality, nondiscrimination, and respect for identity differences intersect with the values of freedom of expression, freedom of association, and autonomy. It is one of the most difficult and fascinating points of tension within the constitutional scheme, and a point of recurring tension within American universities. The assertion of the rights of association and non-association in the context of higher education often involves the rights of student groups.

Consider this problem: When a student organization refuses to grant membership to students who are not of a particular race, gender, or sexual orientation, in violation of a school or university policy forbidding such discrimination, does the student group's right of disassociation prevail over the institution's interest in prohibiting discrimination and promoting inclusion?

One of the most significant Supreme Court precedents germane to the issue is *Healy v. James* (1972).[35] In *Healy*, the President of Central Connecticut State College denied official recognition to a local chapter of Students for a Democratic Society, a group famous as a catalytic force for everything ranging from passive civil disobedience to more aggressive acts of seizure of campus buildings, vandalism, and arson, in pursuit of the SDS mission of protest against the Vietnam War and social injustice in the United States.

The decision of the Supreme Court, written by Justice Lewis Powell, was a somewhat mixed bag. "Among the rights protected by the First Amendment is the right of individuals to associate to further their personal beliefs," the Court proclaimed. "While the freedom of association is not explicitly set out in the Amendment, it has long been held to be implicit in the freedoms of speech, assembly, and petition." The Court then made it clear that denying recognition to a student group clearly impinged on that group's First Amendment freedoms by creating practical impediments to the group's ability to gather and function on campus.

In remanding the case to the district court, however, the Supreme Court in *Healy* did not stack all the cards with the students. The Court *also* directed the lower court with the admonition that if there was evidence to support the conclusion that the SDS chapter at Central Connecticut State posed "a substantial threat of material disruption," then the President's decision to deny official recognition to the SDS group should be affirmed. "Associational activities," the Court warned, "need not be tolerated where they infringe reasonable campus rules, interrupt classes, or substantially interfere with the opportunity of other students to obtain an education." What was critical, the Court explained, was that the decision against the student group be "directed at the organization's activities, rather than its philosophy." The Court admonished that "the critical line for First Amendment purposes must be drawn between advocacy, which is entitled to full protection, and action, which is not." The Court concluded with the somewhat opaque warning that "the benefits of participation in the internal life of the college community may be denied to any group that reserves the right to violate any valid campus rule with which it disagrees."

The delicate balance struck by Justice Powell's opinion in *Healy* does little to clearly resolve the question of whether a student group may be denied recognition for discriminating in its rules governing eligibility for membership. For in *Healy* the counterweights to the student group's rights of association were hefty—the university clearly had a powerful interest in preventing violence and property damage of the sort often associated in those times with the national SDS organization and movement. *Healy*, however, merely establishes the fact that student groups do possess associational rights protected by the First Amendment, which may in turn be regulated by colleges and universities to protect certain vital institutional interests. *Healy* did not address, let alone decide, the forced inclusion issue. In contrast, when a student group does not engage in violence but rather in exclusion, it runs afoul of powerful university values against discrimination. Yet unlike violence to persons and property, a university's values against discrimination are *inherently* contrary to the very right of disassociation itself. Disassociation *is* discrimination, and there's the rub.

A line of First Amendment freedom of association cases explore what might better be called the right of "disassociation": the right of a private group to decide for itself what members it will include or exclude. The exercise of the right of disassociation may be in direct conflict with laws that forbid discrimination. If a group refuses to allow women, Jews, African Americans, Roman Catholics, or gays and lesbians within its membership, for example, such exclusions may run afoul of laws that prohibit discrimination on such grounds. One person's freedom of disassociation is another person's act of discrimination.

This tension has been the subject of numerous judicial decisions, with mixed results. The conundrum is a difficult one. How are we to reconcile the profound commitment in the Declaration of Independence to the ideal that "all men are created equal" with our robust national conception of individual liberty, which includes the right to choose one's affiliations and associations? The Declaration's expression of equality was unheeded through the Civil War. In the modern United States, however, our commitment to equality and inclusion has powerfully evolved, as manifest in the Thirteenth Amendment's abolition of slavery, the Fourteenth Amendment's Equal Protection Clause, the prohibitions on discrimination in voting in the Fifteenth Amendment (race) and the Nineteenth Amendment (gender), in civil rights laws such as Title VI and Title VII of the Civil Rights Act of 1964,[36] the Fair Housing Act,[37] or Title IX of the Education Amendments of 1972,[38] and the many antidiscrimination laws and policies enacted by state and local governments and government agencies. These prohibitions on discrimination are in direct tension with the freedom to choose the persons with whom one will associate or not associate. When in conflict, which of these two values should prevail?

The Supreme Court case law on the subject is split along several divides. While the cases and articulated doctrines are not always crystalline in their clarity, they do in fact fall into a reasonably coherent pattern. Equality and nondiscrimination principles trump freedom of association principles in two vast *public* spheres of American life: in all aspects of governmental, political, and civic participation, and in all areas of the mainstream commercial and economic marketplace. In contrast, the right of free association, which includes the right to discriminate and exclude, trumps equality and nondiscrimination principles in those *private* realms of life that involve private organizations and relationships formed to express strong group beliefs or intimate personal relationships.

The phrase "expressive association quotient" captures this notion: as the measure of expressive and associational intensity of a group's bonds increase, so does the plausibility and persuasiveness of the group's asserted right to set itself apart from the antidiscrimination norms of the mainstream political and economic marketplace. The higher the group's expressive association quotient, the more likely the First Amendment right of freedom of association will trump the Fourteenth Amendment value of equality. The weaker and more diluted that quotient, the more likely the values of equality will trump the values of association.

In the context of American colleges and universities, we would thus ask whether the group that seeks to exclude others is one with strong ideological, religious, or political belief structures, in which the viability of the group itself as a cohesive organization would be sabotaged by an "open membership" rule that required the group to accept all comers, particularly as voting members. On the other hand, when the student group is intended to be broadly inclusive and representative of the student body, the case for exclusion is diluted, and must give way to values of equality and nondiscrimination.

When it comes to characteristics such as race, ethnicity, gender, or religion, we no longer tolerate discrimination and exclusion in voting, in qualification for elected or appointed office, in participation in juries, in public schools, or in any other exercise of participation in our political and civic institutions. Nor do we tolerate such discrimination in the mainstream channels of modern commerce—in employment, housing, transportation, lodging, dining, or the vast marketplace of products and services. When the operator of Ollie's Bar-B-Que restaurant in Birmingham, Alabama, or the operator of the Heart of Atlanta Motel in Georgia sought to exclude black patrons, the Supreme Court held—in *Katzenbach v. McClung* (1964),[39] and *Heart of Atlanta Motel v. United States* (1964),[40] respectively—that the prohibitions on discrimination in interstate commerce enacted in the Civil Rights Act reached into every small vein and capillary of the American stream of commerce.

At the opposite extreme, when the group that seeks to engage in discrimination is bound by intense ideological, political, or spiritual bonds, our equality principles yield to the superior force of freedom. Religious organizations provide a ready example of groups with a high expressive quotient, through which individuals bond in intense expressions of faith and community. We do not use our laws to force the Catholic Church to ordain women as priests. We do not force a church to accept members of racial groups that they refuse to accept, or to admit gays or lesbians if they choose not to do so. In the religion example, of course, there is no need to resort to the implied First Amendment right of association to find the textual constitutional authority that trumps equality values, for this right of "religious association" may be inferred as an element of the clause that protects the free exercise of religion. Indeed, the Constitution's strong focus on religion seems to contemplate the very associational divide described here. The Constitution explicitly prohibits the creation of any religious oath or qualification for office. Our government may not require an oath of allegiance to God as a precondition of public office, nor forbid a cleric from serving. (The Supreme Court in *McDaniel v. Paty* [1978][41] struck down a law that prohibited clerics from serving in the state legislature.)

Non-religious examples are also plentiful. For groups with high expressive association quotients that we despise as well as those we respect, freedom of association requires our laws to bend to the identity and autonomy of the group in deciding whom to admit or reject as members. The Ku Klux Klan, a group widely and justly despised by society, is guaranteed the right, under our First Amendment, to exist. Our Constitution does not empower us to ban the Klan. The Klan, which is largely organized around a belief structure of prejudice, may choose to decide for itself whom to admit as members. If the improbable black, Catholic, or Jew seeking Klan admission were to bring suit against a local Klan chapter, claiming its refusal to grant membership violated the civil rights laws, the Klan would prevail.

Even some large and vastly inclusive organizations may lay some claim to a right to discriminate as to the characteristics that define their core character. The two great modern political parties in the United States, the Republicans and the Democrats, comprise between them a large percentage of the national electorate. The Supreme Court has held, however, that those parties may exercise a degree of dominion over their membership and identity. The Court has ruled unconstitutional state laws that prohibit "closed primaries," laws that sought to prevent Republican or Democratic parties at the state level from deciding for themselves whether to allow persons not registered as Republicans or Democrats to "cross over" and vote in their primary elections. But the political party example also introduces the subtlety and complexity of the legal balance our society has struck between equality and liberty.

While there may be a constitutional right for Democrats to hold a "Democrats-only" primary, there are cases that have held that Democrats do not have a right to hold a "whites-only" primary. In the early days of the civil rights struggle, the Supreme Court in two consecutive decisions refused to allow the Texas Democratic Party and then the "Texas Jaybird Party" to exclude blacks from primary elections. The first decision, *Smith v. Allwright* (1944),[42] arose when Texas was still essentially a one-party state, so that whoever was nominated for statewide office in the Texas Democratic primary essentially was guaranteed that office in the general election. The Supreme Court ruled that the Texas Democratic Party's whites-only policy was, as a practical matter, "state action" for purposes of the Fourteenth and Fifteenth Amendments, in that it effectively excluded blacks from the Texas electoral process.

At least with regard to race, the Supreme Court placed the Texas Democratic Party on the "governmental political marketplace" side of the constitutional divide, and not on the private "expressive association" side. In the wake of this ruling, the undaunted Texas Democrats sought to game the system by creating a new, nominally "private" party, the Texas Jaybirds, which would hold its own political processes, for whites only, and nominate its Jaybird slate for the Texas Democratic primary. The Supreme Court in *Terry v. Adams* (1953)[43] also struck down this "party within a party" device, treating the Jaybirds as simply the reincarnation of the Texas Democratic Party. The Supreme Court refused to be fooled by this shell game, piercing the surface formalities to reach the authentic reality, which was the systematic disenfranchisement of black voters in Texas.

The learning of these cases, however, remains both subtle and supple. For we ought not extrapolate from the Texas decisions a general rule that no political party in the United States could ever organize along grounds that discriminate on the basis of race, gender, religion, or sexual orientation. While we do have the Congressional Black Caucus and the National Women's Political Caucus and legislative prayer breakfasts and various other forms of cohesive identity groups in American politics, the United States has yet to witness the rise of large and influential political parties that openly discriminate on the basis of race, gender, or religion. One may hope that we never do. It would probably be reading too much into our constitutional norms, however, to suggest that the formation of such identity parties could be entirely prohibited.

In cases where a private club or organization has a broad and diffuse membership, and the expressive content of the organization is relatively unfocused and amorphous, the Supreme Court has tended to subordinate the First Amendment disassociation right to the compelling governmental interest in the enforcement of civil rights laws. Conversely, when the discrimination that is practiced stems from some value or belief that is central to the group's identity, reason for existence, or belief structure, the enforcement of civil rights laws will be subordinated to the First Amendment.

The two most visible examples of equality trumping the First Amendment involve the Rotary Club and the Jaycees. In *Board of Directors of Rotary International v. Rotary Club of Duarte* (1987),[44] the Supreme Court held that a civil rights law prohibiting discrimination against women could be applied against the Rotary Club. In *Roberts v. United States Jaycees* (1984),[45] the Court reached the same conclusion in reference to the Jaycees. With regard to both the Rotary Club and the Jaycees, the expressive association quotient was relatively low. It would be an insult and an inaccuracy to say that the Rotary Club and the Jaycees didn't stand for anything or share any bonding. Of course they did—but what they stood for (values such as public service and civic participation) and how they bonded (lunches and service activities involving a broad spectrum of the community) were not so intense to offset the strong role each group played in the channels of commerce. Many people joined the Jaycees or the Rotary Club to make business, political, and community contacts, and to systematically exclude women from those large networking societies was the business and social equivalent of excluding blacks from the Texas primaries.

On the surface, one might have thought that the Rotary Clubs and the Jaycees should have won, for they were plainly "private groups." Much like the Texas Jaybirds, however, they lacked a strong expressive association quotient on anything *other than* their discriminatory mantras—"no blacks allowed" and "no women allowed." This both diminished the force of their free association claims and increased the importance to society of enforcing equality values. So too was there a disconnection between the identities and belief structures of the Jaycees and the Rotary Club and their practices of excluding women. The values traditionally associated with the two groups, such as public service, charity, community engagement, and internationalism, were not special "guy things." Unlike college fraternities and sororities, discussed later, which can make at least a colorable argument that their single-gender membership is central to their identity and purpose, the Jaycees and Rotary had a difficult time explaining how what they did or stood for was in any very intense sense gender-based.

If the Jaycees and the Rotary Club may be forced not to discriminate, however, what about the Boy Scouts, the Girl Scouts, the Young Men's or Young Women's Christian Associations, or the organizers of a private St. Patrick's Day parade?

In *Hurley v. Irish-American Gay, Lesbian, and Bisexual Group of Boston* (1995),[46] the Supreme Court held that the free association rights of the private organizers of a St. Patrick's Day parade in South Boston took priority over a Massachusetts civil rights law that prohibited discrimination on the basis of sexual orientation. The St. Patrick Day's parade in South Boston was not run by the city, but instead by a private group, which obtained a permit from the city to use city streets for the parade. This group refused to allow a gay, lesbian, and bisexual group of Irish Americans to march, which violated the Massachusetts law. The Supreme Court held that the parade organizers were engaged in activity that had a strong expressive associational element. It was the group's parade, and the group was entitled to bar others from raining on it. To permit the gays and lesbians to participate could have been interpreted as an expression of approval of the group's message, which was in direct contradiction to what the parade organizers wished and intended.

Similarly, in *Boy Scouts of America v. Dale* (2000),[47] the Supreme Court held that the Boy Scouts could exclude a gay person from the role of scoutmaster. As in the Massachusetts case, a New Jersey civil rights law prohibited discrimination on the basis of sexual orientation. The Supreme Court held that the disassociation rights of the Boy Scouts trumped the enforcement of the New Jersey law. The Court distinguished its earlier decisions in the *Rotary Club* and *Jaycees* cases, holding that the Boy Scouts had much more elaborate and intense systems of beliefs and practices than the Rotary Clubs or Jaycees, thereby upping their expressive association quotient.

The Supreme Court resolved the competing constitutional values posed by these decisions in *Christian Legal Society Chapter of the University of California–Hastings v. Martinez* (2010).[48] The case involved a challenge by the Christian Legal Society to a policy of the Hastings Law

School, a state institution in San Francisco that is part of the University of California system. The directive, which the Supreme Court described as an "all-comers" policy, imposed an open membership rule on all officially recognized student groups, requiring a student group to accept all comers as voting members even if those individuals disagree with the mission of the group. The Hastings chapter of the Christian Legal Society, a national organization, required its members to sign a "Statement of Faith" and to live their lives according to certain tenets, including the principle that sexual activity should not occur outside of marriage between a man and a woman. Consistent with this belief, the organization would not accept gay and lesbian members, placing it in conflict with the nondiscrimination policy that Hastings mandated for all its registered student organizations. The Christian Legal Society sought a waiver from Hastings, arguing that to force it to accept gay and lesbian members violated its First Amendment rights of freedom of speech and freedom of association, relying on decisions such as *Boy Scouts of America v. Dale.*

By a 5–4 vote, in a decision written by Justice Ruth Bader Ginsburg, the Supreme Court rejected the Christian Legal Society's claim, holding that the Hastings Law School could require adherence to its all-comers nondiscrimination policy as a condition of official recognition as a registered student organization. Justice Ginsburg's opinion for the Court held that the First Amendment rights of the Christian Legal Society had to be measured in light of the special deference that courts pay to the pedagogical judgment of public universities in making judgments germane to the educational process—judgments that are not limited to the classroom, but that extend to extracurricular activities as well. Exclusion, Justice Ginsburg reasoned, has two sides: "Hastings, caught in the crossfire between a group's desire to exclude and students' demand for equal access, may reasonably draw a line in the sand permitting *all* organizations to express what they wish but *no* group to discriminate in membership."[49]

The Court observed that just as Hastings would not allow its professors to teach only classes to those students who adhere to certain beliefs, it could reach the educational judgment that it should not grant official status to student groups that engage in similar discrimination. Moreover, the Court reasoned, it would be difficult for Hastings to police student groups to determine which forms of discrimination were truly belief-based, and which were mere cover for discrimination. The Court held that the Hastings Law School was entitled to reach the judgment that an all-comers policy would advance the valid educational goals of encouraging tolerance, conflict-resolutions skills, and a readiness to find common ground. Finally, the Court reasoned, the nondiscrimination policy followed by the Hastings Law School was consistent with the broader nondiscrimination policies of the state of California. Hastings, the Court reasoned, could make the judgment that it would not subsidize discrimination that ran contrary to the state's declared public policies.

The Court in *Christian Legal Society* made much of the fact that the Hastings policy did not force the organization to accept gay and lesbian members; rather, it merely conditioned status as a registered student organization on such acceptance. The Christian Legal Society could still exist, and could even gain access to school facilities and enjoy the use of chalkboards and bulletin boards to advertise Society events. All the Hastings rule did was prevent the group from receiving the other benefits that came with recognition as an official registered student organization, such as eligibility for financial assistance through the funds generated by required student fees, use of the school's name and logo, participation in a student organization fair, access to the school's official student services newsletter, and use of the school's e-mail service with an official Hastings organizational e-mail address. As the Court saw the matter, the Christian Legal Society could remain true to its principles if it chose, and reject these fringe benefits of official recognition, but still function within the law school as an unofficial student organization; or it could accept the benefits and agree to adhere to the Hastings policy.

Indeed, the Court appeared to concede that the First Amendment rights of the Christian Legal Society would have been violated if the government had forced the Society to accept gay and lesbian members against its will, through an outright criminal prohibition. The Court noted, however, that "in diverse contexts, our decisions have distinguished between policies that require action and those that withhold benefits." A less restrictive First Amendment standard applied, to the Hastings registered student organization program, the Court reasoned, because through it Hastings was "dangling the carrot of subsidy, not wielding the stick of prohibition."[50]

This principle articulated by Justice Ginsburg in *Christian Legal Society*, that it mattered whether the Hastings Law School was using a carrot instead of a stick, conjured one of the oldest and most vexing conundrums of constitutional law, the distinction between "rights" and "privileges." It is a distinction that constantly surfaces in the context of American universities. As demonstrated by *Christian Legal Society*, student groups may have a constitutional right to exclude others from membership, but they do not necessarily have a constitutional right to engage in such exclusion and still receive university subsidies. In turn, universities may have a constitutional right to pursue their own policies, but it does not necessarily follow that they have a constitutional right to pursue those policies and still receive government funds conditioned on adherence to alternative policies. In these and myriad other contexts in higher education, it may matter a great deal whether the device used by government is a "persuader" or an "enforcer," a carrot or a stick. It is to these issues that we now turn.

4

Rights and Privileges

The petitioner may have a constitutional right to talk politics, but he has no constitutional right to be a policeman.
—Justice Oliver Wendell Holmes, writing for the Supreme Judicial Court of Massachusetts in *McAuliffe v. City of New Bedford* (1892)

For at least a quarter-century, this Court has made clear that even though a person has no "right" to a valuable governmental benefit, and even though the government may deny him the benefit for any number of reasons, there are some reasons upon which the government may not rely. It may not deny a benefit to a person on a basis that infringes his constitutionally protected interests—especially, his interest in freedom of speech. For if the government could deny a benefit to a person because of his constitutionally protected speech or associations, his exercise of those freedoms would in effect be penalized and inhibited.
—Justice Potter Stewart, writing for the Court in *Perry v. Sindermann* (1972)

Holmes and the Right-Privilege Distinction

One of the principal intellectual architects of the distinction between rights and privileges was Justice Oliver Wendell Holmes. In 1892, when he was still a state Supreme Court Justice on the Supreme Judicial Court of Massachusetts, Justice Holmes was faced with a case involving an Irish constable from New Bedford, Massachusetts, named John McAuliffe, who was fired for talking politics while walking his beat. McAuliffe argued that his dismissal violated the First Amendment. Justice Holmes disagreed. He tossed out McAuliffe's free speech claim in *McAuliffe v. City of New Bedford* (1892) with the gruff observation that "the petitioner may have a constitutional right to talk politics, but he has no constitutional right to be a policeman."[1]

As Justice Holmes saw the matter, McAuliffe signed on to keep his mouth shut when he signed on to be a policeman. No one forced him to take the job. In almost any job, Holmes noted, the employee signs away certain freedoms as a condition of employment, including freedom of speech. As Holmes put it, there are "few employments for hire in which the servant does not agree to suspend his constitutional rights of free speech as well as of idleness by the implied terms of his contract." Holmes had a ruthlessly logical mind, and it was difficult to quarrel with his ruthless logic: A person has a constitutional right to sit around and do nothing, and a person has a constitutional right to speak his or her mind. When a person takes a job, however, the standard understanding is that one usually must agree to do the work while working and not spend the day jabbering, in defiance of the boss's rules. This is true whether the boss is a private business or the government. McAuliffe, Holmes wrote, was like any other employee: "He takes the employment on the terms which are offered him."

The Holmes logic, if extended to the modern public university, would allow public universities to decide for themselves how much "academic freedom" to grant administrators, professors, and students. The university president may have a constitutional right to talk politics, but he or she has no constitutional right to be a university president. The professor may have a constitutional right to talk politics, but no constitutional right to be a professor. Even the student, though not an employee—like Officer McAuliffe, the university president, or the professor—is nevertheless a contractor with the university. When the student accepts the university's contractual offer of admission, and agrees to pay the contractual tuition, board, and fees, the student also accepts all the fine print that comes with the deal. This may include certain restrictions on liberties that the student would otherwise enjoy, such as restrictions on freedom of speech.

In another Holmes decision written while he was on the Massachusetts Supreme Judicial Court, *Commonwealth v. Davis*,[2] Holmes upheld an ordinance that prohibited public speaking in a municipal park without a permit from the mayor. Holmes reasoned that because the city owned the park, it could establish rules for use of the park just as if it were a private landlord. The city, as Holmes saw it, could forbid all public speaking in its parks. Since the city held the greater power to ban all speeches in the park, it logically also held the lesser power to allow public speaking, but on such conditions as the city might prescribe, such as requiring advance permission from the mayor. Holmes did not view this as a restriction on Mr. Davis's freedom of speech. As Holmes saw it, Mr. Davis was perfectly free to speak to his heart's content. He was not free, however, to enter a public park and speak without permission from the city landlord. The decision of Justice Holmes on the Massachusetts Supreme Judicial Court was appealed to the Supreme Court of the United States, which affirmed the decision of Holmes, adopting the landlord analogy that Holmes had employed. "For the legislature absolutely or conditionally to forbid public speaking in a highway or public park," the Court stated, "is no more an infringement of the rights of a member of the public than for an owner of a private house to forbid it in his house."

Again, it is easy to see the potential power of Holmes's line of right versus privilege thinking if pressed to the service of the modern public university. Students and faculty may have a right to speak their minds, but they have no right to speak their minds on university property. The university may require permission for students or faculty before they pass out leaflets, carry signs, or make speeches on the campus green, just as a landlord (such as a private shopping mall owner) might require such permission on private property. The Holmes logic has a certain pristine appeal. A contract is a contract, unencumbered by moral baggage, and a court's job is to enforce the contract, period, and not get into questions of whether the bargain was "fair."

The Right-Privilege Distinction and Higher Education

The right-privilege distinction was visibly at work in the context of higher education in *Hamilton v. Regents of the University of California* (1934).[3] Two applicants to the University of California sought an exemption from a California law that required all University students to take a course in military science and training. The students were members of a religious denomination, the Southern California Conference of the Methodist Episcopal Church, which had adopted a pacifist religious position opposed to all war. The students thus sought to be excused from the military science academic obligation on the grounds that they were conscientious objectors. Their petition was refused, thereby preventing them from attending the University of California. The Supreme Court was unsympathetic, rejecting the argument advanced by the students that the rule violated their constitutional rights. Invoking the language of the right-privilege distinction, the Court observed that the "'privilege' of attending the University as a student comes not from federal sources but is given by the state."

The Court did not attempt to analyze the *Hamilton* case under the Religion Clauses—this was only 1934 and virtually all of what is now the densely developed body of law dealing with freedom of religion had yet to evolve. The Court instead approached the question as to whether the students had been denied any element of "liberty" protected by the Due Process Clause. The Court saw no such denial. While undoubtedly, the Court conceded, the students did possess the liberty to entertain the beliefs that drove their objections to military training, this did not mean they were entitled to a publicly funded education by the state of California on terms of their own choosing. It did not matter that the students might not be able to afford any other college education. California was not "drafting" them and forcing them into military training. Rather, the Court reasoned, California was merely imposing its own educational rules for attendance at its own universities. The students were "seeking education offered by the state and at the same time insisting that they be excluded from the prescribed course solely upon grounds of their religious beliefs and conscientious objections to war, preparation for war, and military education."

The students' theory, that they were constitutionally entitled to a conscientious objectors exemption, was untenable, the Court held. The state of California, like the federal government, was entitled to take measures "to preserve itself in adequate strength to maintain peace and order and to assure the just enforcement of law. And every citizen owes the reciprocal duty, according to his capacity, to support and defend government against all enemies." If the students were not willing to follow the generally prescribed curriculum, it was within the purview of the state to deny them admission.

More recently, Judge Michael Luttig, a prominent conservative legal intellectual, used this line of thinking in the opinion he wrote in *Urofsky v. Gilmore* (2000),[4] while on the United States Court of Appeals for the Fourth Circuit. (Judge Luttig since resigned from the Court of Appeals to become General Counsel of the Boeing Company.) A group of state university professors in Virginia brought a suit against the state of Virginia, challenging a rule that prohibited all state employees, including state university professors, from accessing sexually explicit materials on their state-owned computers without prior permission from their department supervisors. The professors claimed the restriction violated the First Amendment. The requirement of advance permission was a kind of digital-age version of the permission-to-speak-in-the-park dispute that Holmes had faced in the old *Commonwealth v. Davis* case. If "academic freedom" is understood as a freedom that exists *over and above* the freedom of speech that all citizens enjoy under the First Amendment, then it was Judge Luttig's view that the decision of a state to grant or not grant state professors "academic freedom" was entirely a matter of contract and free-market economics. In the competition for first-rate professors, both public and private universities are under economic pressures to grant prospective professors any number of benefits, from high salaries to tuition waivers for their kids to free parking to academic freedom. The "academic freedom" of a professor to use his or her university computer for any purpose, without running to procure special permission from the dean, was just like any other job benefit. In that sense, different professors might value it more or less highly, and be more or less willing to trade it for other benefits. Some professors might be willing to sacrifice a measure of academic freedom for a higher salary or better health benefits, and others might not.

This argument is essentially a reprise of the argument of Oliver Wendell Holmes. Indeed, the professor may always access the Internet from his or her own home, on the his or her own computer. But in choosing to accept a job with the government of Virginia, the argument goes, the professor must accept the terms Virginia chooses to impose on its employees. The professor who does not like it may move to another state or to a private university with no such restrictions. For, as Holmes admonished, "in order to enter into most of the relations of life people have to give up some of their Constitutional rights."

Inroads on Right-Privilege: Unconstitutional Conditions

The Holmes view has not prevailed over time—at least not in pristine form. The doctrine of "unconstitutional conditions" has evolved as a *partial* restraint on the right-privilege argument. If Holmes's right-privilege distinction were accepted as sound, then the solutions to all free speech issues involving governmental affiliation would be relatively effortless. In contemporary times, free speech disputes constantly arise in the context of conditions attached to public benefits. Conscientious and consistent application of the right-privilege distinction would make these disputes easy to resolve: the government would always win. But if the government is not always to win in challenges to the conditions it has attached to affiliation with governmental programs, somehow holes must be punched in the seemingly seamless logic of the right-privilege distinction. Could Holmes be wrong?

In *Goldberg v. Kelly* (1970),[5] the Court held that a welfare recipient was entitled to a hearing and an opportunity to be heard before the state can terminate welfare benefits. *Goldberg* was a decision influenced in part by the writings of Professor Charles Reich, who had written *The Greening of America*[6] and an influential *Yale Law Journal* article titled "The New Property."[7] Reich's thesis was that public benefits had emerged as a major source of wealth in contemporary American society—a new form of "property." Public education; welfare benefits; programs such as Medicaid, Medicare, and social security; and public jobs, franchises, contracts, or licenses might all be conceived as occupying a position in the lives of Americans every bit as central to their pursuit of happiness as traditional real estate and personal property in older, simpler times. In "The New Property," Reich wrote that "forms of largess . . . must be deemed to be held as of right," and that like "property, such largess could be governed by a system of regulation plus civil or criminal sanctions, rather than a system based upon denial, suspension and revocation."[8] This "new property," Reich argued, should be treated as "vested."

In *Goldberg*, through an opinion by Justice William Brennan, the Supreme Court seemed persuaded by Reich's reasoning. But the theory underlying the notion that government largess should be understood as a "vested right" of some sort was in powerful tension with a basic understanding of the nature of rights and property. While it certainly might be true that government could, through legal enactment or contractual arrangement, create vested interests in certain public benefits, the Supreme Court was understandably chary of reading the Constitution as if it *required* government to create such vested entitlements. Indeed, American constitutional law had traditionally eschewed the notion that *substantive* interests, such as employment, medical care, education, or housing, were "civil rights" or "civil liberties" in an American constitutional sense. These substantive interests might work their way through the political marketplace into laws passed that create social security or universal health care, and they might achieve legal protection through the contractual bargains struck in the economic marketplace, but they do not come directly from the Constitution. In two important decisions involving higher education, *Board of Regents v. Roth* (1972)[9] and *Perry v. Sindermann* (1972),[10] the Supreme Court supplied a complicated answer to this problem.

The *Roth* case involved a dismissal of an assistant professor at what was then called Wisconsin State University–Oshkosh. Professor Roth had been hired for only a one-year term and was not tenured. His contract was not renewed. Under the University's rules, it was not required to give a reason for a decision not to renew the contract of an untenured faculty member. Roth sued under two theories. First, he argued, the failure of Wisconsin State to provide him with any hearing, explanation, opportunity to be heard, or other process violated the Due Process Clause. Second, he argued, the real reason he had been fired was in retaliation for certain statements he had made critical of the Wisconsin State administration, allegedly violating his free speech rights.

The case ultimately reached the Supreme Court of the United States, though the free speech issue was not adjudicated in the Supreme Court. Roth argued, however, that his dismissal was procedurally flawed, regardless of whether he could prove that his free speech rights were violated. The Supreme Court, in an opinion by Justice Potter Stewart, rejected

Roth's claim. The key issue, Justice Stewart reasoned, was whether Roth's interest in maintaining his job at the University was "property" of the sort protected by the Due Process Clause. While the Due Process Clause protects property, Justice Stewart held, the Constitution does not *define* or even *create* property. The legal entity we know as "property," he reasoned, is essentially a creature of *state* law.

Is a job "property"? That depends, the Court in *Roth* held, on whether state law, through statute, regulation, or contractual arrangements, creates some hard, legally enforceable *entitlement* to the job. The mere subjective hope of the employee that employment will continue is not enough. For the job to be "property" it had to be in some sense solidly vested. Roth, an untenured professor, had no such legal anchor. Wisconsin law gave university officials "unfettered discretion" to renew or not renew the contract of an untenured professor. This was not "property," the Court held, and therefore Roth was not entitled to any "due process of law" whatsoever.

The tough-minded decision in *Roth* was tempered in part by a companion case, *Perry v. Sindermann*. Robert Sindermann, like Roth, brought suit claiming violation of his free speech and due process rights when his teaching contract was not renewed. Sindermann had taught in the Texas system of higher education for ten years. After two years at the University of Texas and four years at San Antonio Junior College, he was hired as a professor of government and social science at Odessa Junior College. After four successive one-year contracts at Odessa, his contract was not renewed, allegedly for insubordination. Sindermann maintained that he had been fired because he had given legislative testimony and made other public statements critical of the Texas Board of Regents. The Supreme Court, in another opinion written by Justice Stewart, held that these statements qualified as speech on issues of public concern, and that Sindermann was entitled to attempt to prove that his free speech rights were thus violated, remanding that part of Sindermann's claim back to the lower courts for trial.

Odessa Junior College had not adopted a formal tenure system, and given the holding in *Roth*, one might have thought that Sindermann's second claim, that he had been denied "life, liberty, or property, without due process of law," would thus be doomed. Sindermann, however, had worked at the college for many years, and could point to an alleged custom, a kind of "de facto tenure," which allegedly rose to the level of an implied agreement that employment would be ongoing in the absence of misconduct or malfeasance. As Justice Stewart described Sindermann's claim: "The respondent's allegations—which we must construe most favorably to the respondent at this stage of the litigation—do raise a genuine issue as to his interest in continued employment at Odessa Junior College. He alleged that this interest, though not secured by a formal contractual tenure provision, was secured by a no less binding understanding fostered by the college administration. In particular, the respondent alleged that the college had a de facto tenure program, and that he had tenure under that program."[11] Sindermann further reinforced his argument by claiming that he and other colleagues had legitimately relied on an unusual provision that had been in the college's official Faculty Guide for many years, which stated: "Teacher Tenure: Odessa College has no tenure system. The Administration of the College *wishes the faculty member to feel that he has permanent tenure* as long as his teaching services are satisfactory and as long as he displays a cooperative attitude toward his co-workers and his superiors, and as long as he is happy in his work."[12]

If it looks like tenure, and it feels like tenure, perhaps it *is* tenure. Sindermann could also point to additional guidelines promulgated by the Coordinating Board of the Texas College and University System, which provided that a person who had been employed as a teacher in the state college and university system for seven years or more had some form of job tenure. Against this backdrop, the Supreme Court appeared to leaven the holding in *Roth*, adding a degree of flexibility to the analysis by warning that "interests subject to procedural due process protection are not limited by a few rigid, technical forms." Justice Stewart wrote that "a person's interest in a benefit is a 'property' interest for due process purposes if there are such rules or mutually explicit understandings that support his claim of entitlement." Drawing a comparison to the concept of "implied contracts," Justice Stewart held that "there may be an unwritten 'common law' in a particular university that certain employees shall have the equivalent of tenure." Justice Stewart explicitly rejected the simplistic notion that the government had unfettered power to place any conditions it pleased on its dispersal of largess, explaining that even when a person has no right to a government benefit, the Constitution still imposes restraints on the reasons the government may invoke in denying the person that benefit.

This principle articulated in *Perry*, expressing what has come to be known as the doctrine of unconstitutional conditions, is driven by the rationale that, given the enormous leverage that modern governments possess over the various forms of public benefits that we historically regard as "privileges," we must devise constitutional principles that deter the government from using that leverage in a manner that effectively squelches constitutional rights. The Supreme Court in modern times has applied the doctrine in many circumstances to defeat application of the right-privilege distinction. Teachers may not be compelled to relinquish First Amendment rights that, in the words of the Supreme Court in *Arnett v. Kennedy* (1974),[13] "they would otherwise enjoy as citizens to comment on matters of public interest in connection with the operation of the public schools in which they work."[14] A rank-and-file government employee may not be discharged simply because he or she is not a member of the political party currently in power. Welfare recipients and persons seeking unemployment compensation may not be forced to surrender First Amendment rights as a condition of the receipt of their benefits.

In the context of colleges and universities, what the doctrine of unconstitutional conditions teaches is that professors and students (and perhaps, to lesser degree, some university administrators) may not be subjected to *automatic* forfeiture of their constitutional rights as a condition of affiliation with the university. A state college or university may not say, in absolute terms, that when you accept a position here, you forfeit all your First Amendment rights—love it or leave it. By the same token, however, the doctrine of unconstitutional conditions *does not mean* that the same free speech rights that apply in the general marketplace apply with undiminished force in all places and contexts within the university. As an employer there may be instances in which regulation of speech is justified by the university's need to conduct its business as an employer in a manner consistent with civil rights laws, which require a working environment free from discrimination, in which individuals are treated with elemental human dignity. As an educator, a university may justify some regulation of speech to ensure that faculty, students, and administrators conform to norms of professionalism and academic integrity. We might think of entry into a college or university community as an entry into a special "social compact" of sorts, one more specialized than the broad social compact that defines our relationships to one another as citizens.

Conditions on a University's Receipt of Government Money

The right-privilege distinction is also central to one of the principal vehicles by which governments at the federal and state level seek to force universities and colleges to conform to norms imposed by the government. While *private* universities undoubtedly enjoy academic freedom to fashion their own educational policies, governments may use the fulcrum of financial assistance to force institutions to bend their academic judgments to the government's will. In the logic of Holmes's right-privilege distinction, the university is always free to reject the offer by telling the government to keep its money.

At the federal level, the power of the purse has been used as a vehicle to enforce norms of equality, as with Title IX. In *Grove City College v. Bell* (1984),[15] the Supreme Court held that the constitutional rights of Grove City College, a private college, were not violated by provisions of Title IX, which withheld federal funds from colleges that violated the legislation's anti-gender-discrimination provisions. Grove City was a private, coeducational liberal arts college, and it sought to preserve its institutional autonomy by taking a strong position against the receipt of any state or federal government assistance, generally refusing to accept governmental grants or to participate in most federal student assistance programs.[16] Grove City did, however, enroll a large number of students who received federal assistance through Basic Educational Opportunity Grants, now known as Pell Grants, which were awarded to students, not institutions. The federal Department of Education took the position that because there were Grove City students receiving federal financial aid, Grove City was required by federal law to sign an "assurance" that it complied with all provisions of Title IX prohibiting sex discrimination. Grove City refused to sign this assurance. It does not appear that Grove City would have been in violation of Title IX—that is to say, it does not appear that Grove City's refusal to sign was grounded in any defensive concern that it was in fact guilty of sex discrimination. Rather, for Grove City it was the principle of institutional autonomy from government interference that animated its refusal to sign the government form. Grove City argued that these grants to students did not constitute grants to Grove City itself, but were more in the nature of general welfare distributions, such as food stamps, social security payments, or other forms of welfare to low-income families. The college thus asserted that it could not be forced to adhere to the requirements of Title IX, because as an institution it was not receiving federal financial assistance.

The Supreme Court rejected Grove City's argument, reasoning that the financial aid to Grove City's individual students was economically indistinguishable from aid to Grove City as an institution, and that Congress intended for Title IX to be triggered by a private college's enrollment of students who received federal financial aid. More significantly, however, the Supreme Court also rebuffed Grove City's attempt to resist Title IX on constitutional grounds. Grove City argued that its institutional First Amendment rights—its institutional academic freedom, if you will—was violated by the imposition of Title IX norms upon it. Grove City had jealously guarded its institutional autonomy, and claimed it was unconstitutional for the federal government to encroach on that autonomy by virtue of the fact that Grove City students received federal financial aid. In a straightforward application of the right-privilege distinction, the Supreme Court stated bluntly that "Congress is free to attach reasonable and unambiguous conditions to federal financial assistance that educational institutions are not obligated to accept."[17] This was a tough-minded assertion by the Court, for obviously Grove City would be at a severe competitive disadvantage if it could not enroll students who received federal aid. The Court was unfazed by this, stating that "Grove City may terminate its participation in the BEOG program" if it wished to avoid Title IX, and the "students may take their BEOGs elsewhere or attend Grove City without federal financial assistance."[18] Its ruling, the Court stated adamantly, "infringes no First Amendment rights of Grove City or its students."[19]

But the power of the purse may also be used to enforce governmental interests not as popular on campuses as Title IX. In *Rumsfeld v. Forum for Academic and Institutional Rights Inc.* (2006),[20] the Supreme Court considered a challenge brought by a group of American law professors and law schools called the Forum for Academic and Institutional Rights (FAIR) to the "Solomon Amendment."[21] The Solomon Amendment, an amendment to the federal statute dealing with the ROTC program, was enacted by Congress 1996 in response to restrictions imposed by law schools on the access of military recruiters to their students because of those institutions' disagreement with the government's "don't ask, don't tell" policy on gays and lesbians in the military. Congress barred a college or university from receiving certain federal funding if it prohibited military recruiters from gaining access to campuses in a manner equivalent to that granted to other employment recruiters.

The Supreme Court, in a unanimous 8–0 decision written by Chief Justice Roberts, rejected the argument advanced by the law professors and law schools that the Solomon Amendment violated their free speech or free association rights under the First Amendment.(Justice Samuel Alito did not participate in the case.) The Court emphasized the fundamental fact that the "Solomon Amendment neither limits what law schools may say nor requires them to say anything." Law schools, the Court reasoned, remained free under the statute to express whatever views they may have on the military's congressionally mandated employment policy, all the while retaining eligibility for federal funds. The Court held that the principle that the First Amendment prohibits the government from telling people what they must say—established in such landmark cases as *West Virginia State Board of Education v. Barnette* (1943)[22] (striking down a law requiring schoolchildren to recite the Pledge of Allegiance and to salute the flag) and *Wooley v. Maynard* (1977)[23] (holding unconstitutional a law that required New Hampshire motorists to display the state motto— "Live Free or Die"—on their license plates)—simply was not infringed in any serious way by the Solomon Amendment. While recruiting assistance provided by the schools often includes elements of speech, such as e-mails or notices on bulletin boards, this sort of recruiting assistance was nonetheless "a far cry from the compelled speech in *Barnette* and *Wooley*." The Solomon Amendment, unlike the laws at issue in *Barnette* or *Wooley*, did not dictate the content of speech at all. The Court noted that "it has never been deemed an abridgment of freedom of speech or press to make a course of conduct illegal merely because the conduct was in part initiated, evidenced, or carried out by means of language, either spoken, written, or printed." As the Court noted, Congress may prohibit employers from discriminating in hiring on the basis of race: "The fact that this will require an employer to take down a sign reading 'White Applicants Only' hardly means that the law should be analyzed as one regulating the employer's speech rather than conduct." Compelling a law school that sends scheduling e-mails for other recruiters to also send one for a military recruiter, the Court held, "is simply not the same as forcing a student to pledge allegiance, or forcing a Jehovah's Witness to display the motto 'Live Free or Die,' and it trivializes the freedom protected in *Barnette* and *Wooley* to suggest that it is."

The Supreme Court also held that the Solomon Amendment did not violate the First Amendment principle that in some circumstances limits the government's ability to force one speaker to host or accommodate another speaker's message. In all such prior cases, the Court reasoned, the complaining speaker's own message was affected by the speech it was forced to accommodate. In contrast, accommodating the military's message did not affect the law schools' speech, because the schools are not speaking when they host interviews and recruiting receptions. Unlike a parade, the Court held, a law school's decision to allow recruiters on campus is not inherently expressive. "A law school's recruiting services lack the expressive quality of a parade, a newsletter, or the editorial page of a newspaper; its accommodation of a military recruiter's message is not compelled speech because the accommodation does not sufficiently interfere with any message of the school."

The Supreme Court dismissed the argument of the law schools that if they treat military and nonmilitary recruiters alike, they could be viewed as sending the incorrect message that they see nothing wrong with the military's policies. Such an argument had previously been rejected in *Pruneyard Shopping Center v. Robins* (1980),[24] in which the Court upheld a state law requiring a shopping center owner to allow certain expressive activities by others on its property, holding that there was little likelihood that the views of those engaging in the expressive activities would be identified with the owner, who remained free to disassociate himself from those views. "Nothing about recruiting suggests that law schools agree with any speech by recruiters," the Court insisted, "and nothing in the Solomon Amendment restricts what the law schools may say about the military's policies." The Court noted that it had held that high school students can appreciate the difference between speech by school sponsors and speech the school permits because legally required to do so, pursuant to an equal access policy, and that surely law students could make these distinctions as well.

The Supreme Court in *FAIR* also held that the Solomon Amendment did not violate law schools' right of freedom of association, for which claim the law schools relied on *Boy Scouts of America v. Dale* (2000).[25] As discussed in chapter 3, in *Dale* the Court upheld the right of the Boy Scouts to exclude gay scoutmasters. The right of freedom of association includes a right of disassociation—a right to exclude as well as to include. The law schools reasoned that they had a right to decide with whom they would associate, and that this right was being violated when they were forced to host military recruiters, just as it was when the Boy Scouts were forced to accept gay scoutmasters. There were huge flaws in this analogy, and the Supreme Court saw right through them. In *Dale*, the Boy Scouts were being forced to accept a member of the group—indeed, a leader of the group. But employers who recruit in a law school do not become members of the law school, much less leaders of those institutions. Perhaps if Congress had attempted to dictate who the law school dean would be, that would have resembled dictating a Scout troop's choice of scoutmaster. But as the Supreme Court pointed out, nothing in the Solomon Amendment prevented law students, law professors, or even law schools from associating with one another to express their disagreement with the "don't ask, don't tell" policy, and nothing forced them to include military recruiters as *insiders* or *members* of the law school community: "Recruiters are, by definition, outsiders who come onto campus for the limited purpose of trying to hire students—not to become members of the school's expressive association."[26]

There is an important parallel worth noting between the Supreme Court's treatment of law schools in *Rumsfeld v. FAIR* and its treatment of law schools in *Christian Legal Society v. Martinez*, discussed in chapter 3. Both involved law school policies designed to prohibit discrimination against gays and lesbians. In *Christian Legal Society*, the antidiscrimination policy prevailed, while in *Rumsfeld* it did not. The critical parallel is that in both cases, the winning side used a carrot and not a stick; in both cases, the entity controlling the purse strings won. After *Rumsfeld*, law schools remained free to deny access to military recruiters as a means of expressing disagreement with the military's policies regarding gays and lesbians, but at the price of giving up receipt of federal funds. In *Christian Legal Society*, student groups remained free to exclude gays and lesbians, but at the price of giving up university funds. In neither case did the Supreme Court heavily emphasize the distinction between rights and privileges, though the Court in *Christian Legal Society* was more open in invoking the distinction between the carrot and stick in explaining why a less rigorous First Amendment standard applied. There is no question, however, that the distinction between rights and privileges played an important role in both cases and, more than any other principle of constitutional law, best accounts for the results both cases reached.

If *Rumsfeld v. FAIR* was a sound rejection of the free speech and free association arguments advanced by law schools, a sequel to the case, brought by the Yale Law School faculty, was an equally strong rejection of the notion that the First Amendment includes a distinct right of academic freedom. That sequel was *Burt v. Gates* (2007),[27] decided by the United States Court of Appeals for the Second Circuit. In *Burt*, members of the Yale Law School faculty argued that the Supreme Court's decision in *FAIR* did not resolve the question of whether the Solomon Amendment violated the constitutional academic freedom rights of the faculty members. The Yale faculty members maintained that while the Supreme Court decision in *FAIR* had clearly held that the Solomon Amendment did not violate any of the free speech or free association rights of law school faculty members or law schools, the law school faculty members nonetheless possessed a distinct constitutional right of academic freedom, which was not adjudicated in *FAIR*. That distinct academic freedom right, they argued, was violated by the Solomon Amendment. In short, the Yale law faculty were arguing for recognition of academic freedom as a First Amendment right that gave them constitutional protections over and above the protections of the Free Speech Clause.

The Yale faculty members in *Burt* advanced two claims. They first argued that excluding employers that engage in invidious discrimination was crucial to their "educational mission of inculcating a commitment to equal justice among their students, ensuring a diverse student body, and helping students find appropriate careers." In denying the validity of this claim, the Court of Appeals in *Burt* emphasized that the "Solomon Amendment places no restriction on the content of teaching, the membership of teachers in organizations, the selection of students, or evaluation and retention of students." Even accepting that requiring a university to grant military recruiters, who discriminate in hiring, equal access to their campuses and students could incidentally detract from the academic mission of inculcating respect for equal rights, the court reasoned that the Solomon Amendment's impact on this mission was still largely indirect, attenuated, and speculative.

The Second Circuit in *Burt* similarly rejected the other theory pressed by the Yale faculty members, which attempted to analogize their actions to a constitutionally protected boycott. In exercising their right to boycott military recruiters, the Yale faculty members maintained that they were exercising their "right of disassociation, which is reciprocal to the right of association." The Court of Appeals reasoned that the Supreme Court in *FAIR* had already rejected what was, in essence, the identical "right of disassociation" style claim, holding that the Solomon Amendment did not force the plaintiffs to associate with the military in any sense that would violate the First Amendment.

The Yale law faculty was asserting the academic-freedom-as-a-freestanding-right argument. As explained in chapter 2, that assertion predictably gained no traction with the court. To be sure, some of the language used by the Court of Appeals in *Burt* did speak of the "First Amendment guarantee of academic freedom"—language that one might press to the service of establishing a distinct and freestanding First Amendment right. But the holding and analysis of the Court of Appeals in *Burt* cut in exactly the opposite direction, supporting the conclusion that enforceable academic freedom rights, which would create constitutional entitlements not cognizable under free speech or free association principles, simply do not exist.

The Court of Appeals expressed skepticism that the Supreme Court's decision in *FAIR* had not rejected the "academic freedom" claim already, noting that there were many references to "academic freedom" made in the briefs of the parties and those of "friends of the court" filed with the Supreme Court in *FAIR*, and that "it would defy reason to assume that the Supreme Court ignored plaintiffs' status as academics in rejecting their First Amendment arguments." Yet the Second Circuit's analysis did not stop there. Turning squarely to the merits, the court held that "even if the Supreme Court did not reject the *FAIR* plaintiffs' academic-freedom argument, we would reject it based on the merits."

Government Aid and Religion

The right-privilege distinction frequently comes into play in the context of higher education in disputes involving government aid and religion. The decision in *Rosenberger v. Rector of the University of Virginia*,[28] discussed in chapter 3, indicates that public universities may not withhold funds from student groups and student publications purely because of their religious message.

The flip side to the issue of whether the government may withhold money from universities to pressure them to conform to government policy is whether the government may *grant* money to universities engaged in religious activity. There is broad consensus in the United States that government may not impose a tax on the general populace specifically to generate money for one established church, forcing those who are not adherents of that church to support it.

There is a striking difference between the application of the aid to religion principle in the context of elementary and high school education and its application in the context of higher education. There have been over twenty Supreme Court decisions dealing with aid to public elementary and high school programs, and the results are not always consistent, often turning on fine nuances. Speaking broadly, however, it is a fair generalization to say that a relatively higher barrier to government aid to schools has been erected in the context of the lower public schools than in the context of higher education.[29]

The most notable exceptions with regard to lower grades have been programs that provide parents or schoolchildren with education subsidies, such as tax breaks or voucher grants, which may then be used for any public or private school, including religious schools. The Supreme

Court in *Zelman v. Simmons-Harris* (2002),[30] for example, upheld an Ohio voucher program that provided tuition assistance that families could use to send their children to public or private schools of their choice, religious or nonreligious. Chief Justice Rehnquist, writing for the majority, emphasized the distinction between those programs giving assistance directly to religious schools and programs in which the aid reaches the religious school as a result of a truly independent choice made by a private individual. Similarly, in *Mueller v. Allen* (1983),[31] the Court upheld a Minnesota program allowing tax deductions for education expenses, including tuition, at private schools, many of which were religious.

A very different pattern, however, has emerged when it comes to colleges or universities. As explained through the cases discussed below, the Supreme Court's Establishment Clause jurisprudence has tended to be less stringently separationist in the context of higher education than in the context of public elementary and secondary schools. Unlike aid to religious elementary and secondary schools, enterprises in which the school's mission may include religious instruction and indoctrination of impressionable children, the students at colleges and universities are young adults, with greater intellectual and spiritual maturity and independence. So too, many religiously affiliated universities and colleges maintain a robust commitment to principles of academic freedom, thereby mitigating the concern that government grants to those institutions directly advance a pervasively religious mission.

The Supreme Court in *Tilton v. Richardson* (1971),[32] for example, upheld a federal program providing grants to both public and private universities and colleges, including religious institutions, for the construction of academic facilities, provided those facilities were not used for sectarian purposes. In an opinion by Justice Potter Stewart, the Court in *Tilton* applied the *Lemon* three-part test, finding that the purpose of the federal grant program was entirely secular, and that it did not have the effect of advancing religion, even at religious schools, because the facilities were not themselves used for religious purposes. Two of the five facilities were libraries; there was also a language laboratory at Albertus Magnus College, a science building at Fairfield University, both religiously affiliated schools, and a music, drama, and arts building at Amherst College. In reaching its judgment, the Court injected a special nuance to the examination of aid to religious enterprises in the college and university setting, asking whether religion entirely permeated the college's enterprise. The rationale for this inquiry was to determine if it was possible to separate the grant of money to assist with construction of nonreligious facilities from the religious elements of the institutions. The Court found that religion did not so permeate the colleges that their religious and secular functions were inseparable. Indeed, the Court emphasized that the colleges were faithful to traditions of academic freedom, noting that courses at the colleges were "taught according to the academic requirements intrinsic to the subject matter," and that "an atmosphere of academic freedom rather than religious indoctrination" was maintained. As evidence of this, the Court specifically noted, with approval, that the institutions at issue all subscribed to the 1940 *Statement of Principles on Academic Freedom and Tenure* endorsed by the American Association of University Professors and the Association of American Colleges. Justices Douglas, Black, and Marshall dissented.

In *Hunt v. McNair* (1973),[33] the Court, in an opinion written by Justice Powell, again rejected an Establishment Clause challenge to a South Carolina state program that permitted private universities, including religious universities, to partake in the benefits provided by state revenue bonds. The case challenged the extension of the state financing scheme to the Baptist College at Charleston, for the purpose of financing a dining hall facility. The college serviced and repaid the bonds, but at a lower cost resulting from the tax-free status of the interest payments under the state program. In upholding the program, the Court followed the lead suggested by *Tilton*. Even though the Baptist College was subject to substantial control and supervision by the Southern Baptist Convention of South Carolina, the Court did not find that the college was "pervasively sectarian," noting that there was no discernable difference between the Baptist college in the case and the Catholic colleges and universities that had been the subject of the litigation in *Tilton*.

A similar result was reached three years later in *Roemer v. Board of Public Works of Maryland* (1976),[34] in which the state of Maryland provided aid to private colleges and universities, including religiously affiliated institutions. The state used a formula by which each institution's entitlement to a subsidy was computed by providing a sum equal to 15 percent of Maryland's per-full-time-pupil appropriation for a student in the state college system. The grants were essentially unrestricted, with the sole caveat that they not be utilized for sectarian purposes. *Roemer* originally focused on one Methodist and four Catholic universities, though by the time the case reached the Supreme Court only the four Catholic universities remained active parties in the litigation. Applying the "pervasively sectarian" litmus test, the Supreme Court again upheld the state aid program.

To underscore the unpredictability and the volatility of American constitutional law with regard to religion, however, the results in *Rosenberger, Tilton, Hunt,* and *Roemer* were counterbalanced by a decision in 2004, *Locke v. Davey.*[35] In *Locke,* the Supreme Court upheld a provision of Washington state law that excluded students pursuing degrees in theology from a statewide Promise Scholarship Program created to assist academically gifted students with college expenses. Joshua Davey was awarded a Promise Scholarship and chose to attend a private Christian college affiliated with the Assemblies of God denomination, to prepare himself for the ministry and life as a church pastor. Under the terms of the Washington law, this meant he forfeited his Promise Scholarship. Davey argued that to exclude him from the general scholarship program merely because he chose to study theology violated the Free Exercise Clause.

The Supreme Court, in a 7–2 ruling written by Chief Justice Rehnquist, rejected Davey's argument. The Chief Justice wrote that the case fell within the dictum that "there is room for play in the joints" between the Establishment and Free Exercise Clauses. Chief Justice Rehnquist noted that since "the founding of our country, there have been popular uprisings against procuring taxpayer funds to support church leaders, which was one of the hallmarks of an 'established' religion." He rejected the argument that the exclusion of Davey was an example of discrimination against religion. Invoking a theme that he often utilized in his judicial career, Chief Justice Rehnquist distinguished between laws that persecute on the basis of expression or belief, such as laws that impose criminal or civil penalties, and ones that merely choose not to subsidize. Washington, the Chief Justice argued, had "merely chosen not to fund a distinct category of instruction." Thus, while decisions such as *Roemer* indicate that the Supreme Court is generally willing to allow government assistance to religious higher education institutions, save those that are "pervasively sectarian," *Locke* balances this doctrine with the principle that government is not required to extend such aid.

The *Locke* ruling is, at the very least, in tension with religious free exercise principles, and the notion that government may not discriminate against religion. Justice Scalia, joined by Justice Thomas, dissented in *Locke* on precisely this theory. "When the State makes a public benefit generally available," Justice Scalia argued, "that benefit becomes part of the baseline against which burdens on religion are measured; and when the State withholds that benefit from some individuals solely on the basis of religion, it violates the Free Exercise Clause no less than if it had imposed a special tax." Justice Scalia argued that this was precisely what Washington had done. It had created a scholarship benefit based entirely on academic performance, and then carved out one subject matter for exclusion—theology.

The majority opinion in *Locke v. Davey* would make intuitive sense if the scholarship were available for a narrow range of *favored* disciplines. It would be difficult to argue that the First Amendment would be violated if a state legislature set up a special merit scholarship program for students planning to study science, for example. But when every topic under the sun, save for one, is funded, the merits seem to shift toward Justices Scalia and Thomas. It is difficult to square the decision in *Locke* with that in *Rosenberger*. Both involved broad subsidy programs in which one topic, religion, was excluded. That the framers may have been hostile to laws aimed specifically at funding the clergy, Justice Scalia argued, does not mean they would have been against laws that merely allowed ministers to partake in benefits made available by government to all. "No one would seriously contend," Justice Scalia quipped, "that the Framers would have barred ministers from using public roads on their way to church."

Making Connections

The large constitutional ideas explored in this book—the notion of the living Constitution, the division between the public and private sphere, the right-privilege distinction, the ideal of ordered liberty, competing conceptions of equality, and the system of checks and balances—are interlinked. They are not separate conceptual compartments, hermetically sealed one from another. For example, the subjects of chapters 2 and 3, which dealt with the public and private spheres and the right-privilege distinction, significantly overlap. As explored in this chapter, one of the devices through which the government may seek to extend the norms and values of the public sphere into the private sphere is the attaching of conditions to the receipt of governmental largess. The government tells the private university or private citizen, if you want government money you must abide by the government's values. Conversely, one of the mechanisms by which the private sphere "fights back" to retain its autonomy and jurisdiction is the doctrine of unconstitutional conditions, through which the university or citizen asserts that there are some conditions that cannot be placed on the receipt of government funds, thereby resisting the extension of the public arena at the expense of the private. So too, specific constitutional issues, such as the role of religion in our public and private life, traverse larger constitutional ideas. One of the central tensions of our Religion Clause jurisprudence is the issue of how much the state and the spiritual ought to be separated. This is another way of stating the question of the extent to which religion should be assigned exclusively to the private sphere, or may take some rightful position in the public. Panning back with a wider-angle lens, one may view the evolution of the right-privilege distinction, beginning with the hard-nosed logic of Holmes and then gradually leavened by the doctrine of unconstitutional conditions, as an example of the living Constitution in action.

These crisscrossing connections define our constitutional experience and influence our constitutional unconscious, and in turn shaping the identity of the modern American university. Keep these connections in mind as we turn next to the constitutional idea that, perhaps more than any other, is at the soul of that poetic tension that most powerfully affects the character of campus life—the fusion of freedom and responsibility encapsulated by our constitutional traditions of ordered liberty.

5

Ordered Liberty

On the other hand, the due process clause of the Fourteenth Amendment may make it unlawful for a state to abridge by its statutes the freedom of speech which the First Amendment safeguards against encroachment by the Congress, or the like freedom of the press, or the free exercise of religion, or the right of peaceable assembly, without which speech would be unduly trammeled, or the right of one accused of crime to the benefit of counsel. In these and other situations, immunities that are valid as against the federal government by force of the specific pledges of particular amendments have been found to be implicit in the concept of ordered liberty, and thus, through the Fourteenth Amendment, become valid as against the states.

—Justice Benjamin Cardozo, for the
Court in *Palko v. Connecticut* (1937)

It simply does not follow under any of our decisions or from the language of the First Amendment itself that because petitioner could not be criminally prosecuted by the Missouri state courts for the conduct in question, she may not therefore be expelled from the University of Missouri for the same conduct. A state university is an establishment for the purpose of educating the State's young people, supported by the tax revenues of the State's citizens. The notion that the officials lawfully charged with the governance of the university have so little control over the environment for which they are responsible that they may not prevent the public distribution of a newspaper on campus which contained the language described in the Court's opinion is quite unacceptable to me and I would suspect would have been equally unacceptable to the Framers of the First Amendment. This is indeed a case where the observa-

tion of a unanimous Court in *Chaplinsky* that "such utterances
are no essential part of any exposition of ideas and are of such
slight social value as a step to truth that any benefit that may be
derived from them is clearly outweighed by the social interest
in order and morality" applies with compelling force.
—Justice William Rehnquist, dissenting in *Papish v. Board
of Curators of the University of Missouri* (1973)

Thomas Friedman Meets Albert Einstein

"Honey, I think the world is flat." Thomas Friedman, author and colum-
nist for the *New York Times*, shared these words with his wife, and a book
was born. In *The World is Flat*,[1] Friedman argued persuasively that the
story of the new century was not the terrorist attacks on the World Trade
Center, not the wars in Afghanistan and Iraq, but the "flattening" of the
earth—the exploding forces of globalization driven by changes in tech-
nology, business, and politics that have fueled the economies of India,
China, and other nations, placing enormous stress on all our moral, social,
political, and economic systems. In the new flat earth, countries, companies, communities, and individuals must all learn to do things differently.

The earth may be flat, but the universe is curved, at least if you believe
Albert Einstein. When Einstein began his contemplations on theoretical
physics, the received understanding of the universe was that explained by
Isaac Newton. Newton's version posited the existence of both absolute
time and absolute space. Time and space were inviolable and universal
realities, independent of each another. Time, for Newton, existed in all
spaces and in all places in perfect synchronization. Time was an omni-
present ticktock, ticktock, ticktock, existing always and everywhere.
So too, for Newton, there existed absolute space, the place in which all
things were contained. All things happened in space, as all things happened in time, and both were immutable and constant. Existing both in
time and in space was matter.[2]

In Newton's universe, matter behaved according to certain predictable
and measurable laws of movement and mass, those solid, reliable, and
even comforting explanations of how objects in our familiar time and our

familiar space behave. While objects in the real world of matter behaved *in* time and *in* space, they were not *of* time or *of* space. Matter—iron balls or waterfalls—might move across space and in time, but that physical stuff was not itself time, or itself space, and the realms of matter, time, and space were distinct and independent. The universe, as explained by Newton, was pleasingly logical, linear, and compartmentalized.

Albert Einstein, in a brilliant supernova explosion of creative genius, reinvented our understanding of the universe. In Einstein's physics and cosmology, space and time are not absolute and are not disconnected. Einstein imagined a universe in which there is no universal absolute time or space. Space and time were united, forming a space-time continuum. Space and time did not follow the linear laws and logic of Newton, but were instead curved. And perhaps most profoundly, *matter*, the physical stuff that we experience as hard and real, did not simply exist *in* space and time, but was *of* space and time. The curvature of the space-time continuum shaped and bent the behavior of matter, and matter, in equal turn, influenced and shaped the contours of space and time. Einstein's universe was more imaginative than logical, more curved than linear, more connected than compartmentalized.

The modern American university is at once flat and curved. It is flat in the sense Thomas Friedman meant—wired, global, connected, and seemingly moving at the speed of light. Intellectually, politically, economically, and socially, the modern campus is open to the world. Professors and students connect to one another in an extraordinary global marketplace of ideas, a marketplace increasingly impervious to geographic and political boundaries. Socially, the interactions of students that were once confined to dorm rooms, local bars, or fraternity houses are now dispersed worldwide on YouTube or Facebook.

The campus is also curved in the sense Einstein meant. The rules, arrangements, traditions, and values that define the character of the modern campus are woven into the fabric of the larger society. Just as Einstein taught that time, space, and matter were not separate and distinct, but instead part of a larger unity, so too are morality, culture, and law linked, part of larger human unity, and the modern university is a profound expression of all these linkages. The curved space of the university is permeated by a constant tension between the values of order and the values of liberty. This tension, manifest in our competing conceptions of academic freedom, due process, privacy, and human dignity, is the essential stuff of "ordered liberty," a central defining conflict within the American constitutional tradition.

The Death of Socrates

Socrates, as revealed to us in the writings of Plato, was one of the first martyrs to academic freedom. Plato tells us in the *Apology* that Socrates, a philosopher and teacher, was condemned to death by Athens for his "impiety," in denying the gods recognized by the state. He was also condemned for his "corruption of youth."[3]

Aristotle, a graduate of Plato's academy, injected a measure of counterpoint and balance to Socrates and Plato. Aristotle famously argued that man is by nature a "political" or "civic" animal, by which he meant that it is only through society, community, and law that humans rise above being *mere* animals and achieve virtue. We form society and the state not merely to survive, but to become elevated. Aristotle thus argued that "the state comes into existence, originating in the bare needs of life, and continuing its existence for the sake of the good life."[4]

Centuries later, in *On Liberty*, John Stuart Mill would cite the death of Socrates in arguing forcefully for freedom of thought and opinion. Emphasizing the constant of human fallibility, Mill maintained that *for all we know* unpopular opinions may be true, or at least contain a portion of truth. Even if received wisdom is accepted as entirely true, it will still become dead dogma if not freely and openly contested. Mill argued that even if one man's opinion stood alone against the opinions of the rest of humankind, society would have no more right to suppress the solitary dissenter than the dissenter would have the right to repress the opinions of humankind. Mill rejected the view that opinions should be free only to the extent that they were "temperate," or consistent with "fair argument," arguing that it is impossible to avoid confusing disagreement with the substance of an argument with claims that the argument is intemperate or unfair.[5]

A modern university struggles to balance the lessons of Plato's story of Socrates, the libertarianism of John Stuart Mill, and the balanced and optimistic vision of society suggested by the "good life" of Aristotle.

We want no professors forced to drink hemlock because they deny the gods of the state, whether those gods are divine, political, or economic. John Stuart Mill's fierce defense of open discourse, published ten years after Charles Darwin's *On the Origin of Species*, has rightly taken hold in both American constitutional law—as expressed in the writings of early champions such as Justice Oliver Wendell Holmes and Justice Louis Brandeis[6]—and in the fundamental values of higher education.

Yet Aristotle must also be accommodated. A university is, as Aristotle taught, "established with a view to some good." This "good" for the university community cannot be *entirely* captured in the idea of freedom of thought and an open marketplace of ideas. Even if we believe that Mill is essentially right, his libertarian principles alone are not enough to guide us in the wise conception and administration of a university. Central to the faith of the university is the conviction that it exists both as a community and a marketplace, a moral space as well as a marketplace.

Marketplaces and Moral Spaces

The state may not punish individuals for the gods they adore or the gods they deplore. The university's role, however, is more complex. The relationship of individuals to the university is not the same as the relationship of individuals to the state. While the state has no authority to pass judgments on thought and expression, the university *must* pass such judgments. The enlightened university never punishes opinion merely because it is contrary to orthodoxy. The very idea of orthodoxy is repugnant to the ethos of creativity, invention, and intellectual honesty. Slavish adherence to what has gone before is anathema to the arts and to the scientific method.

Yet this is *not* the same as saying that the university is entirely stripped of moral and legal jurisdiction to *judge* expression and opinion. The "good life" for the university is not entirely determined by the market. Norms of academic and professional rigor, integrity, and quality are core to the university's missions of teaching, research, and service. A university that does not evaluate thought and expression is incoherent. The exercise of judgment on whom to hire to teach and research, whom to grant tenure, whom to admit to study, whom to pass or fail in courses, whom to graduate and certify to society as credentialed with certain levels of academic attainment, must, by its intrinsic nature, partake of intellectual and academic judgment.

For many private universities Aristotle's point can be taken one layer deeper. Private universities have the license to develop unique identities more distinctive than their public university counterparts. Public universities are constrained by egalitarian obligations that prevent them from developing identities that are politically partisan. Public universities are also constrained by the Establishment Clause of the First Amendment, preventing them from adopting any form of religious identity. For many private universities, in contrast, the conception of the university's meaning and mission—the core principles that constitute it as a community—include ideas of the "good life" imbued with moral, political, philosophical, and even spiritual judgments. While these judgments may not be within the "jurisdiction" of the secular state, they are well within the "jurisdiction" of the private university, and are often central to the private university's reason for being. Thus the private university may have strong conceptions of social justice, of moral behavior, of honor and ethics, of theology and the divine, all of which appropriately color its judgments on who shall teach, who shall learn, or what shall be the bounds of permitted civil discourse. Public universities may be tempted to adopt these conceptions as well. When they are not overtly religious or politically partisan, but merely stake out some special claim to the importance of honor or ethical integrity or civility, the public university may seek to strike a judicious balance between operating as a robust and open intellectual marketplace and as a community of scholars with a conception of the common good and the rule of law.

The "marketplace of ideas" metaphor, a notion that can be traced back at least as far as John Milton in *Areopagitica*,[7] will forever be most powerfully represented in the American constitutional tradition by the words Justice Holmes wrote in his dissenting opinion in *Abrams v. United States* (1919).[8] In *Abrams*, dissidents opposed to World War I dropped leaflets written in Yiddish and English denouncing American involvement in the war and praising the Russian Revolution. The activists were found guilty of inciting resistance to the war, and their convictions were affirmed by the Supreme Court. Justice Holmes dissented, writing one of the most famous defenses of freedom of speech in American history:

Persecution for the expression of opinions seems to me perfectly logical. If you have no doubt of your premises or your power, and want a certain result with all your heart, you naturally express your wishes in law and sweep away all opposition. To allow opposition by speech seems to indicate that you think the speech impotent, as when a man says that he has squared the circle, or that you do not care wholeheartedly for the result, or that you doubt either your power or your premises. But when men have realized that time has upset many fighting faiths, they may come to believe even more than they believe the very foundations of their own conduct that the ultimate good desired is better reached by free trade in ideas—that the best test of truth is the power of the thought to get itself accepted in the competition of the market, and that truth is the only ground upon which their wishes safely can be carried out. That, at any rate, is the theory of our Constitution. It is an experiment, as all life is an experiment. Every year if not every day we have to wager our salvation upon some prophecy based upon imperfect knowledge. While that experiment is part of our system I think that we should be eternally vigilant against attempts to check the expression of opinions that we loathe and believe to be fraught with death, unless they so imminently threaten immediate interference with the lawful and pressing purposes of the law that an immediate check is required to save the country.[9]

The above passage lives on in the American constitutional experience in poetic tension with yet another beautifully written paragraph by another Supreme Court Justice, Frank Murphy, in *Chaplinsky v. New Hampshire* (1942).[10] Walter Chaplinsky, a Jehovah's Witness, was making a speech and passing out leaflets from a sidewalk in Rochester, New Hampshire. A crowd gathered and grew hostile toward his message, an attack on organized religion. When a police officer intervened, Chaplinsky verbally blasted the officer, calling him a "damned Fascist" and a "God-damned racketeer." Chaplinsky was arrested and convicted for engaging in offensive conduct. Justice Murphy, writing for a unanimous Court, upheld the conviction, asserting:

There are certain well-defined and narrowly limited classes of speech, the prevention and punishment of which has never been thought to raise any Constitutional problem. These include the lewd and obscene, the profane, the libelous, and the insulting or "fighting" words—those which by their very utterance inflict injury or tend to incite an immediate breach of the peace. It has been well observed that such utterances are no essential part of any exposition of ideas, and are of such slight social value as a step to truth that any benefit that may be derived from them is clearly outweighed by the social interest in order and morality.[11]

These two opposing passages represent the yin and the yang of the constitutional struggle to balance liberty and order. Justice Holmes tells us to tolerate speech we *loathe*, speech we are convinced is *fraught with death*. It is the marketplace, not law, that will decide the value of speech. The government may intervene through the force of law only if there is an *immediate* need to check the speech *to save the country*. Justice Murphy, in contrast, admonishes us to take a stand against the demise of order and the disintegration of morality. His opinion captured elegantly and economically the view that competes against Holmes, the view of all those who believe that in the end, freedom of speech must always be measured against other vital societal interests, namely those of order and morality.

Justice Murphy expresses the "values-conscious" view of freedom of speech, adhered to by those who believe society can and should draw lines between speech of high value and speech of low or no value. Instances of low-value speech, *Chaplinsky* tells us confidently, "are no *essential* part of any exposition of ideas." The Court did not say they play *no* part, but rather no *essential part*. Thus one need not say, "Fuck the draft," in order to express the idea "oppose the draft."[12] One need not burn a flag to express the idea of dissent from the war effort. Reinforcing this theme, *Chaplinsky* speaks of *exposition*, connoting the use of language, reason, and argument—an *intellectual* enterprise, something more than burning two beams of wood to ignite a cross.

Most profoundly, the *Chaplinsky* position is decidedly not the stuff of the marketplace of ideas. *Chaplinsky* does not leave the test of truth to the power of the idea to command the market. Rather, it assumes that the test of truth has already been administered, and that these forms of speech have flunked. They have been certified already as truth retarded, as being of only "slight social value as a step to truth." Perhaps more important, they have been certified already as unfit for decent society, as "outweighed by the social interest in order and morality." *Chaplinsky*, moreover, is not just about keeping order, but also keeping morality. The decision is not limited to the speech that might breach the peace; it extends to speech that offends our moral sensibilities.

Neither the Holmes view nor the *Chaplinsky* view has ever fully dominated free speech law. Like dominant and recessive genes, the Holmes view has ultimately prevailed as the dominant theory in American life. The *Chaplinsky* view periodically reasserts itself, however, in special settings that constitute "carve-outs" from the general marketplace, settings in which the wide-open freedom of the marketplace is displaced by an overriding interest in order or morality.

This tension between the Holmes marketplace position and the *Chaplinsky* moral space position is particularly intense on American campuses. Debates over the meaning of free speech on campus are largely debates over whether the Holmes ethos or the *Chaplinsky* ethos best captures the soul of what an American university should be about. Both views have their appropriate place within American universities, just as they do within wider society. The trick is to articulate a coherent rationale for explaining *when, where,* and for *whom* the Holmes wide-open marketplace view should prevail, and *when, where,* and for *whom* the *Chaplinsky* order and morality view should prevail. When should it be out of order to punish speech, and when should it be permissible to rule speech out of order? When may a university decide that certain speech both contributes nothing of appreciable valuable to the *exposition of ideas* and palpably harms the university's interest in "academic order" and "academic morality"? When may a university appropriately decide that the ethos of the open marketplace is trumped by the university's commitment to integrity in argumentation, in experimentation, in the presentation of data, in traditions of collegial civility, and in the values of an inclusive sense of community and human dignity?

The Neutrality Principle in the General Marketplace

In struggling to answer to these hard questions, it is helpful to begin from the baseline of modern free speech law in the "general American marketplace." This general marketplace is the wide-open-let-'er-rip-free-speech-free-for-all that is modern American culture. The starting point has evolved to a point that modern First Amendment law almost *never* permits the government to censor speech just because the government finds the speech objectionable. Following the views of Holmes, modern free speech principles allow speech that we loathe and believe to be fraught with death to run free, unless it crosses the line that defines imminent incitement or a true threat. Illinois Nazis are allowed to march through Skokie, a Chicago suburb populated by many survivors of the Holocaust.[13] The Ku Klux Klan may burn the cross,[14] antiwar protestors may burn the flag,[15] and abortion protestors may picket abortion clinics with large photographs of dead fetuses.[16] There are limits, of course, but we don't define those limits by revulsion alone. With one notable exception, dealing with the law of obscenity,[17] the mere capacity of speech to cause offense is not enough, standing alone, to justify its abridgement. This is usually captured in fancy First Amendment lawyer talk under the rubric of "content discrimination" and "viewpoint discrimination." When the government comes down on speech because of disagreement with or disquiet over the content of a speaker's message, it violates the speaker's freedom of speech.

This is the modern First Amendment's "neutrality principle." The government must remain neutral in the marketplace of ideas. Setting aside a few rare exceptions, such as expression involving hard-core obscenity or depictions of child pornography, the government must treat all ideas as equal before the law, even when it is convinced that all ideas are not equal in merit.

The "Carve-Outs" from the General Marketplace

If this neutrality principle were all there was to modern free speech law, it would not be all that complicated. Rules and refinements would still be required, but in forming those rules and refinements our judgment would be consistently guided by this core commitment to neutrality. The rules and refinements would largely define situations in which the justification for punishing speech is not grounded in disagreement with the message, but instead with demonstrated linkages in certain clearly defined cases between the message and palpable harm. It is one thing for society to tolerate the *idea* of terrorism, and another thing to tolerate incitement to engage in terrorism, or conspiracy to plan and execute a terrorist plot. So even if the open marketplace and the neutrality principle were accepted as the governing regime, there would still be work to do in defining limits, but there would be no fundamental debate over basic premises.

Yet modern free speech law, as it has evolved, is astonishingly complicated. The principal reason for the complication is that we have come to recognize a number of "special settings" in which the general marketplace rules do not apply. These are what I will call "carve-outs," settings in which we treat the speech as *not part of the general marketplace*, but as a distinct and defined space in which the neutrality principle is abandoned. It is as if the general marketplace of ideas is the great outdoors, subject to all the violent storms of bizarre, irrational, and freakish opinions, to the ideological equivalents of hail, sleet, and damaging winds, and the "special settings" are domed stadiums, built to repel hurricanes, climate controlled, free of rain, snow, and all extreme temperatures.

The principal carve-outs, the domed spaces, if you will, usually involve some form of government participation in the speech activity. These may be settings in which the government is literally "the speaker" itself. These may also be settings in which the government is a direct participant in the expressive enterprise, settings in which the purpose of the expression is to accomplish some government-related goal. Prime examples are settings where the government is acting as an employer or an educator, situations involving captive audiences, and situations involving children.

In attempting to make sense of free speech principles as they apply on a modern campus, *the critical question is whether to treat the campus, or some special setting within the campus, as part of the open marketplace or as a carve-out deemed distinct from the open marketplace.*

The Dual Character of the University

Much of our public and legal rhetoric about the nature of a university does appear to treat the university as the quintessential marketplace. We often consider the university as an "anything goes" sort of place, in which students, professors, administrators, and outside speakers gather in an open marketplace to exchange views from every conceivable viewpoint with no control or regulation imposed by external authority. Indeed, at times we seem to conceive of the university as a "super marketplace," in which freedom from regulation based on content or viewpoint is even more robust than in society generally.

Hypothetically, a university campus might be treated as if there were a giant dome that extended over the entire campus environment, exempting the whole university from general free speech principles. The university, it might be thought, is a community of scholars, with an emphasis on both the concept of community and the concept of scholarship. Traditions of mutual respect, civility, rationality, objectivity, and intellectual rigor may invite us to rule out of bounds certain extremes of expression that are tolerated in the general marketplace. While the university may thus borrow from the "marketplace of ideas" metaphor that has so dominated American thinking about freedom of speech, that metaphor may place special emphasis on the notion of *ideas* when defining the nature of the campus marketplace, so that the university need not accept elements of expression that appear only to communicate vulgarity, hatred, personal attack, *or even ideas blatantly lacking in scientific evidence or accepted norms of argument and evidence.*

Before jumping to the conclusion that any such "grading" of ideas is antithetical to the very notion of freedom of speech, remember that we are testing the hypothesis of whether the classic notions of freedom of speech *should govern* on the campus in the same way they do in the marketplace. And consider as well a broader complication. The university world is all about the content of speech; it is in the content business. In that business we must discriminate. In our daily work on campus, all ideas are not created equal. We make scientific judgments, mathematical judgments, historical judgments, philosophical judgments, legal judgments, creative and artistic judgments, day in and day out. We hire and fire on the basis of content. We assign grades on the basis of content. The notion that *all* content-based judgments presumptively violate the First Amendment is conceptually incoherent when applied to a university.

Neither of these "all or nothing" conceptions of the university accurately captures either the "soul" of modern academic life or the core insights of modern First Amendment doctrine. The best way to conceive of a modern campus is to accept that it is divided between those spaces and programs in which robust open marketplace principles apply, and those that are "carve-outs" in which content-based and viewpoint-based regulation of speech is permitted in order to advance the educational mission of the campus.

While it makes analysis more complicated, it is best to think of a university campus as a microcosm of society as a whole when it comes to free speech principles. This means there will be "free speech zones" on the campus in which the free-for-all of the open marketplace and the neutrality principle govern, and other spaces and settings in which the university is itself speaking, or acting as an employer or educator, or protecting a captive audience. In these carve-out settings the university may legitimately insist on minimum standards of academic professionalism. The next task is to define the boundaries of these marketplaces and moral spaces, and the rules that apply within each.

Captive Audiences

In the open marketplace the burden is normally on those who are exposed to speech they deem offensive because it is lurid, violent, tasteless, or ideologically unpalatable to avert their eyes or close their ears. Any of us may for a fleeting moment be unwittingly exposed to offensive speech, but the prevailing ethos of First Amendment law is that we put the burden on individual citizens to avoid or shun the messages they do not like, rather than enlist the power of government to censor the message, preventing its receipt by all. *Cohen v. California* (1971),[18] in which the Supreme Court refused to permit censorship of the message "Fuck the Draft" on the back of a jacket worn by an individual in the public corridors of the Los Angeles courthouse, is a graphic example of this principle. Similarly, in *Erznoznik v. Jacksonville* (1975),[19] the Supreme Court struck down an ordinance prohibiting drive-in movie theaters from exhibiting nudity when the screen was visible from a public street or place. This ordinance prohibited mere nudity, not merely material that was legally obscene. The Court placed the burden of eluding exposure to the speech on the viewer: "The plain, if at times disquieting, truth is that in our pluralistic society, constantly proliferating new and ingenious forms of expression, 'we are inescapably captive audiences for many purposes.' Much that we encounter offends our esthetic, if not our political and moral, sensibilities. Nevertheless, the

Constitution does not permit the government to decide which types of otherwise protected speech are sufficiently offensive to require protection for the unwilling listener or viewer. Rather, . . . the burden normally falls upon the viewer to 'avoid further bombardment of [his] sensibilities simply by averting [his] eyes.'"[20]

The same principle was applied by the Court in *United States v. Playboy Entertainment Group Inc.* (2000),[21] a case dealing with sexually explicit programming on cable television. The Court in *Playboy* rejected the government's attempt to justify restrictions regarding "scrambling" of sexually explicit programming on cable merely because adults might inadvertently stumble on fleeting images of naked sexuality (due to a technical phenomenon known as "signal bleed," in which scrambled programs may become slightly visible or audible for brief moments). "Our precedents teach these principles," the Court chided. "Where the designed benefit of a content-based speech restriction is to shield the sensibilities of listeners, the general rule is that the right of expression prevails, even where no less restrictive alternative exists." The answer to such accidental exposure to objectionable speech is to look the other way. "We are expected to protect our own sensibilities 'simply by averting [our] eyes.'"

Sanctuaries from Offensive Speech

The carve-outs to the "avert your eyes" principle have primarily involved society's interests in the protection of children and of certain sanctuaries of privacy, such as the home. Judge Jerome Frank wrote that a "sane, decent society must provide some . . . oasis, some shelter from public scrutiny, some insulated enclosure, some enclave, some inviolate place which is a man's castle."[22] The home is the American castle (for women and men), and by tradition the rights of privacy are especially inviolable there. As Justice John Marshall Harlan explained, the home is a sanctum protected not merely as a piece of private property, but as "the seat of family life."[23]

In *Federal Communications Commission v. Pacifica Foundation* (1978),[24] the Supreme Court sustained the power of the FCC to police "indecent programming" on radio and television, cracking down on a radio station for broadcasting comedian George Carlin's "Seven Words You Can

Never Say on Television" routine, a twelve-minute monologue on "the words you couldn't say on the public airwaves" and "the ones you definitely wouldn't say, ever."[25] Although the offended listener in *Pacifica* was not in his home at the time of the broadcast, but rather riding in his car with his son, the Supreme Court placed significant weight on the fact that radio broadcasts permeate the home. "Patently offensive, indecent material presented over the airwaves confronts the citizen," the Court observed, "not only in public, but also in the privacy of the home, where the individual's right to be left alone plainly outweighs the First Amendment rights of an intruder." While the FCC in recent years has shown some willingness to loosen regulation of the economic aspects of broadcast regulation, it has not loosened its grip over "indecent programming." The FCC has come down hard on "shock jocks" such as Howard Stern for use of vulgar and indecent language. Most famously, the FCC took a dim view of the Super Bowl 38 halftime show "nipplegate" controversy, in which Janet Jackson's bare breast was exposed by Justin Timberlake in a "wardrobe malfunction." Relying on the powers the Supreme Court had granted it in cases such as *Pacifica*, the FCC levied a record $550,000 fine on CBS, for the few seconds in which such "indecent programming" was sent to millions of viewers before CBS could cut to an aerial view of the football stadium. In July 2008, the United States Court of Appeals for the Third Circuit overturned the FCC fine arising from "nipplegate," holding that the agency acted "arbitrarily and capriciously" in changing its policy, which had previously excused broadcasters from the "fleeting" broadcast of indecent material.[26]

Is the University a Sanctuary?

Is the university a sanctuary? Reflecting the dual character of the university, the most principled answer is "in some respects yes, and in some respects no." The university is not simply an academic space; it is also a living space. While the students, faculty, staff, and administrators who populate a university campus are not children, the university does retain some residual responsibilities in loco parentis ("in the place of a parent"), particularly with regard to basic concerns for health and safety. While a university campus is not the "home" in a traditional sense, a campus does typically contain residences, primarily student housing, and often housing for faculty, administrators, and their families, spaces in which the occupants may legitimately demand some reasonable expectation of privacy. To what extent are the sheltering principles that have evolved to protect the privacy of the home and the sensibilities of children transferable to other settings, such as a campus?

In *Public Utilities Commission v. Pollak* (1952),[27] a District of Columbia transit company installed FM receivers in its buses and streetcars. Two passengers argued that they were "captives" when riding the buses and streetcars, and that this coercion, forcing them to listen on the government-operated transit facilities, violated the Constitution. The Supreme Court rejected this captive audience claim, distinguishing between the level of privacy persons enjoy in the home, and the privacy to which they are entitled on a public conveyance. Justice Douglas dissented, pressing strongly for recognition of a "right to be let alone" that would embrace a right to avoid exposure to unwanted messages while riding on public transportation vehicles. "The present case involves a form of coercion to make people listen," Justice Douglas maintained. "The listeners are of course in a public place," Douglas wrote, but "in a practical sense they are forced to ride, since this mode of transportation is today essential for many thousands." Justice Douglas then invoked images of Big Brother forcing a pliant citizenry to consume propaganda: "Compulsion which comes from circumstances can be as real as compulsion which comes from a command. . . . The man on the streetcar has no choice but to sit and listen, or perhaps to sit and try not to listen. When we force people to listen to another's ideas, we give the propagandist a powerful weapon. . . . Once a man is forced to submit to one type of radio program, he can be forced to submit to another. It may be but a short step from a cultural program to a political program."[28]

In contrast to *Pollak*, in *Lehman v. City of Shaker Heights* (1974),[29] the city of Shaker Heights, Ohio, operated a public transit system that sold commercial and public service advertising space for car cards on its vehicles, but permitted no "political" or "public issue" advertising. The Supreme Court upheld the law, holding that the transit vehicles were not "public forums" like streets, parks, meeting halls, or other public property dedicated to wide-open free expression. In the course of its defense of the city's ordinance, the Supreme Court observed that "users would be subjected to the blare of political propaganda. There could be lurking doubts about favoritism, and sticky administrative problems might arise in parceling out limited space to eager politicians. In these circumstances, the managerial decision to limit car card space to innocuous and less controversial commercial and service-oriented advertising does not rise to the dignity of a First Amendment violation."[30]

Justice Douglas, building on his views in *Pollak*, put the matter in even stronger terms. The streetcar or bus, he argued, is not like a street or park—it is simply a mode of transportation. "If we are to turn a bus or streetcar into either a newspaper or a park, we take great liberties with people who because of necessity become commuters and at the same time captive viewers or listeners," Justice Douglas maintained. The "right of commuters to be free from forced intrusion on their privacy," he argued, precluded the city from transforming its public vehicles "into forums for the dissemination of ideas upon this captive audience."

Pollak and *Lehman* are not entirely inconsistent. *Pollak* held that a public transit authority could permit speech on its conveyances, even though passengers were, in a sense, "captive." *Lehman*, by contrast, held that the government is not required to permit all genres of protected speech on its vehicles, but rather is permitted to invoke its concerns for the "captivity" of its passengers to shelter them from partisan politics while riding on its buses and trains.

Defining Campus Spaces, Places, People, and Programs

If we put together these various strains of standard First Amendment doctrine and theory—taking into account the distinction between the neutrality principles that reign in the "open marketplace" and the reduced protection for freedom of speech that operates in the various carve-outs that are well-recognized in First Amendment law—the challenge is to translate this core dichotomy into the context of the university. A college is a collage of people, places, and programs. The people who compose a college or university include students, faculty, staff, administrative leaders, trustees, alumni, parents, and various other supporters and friends, along with myriad transient visitors and guests, all combining to form a complex and dynamic extended community. It is thus impossible to make sense of the free speech rights of the various persons within the university environment in static terms. The linear physics of Isaac Newton won't do; we must invoke the more curved and integrated physics of Einstein. We cannot speak intelligently of the "free speech rights of students" or the "free speech rights of professors" or the "free speech rights of outside speakers invited to the campus" as constants. The *identity* of the speaker—as a student, a professor, a university president, or an outside speaker, for example—is certainly an important factor in assessing the free speech rights that speaker possesses, but it is only one factor.

Similarly, the captive audience cases tell us that there may be certain situations on a campus in which certain persons are in some sense "captive," such as where a staff member is assigned to a specific workstation and might well object to a constant barrage of sexist jokes by her coworker or supervisor in the same workspace, or students in a class are subjected to a steady stream of sexual innuendo or racist language by a professor. There are many other spaces and programs on a campus, however, in which the metaphor of the open marketplace is far more apt, where the onus should be on the offended viewer to simply avert his or her eyes. And finally, the *place* in which the speech occurs is often critically important, as is the *program*, if any, within which the speech occurs. The task is always generally the same: to determine whether we should treat the speech, as spoken by *this* speaker, in *this* place, as part of *this* program, as content within the "general marketplace of ideas," in which case almost anything goes and the power of government to regulate or ban the speech is minimal.

A Funny Thing Happened on the Way to the Forum

In determining whether we are in the open marketplace" or a special setting, a body of doctrines known as "public forum law" often serves as the mediating device. Courts distinguish between "traditional" or "designated" public forums,[31] in which open marketplace rules apply, and "limited forums" or "non-forums," in which lesser levels of First Amendment protection are used.[32] These different categories of spaces and places exist throughout our society—in our cities and states, as well as our *academic* cities and states.

In any American city, for example, there will be traditional public forums, places that have traditionally been dedicated to public expression and therefore constitute the core physical location of the open marketplace (e.g., the National Mall or Boston Common). In a public university, the central campus green would be an analogue. There may be other facilities that have, by official policy or practice, become designated as public forums (e.g., the main city or campus auditorium). There may also be spaces that are open to expression but only on certain topics, such as meeting rooms set aside for student groups. In a limited forum, the government may ban speech that does not fall within the facilities' use definition. Likewise, university rooms set aside for student groups, for instance, may be closed to outsiders. But the government may not discriminate on the basis of the identity of the speaker or the content of the speech if the speech falls within the use definition. The government may not, say, let the campus Democrats use a room but not the campus Republicans.

Finally, there are government spaces that are non-forums—spaces the government uses to conduct its business, but not to permit citizens to engage in expression. The Mayor's Office inside city hall is such a non-forum. While citizens may protest on the street outside city hall (for that is a traditional forum) or in the auditorium inside the hall (a designated forum) or in a meeting room reserved for community groups (a limited forum), the actual office of the mayor is for his or her use alone—a *non-forum*—and citizens may be excluded. State university students may have a constitutional right to protest the actions of the president (of the university or of the United States) on the campus green, in the campus auditorium, or in campus meeting rooms, but there is no constitutional right to enter and occupy the president's office.

The Supreme Court's first application of public forum law principles to the world of colleges and universities came in 1981 in *Widmar v. Vincent*,[33] involving the University of Missouri–Kansas City. Like most universities, the University of Missouri-Kansas City encouraged the activities of student organizations, and it officially recognized more than one hundred of them. The University regularly provided facilities for the meetings of registered organizations, and students paid an activity fee to help defray the costs. From 1973 until 1977, a registered religious group named Cornerstone, an organization of evangelical Christian students from various denominational backgrounds, had regularly sought and received permission to conduct its meetings in University facilities. In 1977, however, the administration informed the group that it could no longer meet in the University buildings. The exclusion was based on a regulation adopted in 1972 by the University, forbidding the use of facilities "for purposes of religious worship or religious teaching."[34] The University defended its regulation on the grounds that the prohibition was necessary to avoid a violation of the Establishment Clause of the First Amendment. The Supreme Court found the Missouri restriction unconstitutional. The University had designated its facilities as open forums, the Court held, and therefore could not discriminate against religious speech. "The Constitution forbids a State to enforce certain exclusions from a forum generally open to the public," the Court stated, "even if it was not required to create the forum in the first place."[35]

Widmar was a clear statement from the Supreme Court that public forum law principles could and would be applied to public university campuses. Any thought that public universities would receive a blanket exemption from public forum principles—and thereby be empowered to act like the Oliver Wendell Holmes landlord in *Commonwealth v. Davis*,[36] establishing whatever limitations a university might please with regard to the use of its lands and facilities—was put to rest.

To say that public forum principles apply to universities, however, is merely to say that certain places and spaces on a campus *may become* designated public forums or limited public forums, and if they do become public forums, they will be subject to First Amendment rules restricting viewpoint- and content-based discrimination. In *Widmar* there was really no contest over whether the University of Missouri–Kansas City had turned its classrooms into designated public forums, albeit ones probably limited to certain uses and users, such as meetings and events sponsored by student groups and other campus organizations.

Widmar didn't tell us how much latitude universities would have in deciding the extent to which its places and spaces would become public forums in the first place. The "traditional public forum," remember, is a space such as a central park, street, or sidewalk that is deemed a public forum through the direct force of the First Amendment itself, on the theory that certain central gathering places in our society are held in trust by the government for the people at large to be used as places for assembly and expression. The analogue to such a space at many universities might be the central campus green or quadrangle, places that have taken on the character of the public square in a typical city. Perhaps such campus spaces are not full-fledged traditional public forums in quite the sense of Boston Common or the National Mall—for example, universities might restrict their use to assemblies by groups affiliated with the university community—but with that minor caveat it stands to reason that such spaces ought to be understood for First Amendment purposes as free speech zones.

Moving from outdoor central spaces to other campus facilities such as auditoriums, the large foyers and atriums of student unions, and other high-traffic public spaces, *Widmar* clearly teaches that universities through policy and practice may turn such facilities into designated public forums (though again, perhaps limited to users affiliated with the university in some way). The essential point is that it is most sensible to think of a modern campus as a mix of various forum classifications, from traditional public forums, to limited public forums, to spaces that are not forums at all, but instead dedicated to the transaction of the university's educational business.

Lower court decisions dealing with the public forum status of state university campuses have not yet yielded any clear and consistent legal principles, and the approach suggested here has yet to work itself into the fabric of American law. In *American Civil Liberties Union v. Mote* (2005),[37] for example, a decision of the United States Court of Appeals for the Fourth Circuit, the court dealt with the public forum status of facilities and spaces at the University of Maryland campus in College Park. As recounted by the court, the College Park location is the University's flagship campus, occupying more than 1,200 acres.[38] The University has more than thirty-four thousand students, approximately a quarter of whom live on campus, and employs approximately twelve thousand faculty and staff.[39]

The case arose from an attempt by Michael Reeves to engage in speech of a political nature in one of the outdoor areas. Reeves was a member of the "LaRouche movement," a group dedicated to the politician Lyndon LaRouche, a third-party perennial candidate for the presidency of the

United States. Supported by several Maryland students, student groups, and the ACLU, Reeves argued that the outdoor areas of the College Park campus should be considered public forums.[40] Access to the outdoor areas was not limited to students, faculty, and staff, but instead was generally open to any member of the public, and the University allowed members of the public to engage in any lawful activity in these open areas, except public speaking and hand billing.[41] The court held, however, that these factors were not determinative, because the government does not create a public forum by inaction or by permitting limited discourse, but only by intentionally opening a nontraditional forum for public discourse.[42] The court held that the College Park campus was a limited public forum. The campus was not akin to a public street, park, or theater, but instead was "an institute of higher learning that is devoted to its mission of public education."[43] This mission necessarily "focuses on the students and other members of the university community."[44] The campus had not "traditionally been open to the public at large, but instead has been a 'special type of enclave' that is devoted to higher education." By implementing its use and access policy, the court held, the University made the campus a limited public forum.[45]

Issues of Safety, Security, and Violence on Campus

On February 12, 2010, Amy Bishop, a biology professor at the University of Alabama–Huntsville, shot six people at a faculty meeting, killing three of her colleagues in the biology department, including the department chair.[46] On April 16, 2007, Seung-Hui Cho, a student at Virginia Tech, murdered thirty-two students and faculty and wounded seventeen more, in the single worst day of student-inflicted violence on campus in American history.[47] On February 14, 2008, Steven Kazmierczak, a former student at Northern Illinois University, entered a lecture hall on the Northern Illinois campus packed with students attending an oceanography class, and opened fire with a shotgun and three handguns, killing six and wounding eighteen.[48]

In the aftermath of such tragedies, the concern for "order" on American college and university campuses, and the balance between the maintenance of order and the preservation of liberty, has taken on a special intensity. These incidents, fresh in the national consciousness, are not entirely new. In 1966, Charles Whitman, a student at the University of Texas, ascended to the observation deck of Austin campus clock tower and began a shooting rampage that lasted for ninety-six minutes, killing sixteen and wounding thirty-one. In 1976, Edward Charles Allaway, custodian at the Cal State Fullerton library, killed seven and wounded two more with a .22-caliber rifle in the morning as the library was opening, in what became known as the "Fullerton Library Massacre." In 1991, a graduate student at the University of Iowa named Gang Lu killed five persons on the campus and wounded two others before taking his own life, reportedly because he was upset about being passed over for academic honors. In 1996, Frederick Martin Davidson, a graduate student in engineering at San Diego State, in the midst of defending his graduate thesis, pulled out a gun and murdered three professors. In 2002, a student who had just been dismissed from the Appalachian School of Law in Virginia, Peter Odighizuwa, returned to the school and killed the dean, a professor, and another student, and wounded three other students. That same year a nursing student at the Arizona Nursing College, reportedly distressed over failing, entered the college with five guns, killing three instructors and then shooting himself. In 2006, five members of the Duquesne University basketball team were shot and wounded by other Duquesne students on campus after a dance, allegedly because one of the two shooters was upset that his date had talked to one of the players. To these and other college incidents we may add scores of notorious shootings at the nation's high schools and elementary schools, including the horrible 1999 mass murder of twelve and wounding of twenty-three other students and teachers by two students at Columbine High School in Littleton, Colorado.[49]

Striking the appropriate balance between the need to maintain physical safety on the campus and preservation of the traditionally open atmosphere of college life requires assessment of many trade-offs. Central among them is the relationship of violent action to violent expression. American law deals with the relationship of speech to harm—physical, psychological, and moral—through a variety of legal doctrines, including doctrines that deal directly with the relationship between speech and violence. They range from doctrines involving "incitement" or "threats," to doctrines that deal with harms to human dignity and reputation, such as "defamation" and "invasion of privacy," to doctrines that deal with speech that "discriminates" in conditions of employment or education, such as speech constituting sexual or racial harassment, to broader doctrines that attempt to regulate speech involving attacks on the basis of identity, such as race, gender, religion, or sexual orientation—usually described as "hate speech." This matrix of doctrines is complex and difficult to sort through in First Amendment law generally, and often becomes even more complex when transported to the environment of a modern campus.

Incitement and Campus Protest

A central conflict of modern free speech law is the relationship of speech to incitement of violence. The early answer to the problem was to err on the side of safety, security, law, and order. Speech that merely had a "bad tendency," meaning that it plausibly *might* lead to violence or lawbreaking, could be penalized, essentially on the theory that it is better to be safe than sorry. Indeed, the early decisions of Justice Holmes seemed to endorse this "bad tendency" test, notwithstanding his famous "clear and present danger" formulation. As explored in the prior chapter, Holmes ultimately abandoned the bad tendency test for his far more stringent emphasis on immediacy and imminence of severe danger in his dissenting opinion in *Abrams v. United States*.[50]

It took six decades for the Holmes view to firmly and finally take hold, in *Brandenburg v. Ohio* (1969).[51] The Ku Klux Klan was conducting a cross-burning ceremony on a farm in Hamilton County, Ohio, outside Cincinnati. The only non-Klan witnesses were members of a local Cincinnati television crew, which filmed the episode for later broadcast on a local station and a national network. The Klan members could be heard on film shouting all sorts of racist bile, such as "the nigger should be returned to Africa, the Jew to Israel," and "if our President, our Congress, our Supreme Court, continues to suppress the white, Caucasian race, it's possible that there might have to be some revengence taken."[52] ("Revengence" is not actually a word in English, but everyone got the message.)

The Supreme Court held that the speech of the Klan members was protected under the First Amendment, and reversed a criminal conviction against Brandenburg, the leader of the Klan group. The prosecution had been brought under an Ohio law that made it a crime to advocate "the duty, necessity, or propriety of crime, sabotage, violence, or unlawful methods of terrorism as a means of accomplishing industrial or political reform," or to assemble "with any society, group, or assemblage of persons formed to teach or advocate the doctrines of criminal syndicalism."[53] The Court emphasized that the ranting of the Ku Kluxers did not pose any immediate physical threat to anyone. While the Klan members had certainly engaged in the "abstract teaching" of the "moral propriety" of racist violence, this was not the same as an immediate incitement to violence. The Court thus held that the constitutional guarantees of free speech and free press "do not permit a State to forbid or proscribe advocacy of the use of force or of law violation except where such advocacy is directed to inciting or producing imminent lawless action and is likely to incite or produce such action."[54]

The *Brandenburg* test remains the governing legal standard. Distilled, it has three elements: intent, imminence, and likelihood. To punish someone for inciting violence, the government must prove that the speech is intended ("directed") to incite "imminent" lawless action and is "likely" to produce that lawless action. *Brandenburg* originated with protection of the evil speech of the Klan, but it would soon be put to the service of protecting speech on the other side of the political and social spectrum.

Brandenburg was applied in the context of a university campus during a 1970s Vietnam War protest, in *Hess v. Indiana* (1973).[55] Gregory Hess was one of the leaders of an antiwar demonstration on the campus of Indiana University. The demonstration spilled into a public street, with roughly 150 demonstrators blocking traffic. The sheriff ordered the protesters to clear the street. As they obeyed, Gregory Hess declared (as the sheriff passed by), "We'll take the fucking street later." Like a basketball referee slapping Bobby Knight with a technical file for dropping an f-bomb while protesting a call, the sheriff immediately laid one on Mr. Hess, arresting him for disorderly conduct.

The Supreme Court reversed Hess's conviction, stating that he could not be convicted merely for having used the word "fuck." More pointedly, the Court held that Hess's statement could not properly be treated as a direct verbal challenge to fight the sheriff or his deputies. There was testimony in the case that Hess was facing the crowd, not the street, and that he did not appear to be addressing any particular person. Relying on the *Brandenburg* test, the Court held that when Hess said, "We'll take the fucking street later," he was not advocating immediate lawbreaking, but rather illegal action "at some indefinite future time."

So too in *Cohen v. California* (1971),[56] in which Paul Cohen wore a jacket in the corridor of a Los Angeles courthouse, with women and children present, bearing on its back the phrase "Fuck the Draft." The Supreme Court, in an opinion by Justice John Marshall Harlan, rejected California's claim that it could use the law to preserve decency and decorum in society by banning public vulgarity and sheltering citizens from offensive language. No longer, the Court made clear, could vulgar words be equated with "fighting words", as that phrase had been used in *Chaplinsky*. Rather, to qualify as "fighting words," the statements must constitute "a direct personal insult" directed at a specific person.

Hate Speech and Threats on Campus

The phrase "hate speech" is widely used in our culture, including our universities. It's a popular term, but a not a legal one. In its broadest usage the phrase "hate speech" is usually understood as speech that attacks, insults, or degrades groups or individuals who are members of communities with a shared identity—such as race, religion, ethnicity, gender, or sexual orientation.[57] The extent to which hate speech should be prohibited and punished is a difficult political and legal question for most societies in the world. It has been an issue of great contention in American law, and is in turn an issue of great contention in American universities.[58] In both politics and law, off and on campus, the hate speech debate tends to be one of the most intense of all, because it places in opposition values that are each enormously weighty and of a constitutional dimension— the values of freedom of speech and the values of equality and protection of human dignity.[59]

If arguments for limiting speech are usually grounded in claims that the speech will pose palpable dangers, such as violence, or claims that the speech offends fundamental values of society, such as equality or respect for human dignity, the arguments for prohibiting and punishing hate speech tend to partake of both. History teaches us the tragic reality that hate speech may lead to murder and even genocide. In the United States, hate speech fueled Ku Klux Klan lynchings against blacks; in Nazi Germany, hate speech ignited the Holocaust. Hate speech may in some circumstances not merely *lead* to lawless action, it may in a direct sense *be* lawless action, as when hateful comments are so severe as to constitute a "hostile environment" in the workplace, and thus be deemed a form of discrimination prohibited by civil rights laws, such as Title VII of the federal Civil Rights Act of 1964.[60] Aside from the risk that hate speech may escalate into hate crime, or constitute a form of discrimination, it is deeply offensive to most people of good will, hurtful and damaging to the peace and human dignity of its victims, and corrosive of community values of equality and respect. Finally, in calibrating the quotient of rational to emotional content, hate speech tends to score low in rationality and high in emotional irrationality, a factor that adds to the case against hate speech in the context of a college campus, where rationality is an especially favored value.

The legal principles germane to the regulation of hate speech are intertwined with both the *Brandenburg* "incitement" standard and its legal cousin, the "true threat" doctrine. A "threat" is a slightly different legal animal than an "incitement." In incitement cases, the speaker is urging someone to do something illegal, and as the *Brandenburg* standard instructs, modern First Amendment law imposes a standard of imminence for the incitement to be illegal. Threats are different, and may take a number of different forms. The classic formulation of a threat is a statement intended to place the victim in reasonable apprehension of bodily harm. To brandish a gun or knife and say "hand me your wallet or I'll kill you" is a clear example. Unlike an incitement, a threat need not pose the specter of *immediate* evil repercussions to be illegal and outside the shelter of the First Amendment. If a mafia boss says "pay your gambling debt by the end of the week or my boys will come and break both your legs," the threat is real and illegal even though contingent on disobedience and not to be consummated immediately. A credible letter, e-mail, or phone call from a disturbed student threatening mass violence on a campus could constitute a "true threat" even though it is unclear when or where the violence will occur.

But "threat law" and "incitement law" do share one common characteristic. Mere fiery rhetoric and abstract hyperbole is protected speech even when cast in the language of a "threat," much as fiery rhetoric and abstract advocacy are protected as freedom of speech even when cast in the language of incitement. One famous example is *Watts v. United States* (1969).[61] Robert Watts was convicted for stating, at a public demonstration in Washington DC, that he would not report for his draft physical, and that "if they ever make me carry a rifle the first man I want to get in my sights is L.B.J. They are not going to make me kill my black brothers."[62] The Supreme Court overturned Watts's conviction for threatening the life of the President of the United States, holding that Watts's statements were not intended as literal incitements to violence, but rather were angry statements of what the Court called "political hyperbole."[63]

In assessing hate speech codes on American campuses, there are three logical steps in the analysis. The first step is to determine the First Amendment "baseline," the rules governing hate speech regulation that apply in the general marketplace. The second step, applicable to public universities, is to determine whether the university as a whole, or some aspect of the university's programs or physical spaces, should be treated as "carve-outs" in which the university has greater latitude to punish hate speech than the government would ordinarily have in the general marketplace. The third and final step, applicable to private universities only, is whether to penalize hate speech more severely than the First Amendment would permit for their public university counterparts.

In the general public spaces of the marketplace, outside a university campus, modern First Amendment doctrine protects hate speech, unless it crosses the line of offensive expression and satisfies the First Amendment standards for incitement or true threats. This was not always the case. In *Beauharnais v. Illinois* (1952),[64] the Supreme Court's first hate speech case, the Court upheld a criminal conviction against the leader of a racist Chicago organization, the White Circle League, for passing out leaflets calling on Chicago's Mayor and City Council "to halt the further encroachment, harassment and invasion of white people, their property, neighborhoods and persons, by the Negro."[65] The White Circle League's racist diatribe exhorted "one million self respecting white people in Chicago to unite," proclaiming, "If persuasion and the need to prevent the white race from becoming mongrelized by the Negro will not unite us, then the aggressions, . . . rapes, robberies, knives, guns and marijuana of the Negro, surely will."[66]

These leaflets were vicious and evil, to be sure, but could the state of Illinois send someone to jail for them? In an opinion written by Justice Felix Frankfurter, the United States Supreme Court affirmed the conviction. The opinion of Justice Frankfurter in *Beauharnais* tracked the reasoning of *Chaplinsky*, and represents the high-water mark of that case's influence on First Amendment law. Justice Frankfurter made an oblique but unmistakable reference to Nazi Germany in his opinion, noting that Illinois did not need to "await the tragic experience of the last three decades"[67] to conclude that laws against racial attacks were necessary to preserve the peace and order of the community. Illinois could thus rightly conclude that purveyors of racial and religious hate "promote strife and tend powerfully to obstruct the manifold adjustments required for free, ordered life in a metropolitan, polyglot community."[68] Illinois did not have to look past its borders to reach these conclusions. Recalling events ranging from the 1837 murder of the abolitionist Elijah Lovejoy to riots in Cicero in 1951,[69] Justice Frankfurter argued that Illinois might reasonably conclude that racial tensions are exacerbated and more likely to flare into violence when racist messages are tolerated. Justice Frankfurter also maintained that an individual's human dignity may reasonably be treated as inextricably intertwined with protection for the reputation of the individual's racial or religious group.[70] While in 1952 the term "hate speech" had yet to enter the American lexicon, Justice Frankfurter in *Beauharnais* elegantly captured the core of the argument for banning hate speech, stating that in "the face of this history and its frequent obligato of extreme racial and religious propaganda, we would deny experience to say that the Illinois legislature was without reason in seeking ways to curb false or malicious defamation of racial and religious groups, made in public places and by means calculated to have a powerful emotional impact on those to whom it was presented."[71] It was not for the Supreme Court, he argued, to deny that the "Illinois legislature may warrantably believe that a man's job and his educational opportunities and the dignity accorded him may depend as much on the reputation of the racial and religious group to which he willy-nilly belongs, as on his own merits."[72]

The decision in *Beauharnais*, however, has been undermined by more recent cases. In *R.A.V. v. City of St. Paul* (1992),[73] the Supreme Court, in an opinion by Justice Antonin Scalia, struck down a conviction under a hate speech ordinance from St. Paul, Minnesota,[74] against a minor who burned a cross on a black family's yard. Of course, the Constitution does not grant anyone the right to enter into someone else's backyard and burn a cross. The issue in *R.A.V.* was not whether the conduct of the minor who burned the cross was constitutionally protected, but rather whether the law under which the minor was convicted was constitutionally flawed. The Supreme Court held that the St. Paul ordinance was indeed flawed, infected as it was with "viewpoint discrimination," an exercise in legislative political correctness that penalized actions taken from one ideological perspective but not another. Displays containing abusive invective, no matter how vicious or severe, were permitted under the St. Paul ordinance unless they were addressed to what Justice Scalia described as "one of the specified disfavored topics."[75] Persons who wished to use fighting words in connection with other ideas, such as the expression of hostility on the basis of political affiliation, union membership, or homosexuality, were not encompassed by the language of the ordinance. Justice Scalia saw this as a fatal flaw, writing that the "First Amendment does not permit St. Paul to impose special prohibitions on those speakers who express views on disfavored subjects."[76] Justice Scalia argued that the ordinance licensed one side of the debate to "fight freestyle," while requiring the other to play by "Marquis of Queensberry Rules."[77]

A decade later, however, the result in *R.A.V.* was somewhat tempered by yet another ruling involving cross-burning, *Virginia v. Black* (2003).[78] (I was the lead counsel in the case, urging the Supreme Court to hold the Virginia anti-cross-burning law unconstitutional, for the reasons articulated in *R.A.V.* and *Brandenburg*.) The Virginia law read:

> It shall be unlawful for any person or persons, with the intent of intimidating any person or group of persons, to burn, or cause to be burned, a cross on the property of another, a highway or other public place. Any person who shall violate any provision of this section shall be guilty of a Class 6 felony.
>
> Any such burning of a cross shall be prima facie evidence of an intent to intimidate a person or group of persons.[79]

The Supreme Court held that the "prima facie evidence" provision of the Virginia cross-burning law violated the First Amendment. The plurality opinion was written by Justice Sandra Day O'Connor, and joined by Chief Justice Rehnquist, Justice Stevens, and Justice Breyer. Justice O'Connor held that the First Amendment permits the government to ban a "true threat."[80] In Justice O'Connor's view, it was permissible under the First Amendment for a state to pass *some* kind of cross-burning law, but that this particular Virginia law was not constitutional. As Justice O'Connor saw the matter, the flaw in the Virginia statute was the prima facie evidence provision.[81] This, Justice O'Connor held, was beyond what the Constitution would allow, for it permitted a jury to find the intent to intimidate with no actual evidence of such intent beyond the burning cross itself.[82] This effectively allowed Virginia to treat this particular symbol, a burning cross, as a threat per se, without regard to the surrounding context. As history indicates, the plurality elaborated, "a burning cross is not always intended to intimidate. Rather, sometimes the cross burning is a statement of ideology, a symbol of group solidarity. It is a ritual used at Klan gatherings, and it is used to represent the Klan itself."[83] Among other contexts, cross burnings have appeared in movies such as *Mississippi Burning*, and in plays such as the stage adaptation of Sir Walter Scott's *The Lady of the Lake.* Justice O'Connor admonished:

> It may be true that a cross burning, even at a political rally, arouses a sense of anger or hatred among the vast majority of citizens who see a burning cross. But this sense of anger or hatred is not sufficient to ban all cross burnings. As Gerald Gunther has stated, "The lesson I have drawn from my childhood in Nazi Germany and my happier adult life in this country is the need to walk the sometimes difficult path of denouncing the bigot's hateful ideas with all my power, yet at the same time challenging any community's attempt to suppress hateful ideas by force of law." The prima facie evidence provision in this case ignores all of the contextual factors that are necessary to decide whether a particular cross burning is intended to intimidate. The First Amendment does not permit such a shortcut.[84]

Justice Souter, joined by Justices Kennedy and Ginsburg, took an even stronger free speech position than Justice O'Connor, relying on *R.A.V.*

Those three Justices would have struck down the entire Virginia law, and all three convictions, because the law was tainted with the same kinds of viewpoint- and content-based distinctions that the Court had found constitutionally impermissible in *R.A.V.*[85] Only Justices Scalia and Thomas dissented from the view that the Virginia law was unconstitutional.[86] Justice Thomas took the strongest position, reasoning that given the unique history of the Ku Klux Klan and cross burning, Virginia could treat all such activity as an inherent threat. Justice Thomas wrote that in "every culture, certain things acquire meaning well beyond what outsiders can comprehend."[87] Justice Thomas argued that this may include both the sacred and the profane, and "cross-burning is the paradigmatic example of the latter."[88]

Where does *Virginia v. Black* leave "hate speech" legislation in the general marketplace? Clearly, absolute bans on the use of particular symbols, such as burning crosses or Nazi swastikas, remain unconstitutional after *Virginia v. Black*. Likewise, a state may still not take a "shortcut" and enact rules that treat the use of certain symbols or language as illegal per se.

If these are the principles that govern the general marketplace, what are the principles that govern hate speech codes on public university campuses? If one accepts that university campuses have a "dual character," then the aspect of the university's character that partakes of general marketplace principles will by extension be governed by the same First Amendment principles that apply in the wider societal marketplace. This means that in those physical spaces of the university that are properly deemed public forums, the university may not impose a blanket ban on "hate speech," prohibiting slurs or degrading speech that does not meet the standards for incitement, fighting words, or true threats. The same hate speech protected by Supreme Court decisions such as *Brandenburg v. Ohio*, *R.A.V. v. City of St. Paul*, and *Virginia v. Black* in the public forums of society will be protected in the public forums of the public state university. And as discussed more fully in the subsequent sections of this chapter, dealing with the speech of faculty members and students, when university faculty and students are speaking "as citizens" on "issues of public concern" in those public forums, they receive, as individuals, robust levels of First Amendment protection.

Lower court decisions that have examined hate speech codes at public state universities have generally struck them down as violations of the First Amendment, usually because the codes extended to a broad range of constitutionally protected expression, protection that would be allowed in the general American marketplace. One of the leading cases, often cited as precedent, is *Doe v. University of Michigan* (1989),[89] in which a federal district court struck down the University of Michigan's hate speech regulations. To its credit, the Michigan policy established a nuanced system of regulation, under which the degree of regulation was dependent on the location of the conduct at issue. As the lower court described the policy, the broadest range of speech and dialogue was "tolerated" in public parts of the campus.[90] Only an act of physical violence or destruction of property was subject to punishment in these settings.[91] Publications sponsored by the University, such as the *Michigan Daily* and the *Michigan Review*, were not subject to regulation.[92] In contrast, a more sweeping standard applied to speech in the University's educational and academic centers, such as classroom buildings, libraries, research laboratories, and recreation and study centers.[93] Yet even so, the court found that the Michigan policy, as interpreted by the University Office of Affirmative Action,[94] still captured and prohibited a wide range of expression protected by the First Amendment, and therefore struck the policy the down.[95]

The Michigan decision exemplifies a relatively consistent judicial hostility to campus hate speech codes. Many of these codes have attempted to draw a parallel between the "hostile work environment" concepts that exist in workplace-related civil rights laws, and the notion of a "hostile educational environment." Drawing on the theories of *Chaplinsky* and *Beauharnais*, for example, the University of Wisconsin in *UWM Post v. Board of Regents of the University of Wisconsin* (1991)[96] defended a hate speech code by arguing that the rule only regulated speech with minimum social value, and that hate speech had demonstrably harmful effects. The federal court pointed out that the rule penalized students whose comments demean others on the basis of characteristics such as race, sex, or religion, but not comments that complement or affirm others based on those characteristics. The court clearly saw this kind of content and viewpoint discrimination as prohibited by modern First Amendment principles, and rejected the principles suggested by the older decisions in *Chaplinsky* or *Beauharnais*. The University's argument was provocative. If the

First Amendment permits government to mandate a "racism-free" work-place, why shouldn't it permit government to mandate a "racism-free" campus? The issue here is a variant of the recurring question that permeates this book, which is whether a university should be thought of as an extension of the general marketplace or a "carve-out," such as the work-place, in which other values trump wide-open free speech principles. The answer suggested by *UMW Post* is that rules governing employment are not necessarily appropriate for education. Universities *are* largely marketplaces of ideas, in ways that typical workplaces are not. And in turn, workplaces are settings driven largely by economic objectives, in ways that universities are not.[97] Title VII's proscription on racist or sexist working environments is directly connected to the Civil Rights Act's goal of prohibiting discriminatory treatment in the workplace. The typical work-place is not a space where people come together to debate and discuss ideas and policies, but rather one where people perform functional tasks in cooperation with one another to accomplish some work-related objective. Title VII thus governs economic transactions between employer and employee in settings where the employee who is the victim of harassment is genuinely "captive." Title VII's purpose in banning hostile work environments is not so much ideological as it is practical, designed to buttress the Act's ultimate goal of eliminating discriminatory conduct by employers.[98]

American public universities ought not be deemed powerless, however, to protect themselves against all speech that is inimical to order and morality. At the very least, public universities may adopt and apply the rules applicable to legal concepts such as incitement, true threats, defamation, and invasion of privacy. At the opposite extreme, blanket bans on "hate speech" or "incivility" in all areas of campus life will clearly be struck down, as courts impose the principles of the marketplace over the desire of some public universities to set themselves off as moral spaces. It would stretch existing constitutional law too far, however, to interpret it as finally and fully declaring that all efforts to enforce moral norms of civility and respect for human dignity on campus are doomed. The University of Michigan standard was rightly struck down by the lower court that tested it, given the flights of political correctness that had been grafted onto the policy by the University's Office of Affirmative Action.

The Michigan policy was on the right track, however, in suggesting that the standards of the open marketplace may appropriately apply to vast aspects of the University's spaces and programs, and that yet-more restrictive standards, perhaps akin to those that apply in "hostile environment" cases under civil rights laws, might apply in other academic settings, such as classrooms. Constitutional rules, in short, may be nuanced, and attuned to the particular programs, spaces, and places in which they are being applied. To explore these possible carve-outs from general marketplace principles that legitimately should apply to public universities, let us turn to the First Amendment principles that govern the speech of faculty members and students. These rules appropriately take into account the setting in which the speech occurs.

The Free Speech Rights of Faculty

University professors do not generally think of themselves as ordinary employees, but they don't work for free. In a literal sense, professors at public universities are public employees, and in a legal sense their free speech rights must begin with an analysis of the free speech rights of government employees. In most employment settings, in both the public and private sectors, employees accept certain limits on their speech while on the job. In the general marketplace, for example, free speech principles protect a citizen in telling dirty sex jokes, making lurid and sexually suggestive comments, or using racist epithets such as "nigger." In contrast, an employee who repeatedly tells dirty jokes, engages in sexual innuendo and come-ons, or uses insulting racial and ethnic language at work may be violating civil rights laws, and consequently may lose his or her job. The employer may fire the employee for alienating customers or coworkers, or even for exposing the employer itself to potential liability for violating civil rights laws, such as the body of law that has evolved under Title VII of the Civil Rights Act of 1964 that makes an employer liable for allowing "a hostile work environment."[99] Universities are employers, and as such may demand that administrators, staff, coaches, and professors check their sexual and racial harassment at the workplace door.

The body of First Amendment law addressing the free speech rights of government employees often goes by the label the "*Connick/Picker-*

ing standard," after two of the main cases in the field, *Connick v. Myers* (1983)[100] and *Pickering v. Board of Education* (1968).[101] In *Connick* the Supreme Court held that the New Orleans District Attorney did not violate the First Amendment when he fired an Assistant District Attorney for insubordination when she responded to an unwanted directive by circulating a questionnaire throughout the office dealing with the office's confidence in its supervisors, transfer policies, office morale, and lack of a grievance committee. In *Pickering* the Supreme Court held that a school board violated the First Amendment when it fired a teacher for writing a letter to a local newspaper critical of how the school board and superintendent had handled revenue bond proposals and the allocation of financial resources within the school district. The standard employs a balancing test to weigh the free speech rights of public employees against the workplace needs of public employers to carry on the public's business.

The challenge posed in the application of the *Connick/Pickering* standard was well captured by the Court in *Pickering*, in which the Court explained, "The State has interests as an employer in regulating the speech of its employees that differ significantly from those it possesses in connection with regulation of the speech of the citizenry in general."[102] The task is to calibrate the right accommodation between these competing interests, and thereby "arrive at a balance between the interests of the teacher, as a citizen, in commenting upon matters of public concern and the interest of the State, as an employer, in promoting the efficiency of the public services it performs through its employees."[103]

The *Connick/Pickering* standard has evolved into a two-step inquiry. When a public employee complains that he or she has been disciplined or discharged in retaliation for the exercise of free speech rights, a court first must ask whether the employee was speaking "as a citizen" on "a matter of public concern." If the answer is no, the employee loses the case. If the answer is yes, the court proceeds to part 2 of the test, in which it weighs the rights of the employee against the government's justification for limiting the speech. The focus of this part tends to be on whether the particular government agency is able to demonstrate that the speech at issue in some palpable sense disrupts or interferes with the agency's functions.

Professors at public universities are public employees, which presents the question of how this two-part *Connick/Pickering* standard should be interpreted in the context of public higher education. More specifically, the question is whether concepts of "academic freedom" require either the application of an entirely different standard than *Connick/Pickering* to the world of public universities, or at the very least a special sensitivity to the special place of academic freedom in the "job description" of a university professor in applying the *Connick/Pickering* balance.

The Supreme Court in *Garcetti v. Ceballos* (2006)[104] curtailed the free speech rights of government employees by narrowing the scope of part 1 of the *Connick/Pickering* test. *Garcetti* involved a claim by a deputy district attorney in Los Angeles, Richard Ceballos, who claimed that his First Amendment rights were violated when he had been subjected to adverse employment actions in retaliation for the positions he articulated during a heated dispute over a search warrant in a pending criminal case being handled by the District Attorney's Office. The Court in *Garcetti* held that in determining whether the speech at issue is speech "as a citizen on matters of public concern," the critical inquiry is whether the speech of a government employee is speech required by the employee's job—speech that falls within the official duties of the employee as part of the job description for the position the employee occupies. If the speech is required as part of the employee's job description, the Court held, the employee will be deemed to be speaking "as an employee" and not "as a citizen." Under *Garcetti*, such "do it for the boss" expression will be deemed subject to the rules and restrictions established by the government in its capacity as an employer, which means an employee can be disciplined or even fired for violating the rules established by the employer's governmental supervisors.

Justice David Souter authored a dissenting opinion generally attacking the Court's ruling in *Garcetti* as too restrictive of the speech rights of government employees. In the course of his dissent he homed in particularly on the speech of one class of government employees: university professors. Noting that the Court's ruling appeared "spacious enough" to sweep within its domain public university professors, Justice Souter stated that he had "to hope that today's majority does not mean to imperil First Amendment protection of academic freedom in public colleges and universities, whose teachers necessarily speak and write 'pursuant to official duties.'"

Justice Souter's point seemed to strike home, and the Court's majority opinion answered Justice Souter's "hope" by appearing to concede *at least the possibility* that he was correct. The Court left open the potential for future recognition of an "academic freedom loophole" that might in the future exempt public university professors from the scope of the ruling in *Garcetti*. "There is some argument that expression related to academic scholarship or classroom instruction implicates additional constitutional interests that are not fully accounted for by this Court's customary employee-speech jurisprudence," the majority opinion conceded. Keeping all options open, the Court stated, "We need not, and for that reason do not, decide whether the analysis we conduct today would apply in the same manner to a case involving speech related to scholarship or teaching."

This intriguing exchange in *Garcetti* signals, at the very least, that the Court remains acutely sensitive to the importance of safeguarding the academic freedom interests of public university professors. It does not signal, however, any willingness by the Court to create an entirely separate First Amendment "right to academic freedom" that would displace the Free Speech Clause and the *Connick/Pickering* standard when university professors are involved. A more modest version of the "academic freedom loophole" would be to concede that the job of a university professor is perhaps unique in the realm of public employment, in that it may not be possible to draw a clean line between expression engaged in "as a citizen" and expression engaged in "as an employee" when crafting the "job description" of the professor.

It is very doubtful that the Supreme Court would entirely scrap *Connick/Pickering* in the context of universities. What is instead more likely to evolve, and what is instead more principled, is an interpretation of *Connick/Pickering* that acknowledges that some (but not all) of the speaking and writing undertaken by university professors must be classified as speech "as a citizen on matters of public concern" even though that speech is simultaneously speech undertaken within the scope of employment.[105] There is, in fact, a nice parallelism between this academic freedom loophole and the common higher education practice of treating the writings of university professors as owned by the professors themselves, and not as "works for hire" owned by the university as employer.[106]

In attempting to bring more nuanced focus to the problem of calibrating the appropriate scope of the free speech rights of academics, it
is helpful to divide the analysis into three inquiries: (1) the free speech
issues that arise from the communication and conduct of professors in
the classroom in their role as teachers; (2) the issues that arise from the
"outward-looking" efforts of professors engaging in research, scholarship,
public speaking, public service, or civic engagement; and (3) the issues
that arise from the expression of professors incident to their participation
in internal university governance and collegial interactions.

Free speech issues regarding the rights of professors in relation to
classroom teaching tend to focus on drawing the line between actions
by professors that interfere in some palpable sense with the educational
mission of the university, such as those that constitute gender or racial
harassment by creating hostile environments within the classroom on
the one hand, and that, on the other hand, merely express unpopular,
controversial, or divisive viewpoints. The traditions of academic culture
and the principles of First Amendment law are simpatico in defining this
line. Principles of free speech and academic freedom certainly should be
understood to give faculty a large measure of independence in how they
present materials in class on matters relating to race, sex, or sexual orientation. Viewpoint discrimination should not be permitted, even when
the university regards the view espoused by the professor as repugnant.
Thus a professor should have the right to espouse bona fide academic
opinions concerning racial characteristics or capabilities, even though
many people of goodwill and good sense on the campus might find the
opinions objectionable. It does not follow, however, that the professor
has the freedom to engage in racist, sexist, or homophobic speech attacks
during class, even though those attacks might otherwise be protected in
the open marketplace. Expression that constitutes harassment or the creation of a hostile environment is not protected under any plausible conception of academic freedom or First Amendment law. Expression that is
offensive or disturbing because of its viewpoint is protected by customs
of academic freedom and First Amendment principle. The standards and
traditions are in alignment. There may be close and difficult cases—there
always are—but the guiding principles and defining lines are relatively
clear and stable.

An illustration of a close and difficult case is *Cohen v. San Bernardino Valley College* (1996),[107] which involved a professor named Dean Cohen, a tenured English and film studies professor at a state institution. In the spring of 1992, Cohen taught a remedial English class to community college students. Cohen used a confrontational teaching style, designed to shock his students and make them think and write about controversial subjects. He assigned provocative materials and discussed subjects such as obscenity, cannibalism, and consensual sex with children. In the course of his teaching he at times used vulgarities and profanity. One of his students was offended by Cohen's repeated focus on topics of a sexual nature, his use of profanity and vulgarities, and by certain comments that she interpreted as directed intentionally at her and certain other female students. She considered the comments humiliating and harassing. As the conflict with Cohen intensified, she filed a grievance against him, claiming that his actions violated the College's sexual harassment policy. Following grievance committee hearings and a review by the College president, it was found that Cohen had engaged in "sexual harassment which had the effect of unreasonably interfering with an individual's academic performance or creating an intimidating, hostile or offensive work environment," that Cohen made "sexually suggestive" remarks to the complaining student, and that several students were offended by Professor Cohen's use of profanity and frequent use of sexual topics in class. These findings were in turn affirmed by the College's Board of Trustees. Cohen filed suit in federal court, arguing that the College's action violated his academic freedom rights. Cohen lost his case in the trial court, and then won on appeal to the United States Court of Appeals for the Ninth Circuit. The contrast between the two opinions is illuminating.

The trial court opinion, written by United States District Judge Ronald S. W. Lew, applied the *Connick/Pickering* test, and held that Professor Cohen's discussion of pornography and sexually oriented topics was speech "on a matter of public concern," but his use of profanity in the classroom was not. Judge Lew ruled that the College had substantial interests at stake in deterring disruption of the educational process. Cohen's confrontational and suggestive discussion of sexual issues led to self-censorship, intimidation, and offense on the part of many of his students, the Judge ruled. While Cohen's teaching methods were effective for some of his students, Judge Lew ruled, they were still an impediment to learning for many. Certainly professors have the right to challenge students, the Judge reasoned, and even shock them and make them uncomfortable at times, but there is a line between the appropriate or tolerable use of such methods and sexual banter and innuendo that becomes abusive and offensive. Ultimately, university officials have the power to sanction professors who cross that line. As Judge Lew observed:

> Colleges and universities must have the power to require professors to effectively educate all segments of the student population, including those students unused to the rough and tumble of intellectual discussion. If colleges and universities lack this power, each classroom becomes a separate fiefdom in which the educational process is subject to professorial whim. Universities must be able to ensure that the more vulnerable as well as the more sophisticated students receive a suitable education. The Supreme Court has clearly stated that the public employer must be able to achieve its mission and avoid disruption of the workplace. Within the educational context, the university's mission is to effectively educate students, keeping in mind students' varying backgrounds and sensitivities. Furthermore, the university has the right to preclude disruption of this educational mission through the creation of a hostile learning environment.[108]

Judge Lew's opinion was reversed on appeal by the Ninth Circuit in an opinion written by Judge Robert Merhige, a famous and highly respected Senior District Judge who was sitting by designation (a kind "visiting judge" role) from his normal home base in Richmond, Virginia. Judge Merhige's ruling for the Ninth Circuit was that the College's policy was "unconstitutionally vague," and thus could not be applied to punish Cohen. Judge Merhige did *not* hold that Cohen's speech was protected by the First Amendment, or that in the future the San Bernardino Valley College or any other state college or university could not bar such speech through a more narrowly and precisely crafted policy. Judge Merhige's opinion for the Ninth Circuit instead simply stated:

> We do not decide whether the College could punish speech of this nature if the Policy were more precisely construed by authoritative interpretive

guidelines or if the College were to adopt a clearer and more precise policy. Rather, we hold that the Policy is simply too vague as applied to Cohen in this case. Cohen's speech did not fall within the core region of sexual harassment as defined by the Policy. Instead, officials of the College, on an entirely ad hoc basis, applied the Policy's nebulous outer reaches to punish teaching methods that Cohen had used for many years. Regardless of what the intentions of the officials of the College may have been, the consequences of their actions can best be described as a legalistic ambush. Cohen was simply without any notice that the Policy would be applied in such a way as to punish his long-standing teaching style—a style which, until the College imposed punishment upon Cohen under the Policy, had apparently been considered pedagogically sound and within the bounds of teaching methodology permitted at the College.[109]

What are we to make of the *Cohen* decision? From the College's perspective, it was a near miss; from Professor Cohen's perspective, a narrow escape. The Supreme Court did not review Judge Merhige's ruling. If today's Supreme Court were to review the decision, there is a strong chance that, given its ruling in *Garcetti v. Ceballos*, it would reverse Judge Merhige and instead adopt the view of Judge Lew. Judge Merhige was a great jurist, but in the *Cohen* case his holding that the policy of the College was unconstitutionally vague was itself vague. The policy was, in fact, quite clear, and should have been deemed consistent with First Amendment standards.

The one strong point Judge Merhige did make was that there was an air of sandbagging to what the College did. Cohen had been engaged in his teaching techniques for years, and the policy had been in place for years, yet Cohen had not been disciplined. To spring this on him suddenly (if that is in fact what happened) did seem unfair. If the College had put him on notice that his behavior violated the policy and told him to tone it down—particularly the techniques that seemed targeted at particular female students—there would have been a chance for Cohen to bring himself within the College's definition of acceptable professional bounds. If he chose at that point to defy the College's admonition, the matter could be tested on the merits in court, but Cohen would no longer be able to claim that he had been sandbagged.

On the whole, most lower courts that have addressed the issue have found that classroom speech by professors that may fairly be characterized as sexual harassment or as creating a hostile environment simply is not protected by the First Amendment or conceptions of academic freedom. Similarly, courts have shown little sympathy for the use by professors of racial slurs or graphic vulgarity toward students in classroom settings. As the United States Court of Appeals for the Sixth Circuit stated in *Bonnell v. Lorenzo* (2001),[110] a First Amendment suit brought by a community college professor contesting his suspension, just "as a university coach may have the constitutional right to use the word 'nigger,' but does not have the constitutional right to use the word in the context of motivating his basketball players, so too, Plaintiff may have a constitutional right to use words such as 'pussy,' 'cunt,' and 'fuck,' but he does not have a constitutional right to use them in a classroom setting where they are not germane to the subject matter, in contravention of the College's sexual harassment policy."

In contrast to cases that involve harassment, hostile environments, or gratuitous vulgarity by professors in classrooms, the free speech rights of professors are at a high point when the complaint arises from the university's disagreement with the ideological viewpoint expressed by the professor. In *Levin v. Harleston* (1991),[111] for example, District Judge Kenneth Conboy began his opinion with the provocative statement, "This case raises serious constitutional questions that go to the heart of the current national debate on what has come to be denominated as 'political correctness' in speech and thought on the campuses of the nation's colleges and universities." The case involved Michael Levin, a professor at City College of New York, a public institution funded in part by the State of New York. Professor Levin was the author of a number of controversial writings on matters relating to race, affirmative action, and the relative intelligence of whites and blacks. Judge Conboy found that as a result of Levin's controversial views, the College had set up "shadow sections" for his courses, to which students could voluntarily switch after having been warned by the College Dean that Levin's views were controversial, and that the creation of these shadow sections operated to abridge Levin's free speech and tenure rights. Judge Conboy further found that the College President had created an ad hoc committee of faculty to investigate Levin's writing, but not his conduct, and that this was an unconstitutional attempt by the college to silence his views through an implicit threat to revoke his tenure. Judge Conboy issued an injunction against the College, enjoining it from commencing disciplinary proceedings based solely on Levin's protected expression of ideas, and from creating shadow sections for Levin's courses. Judge Conboy further ordered the College to take reasonable steps to prevent students from disrupting Levin's classes.

Judge Conboy's analysis was predicated on a distinction between the College's right to regulate in reasonable ways the conduct of a faculty member, and the limitations on the College's right to regulate a faculty member's expression of beliefs, in his or her scholarship and in the classroom. Judge Conboy held that Levin's views on matters relating to race were constitutionally protected forms of expression. Because it was quite clear that the College would not have taken the actions toward Levin that it did in the absence of his controversial positions, Judge Conboy held that the College's activities violated the First Amendment.

On appeal, the United States Court of Appeals affirmed the bulk of Judge Conboy's ruling, holding in a relatively brief opinion that Judge Conboy was correct in finding Professor Levin's constitutional rights violated by "shadow classes," upholding that portion of the Judge Conboy's order enjoining those classes, and further finding that Levin's rights had been violated by the College's implicit threats of discipline against him. The Court of Appeals did hold, however, that Judge Conboy had gone too far in finding that the College had failed to adequately respond to actions of students protesting Levin's activities.

In contrast to the powerful interests that colleges and universities possess in exercising some measure of control over the *inward-looking* actions of professors in classroom environments, interests born of the university's imperative responsibility for the educational well-being of its own students, the interests of universities in regulating the *outward-looking* expression of faculty members is more ephemeral. In their public-facing activity, faculty members engage in a huge variety of expressive endeavors, including research, publications, performances, speeches, public speaking, public service, participation in conferences, membership in outside organizations, leadership in scientific, political, religious, and social causes, and myriad other forms of civic and intellectual engagement.

Unlike the role of the professor in the classroom, in which the *Garcetti v. Ceballos* notion of speech "on the job" is at least a plausible fit, the outward-looking expression of professors does not sit at all comfortably within the *Garcetti* model. Research, scholarship, public service, and the almost infinite array of other externally focused activities conducted by faculty members is certainly often a requirement of their job as university professors, though colleges and universities differ in their emphasis on these different components of academic life. Some follow "teacher-scholar" models, others "scholar-teacher" models; there are examples in which one or the other function entirely predominates, and a wide variety of gradations in between. Virtually all higher education treats external expression as, at minimum, a permissible element of a faculty member's life, and at many of the nation's research-centered institutions, scholarship is the single most important component of decisions to hire, promote, and grant tenure to faculty. At the same time, it has always been the understanding that a professor's research and a professor's outward expression of his or her thought "belongs" to the professor, and is understood as speaking "for the professor," not "for the university." The professor's creative and intellectual efforts are not deemed "work for hire" in copyright law, and the professor's efforts are not understood to be the expression of the university in the marketplace of ideas.

In First Amendment law parlance, it thus seems perfectly apt to describe the external speech of university professors as speech in which the employee is speaking "as a citizen on matters of public concern." Yet even this phrasing is not entirely apt in describing a large part of the external expression of professors. While all the speech in the vast array of the arts, sciences, and professions that compose a complex university should surely qualify as speech on matters of "public concern," the phrase "as a citizen" is in some ways too limiting, too tied to notions of politics and democracy, to capture the role of the professor. The scientist who publishes his or her scientific findings, for example, is not speaking as a member of a scientific discipline—perhaps a "citizen of the scientific world," if you will—rather than as a "citizen" in a political sense.

The one phrase from the classic First Amendment tradition that fits perfectly in describing the outward expression of faculty members is the "marketplace of ideas." Indeed, the scholarship of professors is the quintessential exemplar of participation in the world marketplace of ideas, and, in that sense, it is hard to imagine speech that more heartily qualifies for the highest levels of constitutional protection.

Does this mean the university must take a completely "hands-off" posture in relation to the external expression of faculty members? Of course not. Universities *must* engage in assessment of the quality of the intellectual expression of faculty members, and such assessment is undertaken routinely, in deciding whom to hire, whom to promote, whom to grant tenure, whom to award with research stipends, endowed chairs, raises in salary, and other recognitions of achievement in academic life.

And indeed, the outward expression of university professors may trigger controversies that can lead to serious difficulties. The case of Ward Churchill is a telling example. Churchill, a professor at the University of Colorado, was scheduled to give a speech in 2005 at Hamilton College in New York when the Hamilton student newspaper revealed that he had once described the victims killed in the World Trade Center attacks as "little Eichmanns" (by which he meant the financial-service industry workers who banally served the purposes of global capitalism, which he felt was the primary cause of the attacks). Churchill's comparison of the innocent victims of the terrorist attacks to Nazis made him a national target, especially for conservative bloggers and talk radio hosts. For a period, Bill O'Reilly on Fox News used Churchill as his nightly fodder. Hamilton College canceled Churchill's scheduled speech, and the University of Colorado launched an investigation into whether Churchill had, in the words of the Chancellor, "overstepped his bounds." The University ultimately decided that Churchill's outrageous remarks were protected under the free speech guarantees of the First Amendment. The spotlight shined on Churchill, however, led to such intense scrutiny of his record as a scholar and speaker that old charges of fabricated research, plagiarism, and inadequate research citation were unearthed, ultimately leading to Churchill's dismissal from the University, by an 8–1 vote of its Board of Regents. Churchill sued, and a jury awarded him one dollar in damages (a decision that was under appeal as this book was going to press).[112]

The critical line here is one that most professors and administrators know well, one deeply ingrained in our habits of shared governance, peer review, and professionalism. The task is to evaluate the intellectual output of colleagues for its quality and merit, but not for its "viewpoint," at least not in any crass ideological sense. This line is at times blurry, for in passing judgment on the merit or demerit of work it is *impossible* to avoid evaluation of the positions expressed in the work. We do not award tenure purely on neatness and style points.

An example of the difficulty of drawing these lines is the controversy over a memorandum written by John C. Yoo, a tenured professor of law at the University of California–Berkeley, while he was an official at the Department of Justice's Office of Legal Counsel, offering a detailed legal opinion justifying the use of extreme interrogation techniques and arguing that the President of the United States possessed inherent authority as Commander-in-Chief to override federal law and international treaties during wartime. The memorandum triggered an intense debate over whether Professor Yoo should be dismissed from his position on the law faculty at Berkeley. Advocates for Yoo's dismissal argued that his memorandum was directly intended to facilitate torture, that he was a war criminal, that he intentionally ignored settled principles of law and reasonable standards of academic and legal judgment for the deliberate purpose of aiding and abetting the Bush administration in the commission of war crimes, and that the advice he gave the President fell so extremely far below minimal professional standards of academic credibility and integrity as to bring into question his scholarly credentials and fitness to educate law students. A relatively small number of lawyers and legal scholars defended the gist of Yoo's Justice Department "torture memo" on the merits, arguing that his narrow definition of torture and expansive understanding of the powers of the President were both legally sound and necessary to protect the nation. The vast majority of those who defended Yoo, however, did not defend his positions or the quality of his work, but rather his academic freedom. Yoo's dean at Berkeley, Christopher Edley Jr., for example, asserted that even if there was a strong consensus among legal academics and his colleagues on the law faculty that Yoo's views were wrong, to dismiss him from the University on that basis would render academic freedom meaningless. Other defenders of Yoo's academic freedom noted that he had not been convicted of any crime, that academic lawyers often take positions (in the service of both liberal and conservative causes) that are unpopular or outside the mainstream of orthodox theory or doctrine, that all lawyers, including academic lawyers, at times provide advice to unpopular clients or champion unpopular causes, and that it was perilous precedent to punish Yoo by ruining his academic standing for actions taken in his entirely different role as a government lawyer, effectively making him the scapegoat for the larger national disenchantment with President Bush and his administration's policies.[113]

Yet if the line is at times blurry, our confidence in its vitality is not. In my experience, most conscientious academics intuitively acknowledge and respect this line, and endeavor vigilantly to remain faithful to it. In my life at universities I have heard scores of colleagues in faculty and committee meetings make pronouncements to this effect: "While I approach these issues from a different perspective than 'Professor Smith' and disagree with her conclusions, I think her work is of the highest quality, and I endorse her candidacy for promotion." I have read countless reviews of scholarship during tenure review processes in which scholars outside a tenure candidate's university are asked to review the candidate's work. Again, it is commonplace for reviewers to disclose that they are members of an opposing school of thought from that of the candidate, and to articulate disagreement—sometimes pointed disagreement—with the candidate's conclusions. Yet such reviewers will nonetheless frequently give the candidate the highest marks for quality, and recommend that the candidate be granted tenure or promotion.

But there are times when this norm is violated. I have known colleagues who seem almost constitutionally incapable of separating their intellectual judgment regarding the merits of an advocate's argument with their professional judgment regarding the advocate's merit. More troubling, some allow illegal and unethical bias to influence their academic assessments in a far more sinister sense, voting to grant or deny tenure, for example, for illicit reasons such as racism, sexism, or personal grudges. There are also those who simply take the intellectually arrogant stance that any person who disagrees with them intellectually on some proposition of science, the arts, or the professions must be deficient in academic competence.

If the norm of academic professionalism described here accurately captures the prevailing ethos in academic life, does it also describe an intelligible principle in academic law? Is the touchstone articulated here, which distinguishes "neutral judgments of academic quality and merit" from "viewpoint judgments," also a principle of First Amendment law?

The answer is a resounding yes. In decision after decision, the Supreme Court has held that while government may make content-based qualitative judgments regarding how to best invest its resources with regard to expressive activity, it may not engage in viewpoint-discrimination in the allocation of those resources. Perhaps the strongest doctrinal statement of this principle occurred in a decision involving lawyers who worked for the Legal Services Corporation, titled *Legal Services Corporation v. Velazquez* (2001).[114] In *Velazquez*, the Supreme Court declared that certain viewpoint-based restrictions that Congress had placed on the power of legal services lawyers, limiting the types of cases and arguments they could advance in representing clients, violated the First Amendment. In an opinion by Justice Kennedy, the Court held that while government may engage in viewpoint discrimination when the government itself is speaking, or when government is using private speakers as its "agents" to advance the government's own message, it may not engage in viewpoint discrimination when it is merely subsidizing the speech of others. This rule applies with particular force when the government's purpose in subsidizing speech is to encourage a diversity of views among speakers. In the words of the Court, "viewpoint-based funding decisions can be sustained in instances in which the government is itself the speaker" or in which the government "used private speakers to transmit specific information pertaining to its own program." Thus, when "the government disburses public funds to private entities to convey a governmental message, it may take legitimate and appropriate steps to ensure that its message is neither garbled nor distorted by the grantee."

The Free Speech Rights of Students

The free speech rights of students, like the free speech rights of faculty, again reflects the dual character of the university. There are settings in which students are speaking out on issues of public concern as citizens of society, participating in the marketplace of ideas. In those settings, students partake of the fullest protections of the First Amendment. There are also settings, however, in which student speech is not properly characterized as speech in the general marketplace, settings in which the student is speaking as a student, participating in the academic and programmatic mission of the university. In these settings the university has the right to insist that student speech conform to certain norms of academic integrity and civility, just as it may make such demands on its faculty. While the First Amendment bars a public university from censoring student speech in these academic and programmatic settings on the basis of viewpoint, the First Amendment does not bar a university from requiring that those viewpoints be expressed in a manner that conforms to its academic and community standards. In these special settings, the university may not censor the views a student chooses to express, but it may exert some reasonable regulation on the manner of that expression.

The easiest example of this principle involves pure curricular expression, such as a student's expression in a classroom setting or a class assignment. In such curricular contexts, a student is speaking in his or her capacity *as a student*, not as a "citizen" speaking out on public affairs, and correspondingly, the student's free speech rights are at their lowest ebb, and the corresponding powers of the university at their highest. It is important to recognize that in these settings the student may very well be speaking *about* issues of public concern. Indeed, by hypothesis virtually all the curriculum-related speech that takes place on a college campus involves issues of public concern, such as those concerning science, art, literature, religion, medicine, law, or politics. What matters is not the subject matter of the speech, but the academic setting in which that speech is expressed. No university dedicated to academic freedom should penalize a student for his or her views on affirmative action, the origins of the universe, the war in Afghanistan, or modern art. Any university dedicated to academic freedom may and should, however, enforce norms of academic integrity that require that a student expressing such views not plagiarize from the work of others, not deviate from standards of good grammar and clear writing, or not lace the expression with vulgarity, gratuitous personal insult, or other standards of academic civility and that are properly demanded of students in a rigorous academic setting.

In *Brown v. Li* (2002),[115] for example, a graduate student at the University of California–Santa Barbara, Christopher Brown, had his scientific thesis approved on its academic merits by his thesis committee. After obtaining the approval signatures, he added an acknowledgments section, which he labeled as "Disacknowledgements," and which began, "I would like to offer special Fuck You's to the following degenerates for of being an ever-present hindrance during my graduate career."[116] Brown then identified the Dean and staff of the graduate school, the managers of the library, the former California Governor, Pete Wilson, the Regents of the University of California, and "Science" in general as having been particularly obstructive to his progress toward his graduate degree. Brown later explained that he had not revealed the section to the members of his committee because he feared that they would not approve it.[117]

Well, he got that much right.

The University, finding out about the "Disacknowledgements," flunked him. The Ninth Circuit sided with the University, holding that college and university educators may restrict student speech in curricular matters, provided the limitation is reasonably related to a legitimate pedagogical purpose. Academic work, the court held, was different from freedom of speech in the general marketplace: "The Supreme Court has suggested that core curricular speech—that which is an integral part of the classroom-teaching function of an educational institution—differs from students' extracurricular speech and that a public educational institution retains discretion to prescribe its curriculum."[118]

The court quoted from the Supreme Court's decision in *Arkansas Educational Television Commission v. Forbes* (1989),[119] involving a challenge to a decision by Arkansas public broadcasting stations not to include Ralph Forbes, a "perennial independent candidate," in its televised debates for a congressional seat. The Supreme Court in *Forbes* had noted, "Much like a university selecting a commencement speaker, a public institution selecting speakers for a lecture series, or a public school prescribing its curriculum, a broadcaster by its nature will facilitate the expression of some viewpoints instead of others."[120] The court in *Brown v. Li* reasoned likewise. If the judiciary were to so intrude on academic judgments, it would threaten the *institutional* academic freedom that universities enjoy.[121]

The court in *Brown* engaged in illuminating explorations of the extent to which even viewpoint judgments in an academic setting may be somewhat insulated from a First Amendment challenge by students. Educational assignments, *often by their nature,* involve a certain form of viewpoint discrimination. Schools may not force a student to *believe* a particular viewpoint, or even to *profess* it, but they may at times, as an appropriate academic exercise, require a student to *recite* it. As the court in *Brown v. Li* recognized, "A teacher may require a student to write a paper from a particular viewpoint, even if it is a viewpoint with which the student disagrees, so long as the requirement serves a legitimate pedagogical purpose."[122] For example, "A college history teacher may demand a paper defending Prohibition, and a law-school professor may assign students to write 'opinions' showing how Justices Ginsburg and Scalia would analyze a particular Fourth Amendment question."[123]

Brown v. Li is a good example of the "trumping rules" that apply when the academic freedom or free speech claims of a student clash with the academic freedom or free speech claims of a professor or university, *with regard to academic judgments of the professor or university* in relation to the student's academic performance. While Christopher Brown's vulgar insults to every educational authority figure in sight was surely speech protected by the First Amendment in the general marketplace of ideas, when he included it on his graduate thesis he was violating academic norms. Even though, in a strict sense, those insults did not concern the *subject matter* of his thesis, the Ninth Circuit reasoned that it was within the range of legitimate academic and professional judgment of the university to conclude that its student just can't talk to folks this way in handing in assignments. The point of the assignment was to teach the student how to research within an academic specialty and how to present his results to other scholars in his field. Brown was given reasonable standards for that assignment, including a pedagogically appropriate requirement that the thesis comply with professional standards governing his discipline. He was instructed that he should consult a standard style manual or talk with members of his committee about those requirements.

As the student's own surreptitious placement of the "Fuck You's" in his paper seemed to indicate, his angry "acknowledgment" did not meet these professional and academic norms. This standard, the court held, "does not immunize the university altogether from First Amendment challenges but, at the same time, appropriately defers to the university's expertise in defining academic standards and teaching students to meet them."[124]

The decision in *Brown v. Li,* like most judicial decisions dealing with the free speech rights of public university students, reflects the influence of a series of United States Supreme Court decisions involving the free speech rights of high school and middle school students in public schools. These cases involving public school students in their precollege years do not directly control the outcomes of cases involving university students, because university students are young adults, not children, and universities are very different places than high schools and middle schools. Even so, there are themes from the Supreme Court cases that do transfer from one setting to the other. One of the principal themes, and a dominant mantra of this book, is that the free speech rights of students have a dual character, gaining strength when the student is speaking as a student on public issues, but diminishing in strength as the student participates in the institution's own programmatic activities.

The oldest of these Supreme Court cases is *Tinker v. Des Moines Independent Community School District* (1969),[125] a celebrated Vietnam-era case. Mary Beth Tinker, a thirteen-year-old public junior high school student, joined with other students in her school to wear black armbands to school to protest the Vietnam War. School authorities suspended and sent home the students for violating a school policy against the wearing of such armbands, which had been adopted only two days before, in anticipation of the protest. The Supreme Court took umbrage at the fact that "a particular symbol—black armbands worn to exhibit opposition to this Nation's involvement in Vietnam—was singled out for prohibition."[126] Announcing a rule generously protecting the free speech rights of students, the Court declared that expressive conduct by students may not be prohibited unless it "materially and substantially" interferes with "the requirements of appropriate discipline in the operation of the school."[127] Above all, *Tinker* has been absorbed into the national lore regarding the speech rights of students and teachers for its most memorable passage, declaring that rights are not checked at the gate to the schoolhouse: "First Amendment rights, applied in light of the special characteristics of the school environment, are available to teachers and students. It can hardly be argued that either students or teachers shed their constitutional rights to freedom of speech or expression at the schoolhouse gate."[128]

If *Tinker* established that students do have First Amendment rights while attending school, the next three Supreme Court decisions to deal with student speech rights established that school authorities have significant discretion to limit those rights. In *Bethel School District No. 403 v. Fraser* (1986),[129] Matthew Fraser, a fourteen-year-old public high school student, delivered a "campaign speech" on behalf of a fellow student during a school assembly. The speech was filled with sexual metaphor and innuendo, touting his candidate as "a man who is firm—he's firm in his pants, he's firm in his shirt, his character is firm—but most of all, his belief in you, the students of Bethel, is firm."[130] Fraser also praised his candidate as "a man who takes his point and pounds it in . . . a man who will go to the very end—even to the climax, for each and every one of you." For this ribald oratory Fraser was suspended by the school principal, under the authority of a school rule declaring that "conduct which materially and substantially interferes with the educational process is prohibited, including the use of obscene, profane language or gestures."[131] Chief Justice Burger wrote the opinion of the Supreme Court backing the school principal, holding that Fraser's speech was not protected by the First Amendment. The Court emphasized that the free speech rights of students in public schools "are not automatically coextensive with the rights of adults in other settings."[132] In a passage that seemed to dilute the test articulated in *Tinker*, the Court stated that a school need not tolerate student speech that is inconsistent with its "basic educational mission."[133]

Two years later the Court decided *Hazelwood School District v. Kuhlmeier* (1988),[134] a case involving the student newspaper, the *Spectrum*, at Hazelwood East High School in St. Louis County, Missouri. School officials blocked publication of student articles dealing with teenage pregnancy at the school and the impact of divorce on students at the school. The school principal was concerned that the identities of the pregnant girls who were the focus of the stories would be recognized by fellow students, even though fictitious names were used. He was also concerned about the inclusion of quotations by an unnamed student in the story about divorce. The Court sustained the actions of the school principal, drawing a sharp distinction between the speech in *Tinker*, which was not connected to any school program or activity, and the speech in *Hazel-wood*, in which the school itself was an active participant in the speech enterprise. The Court thus contrasted the situation in *Tinker*, in which the school was forced to tolerate student speech, and the situation in *Hazelwood*, in which the school was being asked to affirmatively support the speech. In this second category of cases, involving the authority of school officials "over school-sponsored publications, theatrical productions, and other expressive activities that students, parents, and members of the public might reasonably perceive to bear the imprimatur of the school,"[135] the Court held, the First Amendment did not impose on school officials the "substantial disruption" standard articulated in *Tinker*. "Educators are entitled to exercise greater control over this second form of student expression to assure that participants learn whatever lessons the activity is designed to teach, that readers or listeners are not exposed to material that may be inappropriate for their level of maturity, and that the views of the individual speaker are not erroneously attributed to the school,"[136] the Court stated.

In *Morse v. Frederick* (2007),[137] the Supreme Court dealt with a controversy arising from a school sponsored event at Juneau-Douglas High School to commemorate the passing of the Olympic Torch Relay through Juneau, Alaska, on its way to the Winter Olympic Games in Salt Lake City, Utah. Deborah Morse was the principal of Juneau-Douglas, and Joseph Frederick was a senior at the school. Principal Morse let everyone out of school to observe the festivities as the Torch Parade passed the school. Teachers and administrators monitored the event, which the school treated as akin to a field trip, and school cheerleaders and the school band were present to contribute to the celebratory mood. As the torchbearers passed the school in full view of television cameras, a group of rambunctious seniors, led by Frederick, unfurled a fourteen-foot-long banner bearing the phrase "BONG HiTS 4 JESUS." Principal Morse thought the message promoted illegal drugs, and the Court found this interpretation perfectly reasonable, holding that Frederick's speech fell on the side of the First Amendment line exemplified by *Bethel* and *Hazelwood*, and not on the side of *Tinker*. The Court's opinion, written by Chief Justice Roberts, reasoned that the speech in *Tinker*, involving protest against Vietnam, was the type of political protest that implicated "concerns at the heart of the First Amendment."[138] "BONG HiTS 4 JESUS" did not.

The *Tinker, Bethel, Hazelwood,* and *Morse* quintuplet of cases yield insights that appropriately apply to higher education every bit as much as they apply to elementary and secondary schools. When pursuing reasonable institutional educational objectives, educators have more authority to regulate student speech in the context of activities connected to an educational institution's programmatic activities, even when they would lack the authority to regulate such speech outside the educational setting. As the United States Court of Appeals for the Sixth Circuit observed in *Settle v. Dickson County School Board* (1995),[139] a case arising from a ninth grader's challenge to a teacher's assignment of a failing grade for the student's refusal to write a paper on an assigned topic, "The bottom line is that when a teacher makes an assignment, even if she does it poorly, the student has no constitutional right to do something other than that assignment and receive credit for it. It is not necessary to try to cram this situation into the framework of constitutional precedent, because there is no constitutional question."[140] The decision of the Sixth Circuit in *Settle* quite eloquently explained why the very nature of teaching requires content-based judgments by teachers, in much the same sense that the very nature of judging requires content-based determinations by judges:

Where learning is the focus, as in the classroom, student speech may be even more circumscribed than in the school newspaper or other open forum. So long as the teacher limits speech or grades speech in the classroom in the name of learning and not as a pretext for punishing the student for her race, gender, economic class, religion or political persuasion, the federal courts should not interfere.

Like judges, teachers should not punish or reward people on the basis of inadmissible factors—race, religion, gender, political ideology—but teachers, like judges, must daily decide which arguments are relevant, which computations are correct, which analogies are good or bad, and when it is time to stop writing or talking. Grades must be given by teachers in the classroom, just as cases are decided in the courtroom; and to this end teachers, like judges, must direct the content of speech. Teachers may frequently make mistakes in grading and otherwise, just as we do sometimes in deciding cases, but it is the essence of the teacher's responsibility in the classroom to draw lines and make distinctions–in a word to encourage speech germane to the topic at hand and discourage speech unlikely to shed light on the subject. Teachers therefore must be given broad discretion to give grades and conduct class discussion based on the content of speech.[141]

In another revealing case, *Axson-Flynn v. Johnson* (2004),[142] the United States Court of Appeals for the Tenth Circuit, in a thoughtful opinion by Judge David Ebel, dealt with the difficult problems posed when Christina Axson-Flynn, a student at the University of Utah's Actor Training Program, refused to say the word "fuck" or take God's name in vain during classroom acting exercises, because such language offended her Mormon faith. The court held that the University of Utah's classes could not reasonably be considered public forums. There are three main types of speech that occur within a school setting, the court reasoned. Following the now-familiar theme, the court contrasted student speech that happens to occur on the school premises, such as the black armbands worn by the students in *Tinker*, with school-sponsored speech. "Pure student expression" of the *Tinker* variety, the court reasoned, must be "tolerated" unless it can reasonably be forecasted that the expression will lead to substantial disruption of or material interference with school activities. School-sponsored speech, in contrast, is "speech that a school affirmatively promotes, as opposed to speech that it tolerates."[143] Colleges and universities, like public schools, may exercise editorial control over school-sponsored speech, the court held, so long as their actions are reasonably related to legitimate pedagogical concerns.

There was no doubt that the University of Utah had sponsored the use of the plays that Axson-Flynn was forced to recite while an actress in the University's instructional program. Echoing what the Ninth Circuit had said in *Brown*, the court in *Axson-Flynn* observed that educators routinely require students to express a viewpoint that is not their own in order to teach the students to think critically. "Accordingly," the court held, "the *Hazelwood* framework is applicable in a university setting for speech that occurs in a classroom as part of a class curriculum."[144] In reaching this conclusion, the court in *Axson-Flynn* adopted the view that has been strongly advanced in this book, that "academic freedom" is not a distinct constitutional right. The court thus noted that the University had relied on "the ill-defined right of 'academic freedom'" in advancing its arguments.[145] "Although we recognize and apply this principle in our analysis," the court chided, "we do not view it as constituting a separate right apart from the operation of the First Amendment within the university setting."[146]

While students participating in curricular and school-sponsored expressive activities may have only weak constitutional rights to second-guess the academic judgments of university professors and administrators, this is not to say they have no rights. The *Hazelwood* standard does require the university, at a minimum, to at least justify its actions as grounded in reasonable pedagogical goals. More fundamentally, colleges and universities are not entitled to hide behind the *Hazelwood* standard to disguise illicit motivations that clearly are banned by the Constitution. Proving such illicit motives is extremely difficult, but there is a slight crack in the door that at least leaves students the opportunity to attack academic decisions as complete departures from academic and professional standards.

In *Regents of the University of Michigan v. Ewing* (1985),[147] the Supreme Court reviewed a decision of the University of Michigan to dismiss a student, Scott Ewing, after he failed a critical written exam. The Supreme Court found that the University of Michigan faculty decision to dismiss Ewing "was made conscientiously and with careful deliberation, based on an evaluation of the entirety of Ewing's academic career."[148] This was enough to satisfy the Court. "When judges are asked to review the substance of a genuinely academic decision, such as this one, they should show great respect for the faculty's professional judgment," the Court pronounced.[149] "Plainly, they may not override it unless it is such a substantial departure from accepted academic norms as to demonstrate that the person or committee responsible did not actually exercise professional judgment."[150]

As the court in *Axson-Flynn* put it, "Although we do not second-guess the *pedagogical* wisdom or efficacy of an educator's goal, we would be abdicating our judicial duty if we failed to investigate whether the educational goal or pedagogical concern was *pretextual*."[151] Only if, as *Ewing* suggests, there is a complete abdication of professional judgment, or, as *Axson-Flynn* suggests, the asserted academic reason is a mere pretext for what was actually race, gender, religious, or political discrimination, may a court presume to override the academic judgment of faculty and administrators against a student.

If the free speech rights of students at public universities are to be calibrated by whether they are speaking as citizens in the general marketplace or as students participating in university programs, on what side of the line do activities such as participation in student publications fall? The configuration of these rights turns to some degree on the status of the particular newspaper on the particular campus. In *Hazelwood* the Supreme Court granted substantial discretion to school officials over high school newspapers. But college newspapers often exist on a far more independent footing than their high school counterparts. College "independent" or "underground" newspapers, for example, which are organized privately by students, not supported by any university funding, nor part of the matrix of officially recognized campus student organizations, have First Amendment freedoms identical to that of any independent newspaper in the nation. A public university may not ban distribution of an independent student newspaper any more than it could ban distribution of the *New York Times* or the *Wall Street Journal*.

In *Papish v. Board of Curators of the University of Missouri* (1973),[152] Barbara Susan Papish, a graduate student at the University of Missouri, was expelled for distributing on the Missouri campus copies of an independent newspaper, *The Free Press Underground*. Material in two issues of the paper precipitated the University decision to kick Papish out of school. On the front cover of one issue was a political cartoon depicting policemen raping the Statue of Liberty and the Goddess of Justice, with a caption reading, "With Liberty and Justice for All." A second issue contained an article with the headline "Motherfucker Acquitted," which described the trial and acquittal on an assault charge of a youth in New York City who was a member of an organization known as "Up Against the Wall, Motherfucker."[153]

The Supreme Court held that the expulsion of Papish violated the First Amendment, holding that "the mere dissemination of ideas—no matter how offensive to good taste—on a state university campus may not be

shut off in the name alone of 'conventions of decency.'"¹⁵⁴ The decision in
Papish is important for its round rejection of the suggestion that the *entire
university* is a special setting outside the general marketplace, thereby
diminishing *in gross* the free speech rights of all students who attend. The
"First Amendment leaves no room for the operation of a dual standard
in the academic community with respect to the content of speech,"¹⁵⁵ the
Court flatly declared.

The full import of the *Papish* ruling is underscored by the decisions of
the three dissenting Justices, Chief Justice Warren Burger, Justice William
Rehnquist, and Justice Harry Blackmun. Chief Justice Warren Burger
directly attacked the notion that a university is a general marketplace of
ideas, instead advancing the view that it is a special place imposing special
obligations of civility on those who enter. "In theory, at least, a university
is not merely an arena for the discussion of ideas by students and faculty;
it is also an institution where individuals learn to express themselves in
acceptable, civil terms,"¹⁵⁶ the Chief Justice wrote. Emphasizing notions
of community and group endeavor over the libertarian marketplace,
Chief Justice Burger argued, "We provide that environment to the end
that students may learn the self-restraint necessary to the functioning of a
civilized society and understand the need for those external restraints to
which we must all submit if group existence is to be tolerable."¹⁵⁷

Justice Rehnquist, in an opinion joined by Chief Justice Burger and
Justice Blackman, developed this theme in even more detail. "It simply
does not follow under any of our decisions or from the language of the
First Amendment itself that because petitioner could not be criminally
prosecuted by the Missouri state courts for the conduct in question, she
may not therefore be expelled from the University. A state university is
an establishment for the purpose of educating the State's young people,
supported by the tax revenues of the State's citizens," Justice Rehnquist
complained. "The notion that the officials lawfully charged with the governance of the university have so little control over the environment for
which they are responsible that they may not prevent the public distribution of a newspaper on campus which contained the language described
in the Court's opinion is quite unacceptable to me and I would suspect would have been equally unacceptable to the Framers of the First
Amendment."¹⁵⁸ Invoking the theory of *Chaplinsky v. New Hampshire*,¹⁵⁹

Justice Rehnquist dismissed the speech for which Papish was expelled as of a piece with those utterances that *Chaplinsky* described as "no essential part of any exposition of ideas" and "of such slight social value as a step to truth that any benefit that may be derived from them is clearly outweighed by the social interest in order and morality."[160]

Justice Rehnquist then explored the relationship of state universities to their ultimate trustees—those who loom even more powerful than state university boards of trustees, visitors, and curators—the taxpayers. If forced to put up with the kind of speech that Papish had exhibited, Justice Rehnquist warned, "there is reason to think that the 'disenchantment' of which the Court speaks may, after this decision, become widespread among taxpayers and legislators."[161] The nation should be proud of its system of public universities, he admonished, but one can scarcely blame taxpayers "if, told by the Court that their only function is to supply tax money for the operation of the university, the 'disenchantment' may reach such a point that they doubt the game is worth the candle."[162]

While in *Papish* the view that general marketplace principles should apply to the distribution of an independent newspaper on a modern campus prevailed, there is a haunting realpolitik quality to Justice Rehnquist's warning. And while it is wise educational policy and sound First Amendment analysis to apply general marketplace principles to the vast public spaces and programs of modern universities, certainly Justice Rehnquist was correct that taxpayers, state legislatures, and state university boards must have a function greater than merely paying the bills. At least in certain carve-out settings—such as regulation of curricular speech—that greater role may justly include the imposition of reasonable academic and professional norms.

Papish involved distribution of outside newspapers by students. More complex, for First Amendment purposes, are the principles governing newspapers written and edited by students within the university. As mentioned above, student newspapers at some colleges and universities are truly independent. *The Independent Florida Alligator*, for example, began in 1906 as a student publication of the University of Florida, but in 1973 severed its official ties to the University, moved off-campus, and became entirely independent. Most campus papers, however, are officially recognized student organizations, receive all or some of their funding from university sources (often generated by student activity fees), are housed on campus, have faculty advisors, and have ties of one kind or another to student government, campus media or publication boards, deans of students, or student affairs offices. On some campuses these entities play some role in the selection of student editorial boards, or retain some power to police the publications or the students involved in them for violations of publishing codes of ethics or general university policies. The models vary widely. In some instances the organic link to the university is relatively strong, in others it is more attenuated. In some cases any oversight by outsiders is limited to supervision by other students, such as agencies of student government; in other cases the supervision extends to the university administration, faculty, or disciplinary boards.

Whatever the precise relationship between a campus newspaper and its college or university may be, virtually all campus newspapers will periodically take editorial positions or publish other material disturbing or offensive to university administrators, governing boards, alumni, faculty, students, or members of the surrounding community. When someone in authority at a state university attempts to do something about it—such as seeking to discipline the student journalists involved, reducing or canceling the paper's funding, or seeking to exert greater editorial control over the paper's decisions—First Amendment conflicts can be triggered. Courts have tended to treat officially recognized (and thus not truly "independent") student newspapers much as they have other student organizations that receive campus funding but express their own private viewpoints.

From the university perspective, there is good news and bad news in this. The good news is that a number of courts have held that because the student newspaper is *effectively* independent, the university is not the "publisher" of the paper for purposes of liability for libel or invasion of privacy. If the paper defames someone, the students who do the defaming may have to pay the victim (and they, of course, will rarely have any money), but the university itself is off the financial hook. In a leading case on this issue, *Mazart v. State* (1981),[163] a New York State Court held that the State University of New York–Binghamton could not be held institutionally responsible for alleged libelous material published in the student newspaper, the *Pipe Dream*. While the university provided financial and administrative support to the paper, such as office space and other services, the court held that the university's lack of any editorial control over the paper prevented the paper from being properly considered the "agent" of the university with regard to its content.

The bad news from the university perspective is that responding to unsavory material printed in the paper puts a university in peril of running afoul of the First Amendment. The very independence that insulates the university from liability also bars it from interference. While university presidents, alumni, professors, and students are free to condemn the paper and counterattack with speech of their own, they can't dismiss the offending student journalists from the campus or take away the paper's funding.

A formidable string of decisions supports this proposition. In *Joyner v. Whiting* (1973),[164] the United States Court of Appeals for the Fourth Circuit held that the President of North Carolina Central University violated the First Amendment when he terminated university funding for the school newspaper, the *Campus Echo*, when it published articles advocating that North Carolina Central return to being an all-black college. In *Bazaar v. Fortune* (1973),[165] the United States Court of Appeals for the Fifth Circuit held that the University of Mississippi violated the First Amendment when it stopped the publication of a student literary magazine, *Images*, because the magazine contained two short stories, written by students, describing interracial marriage and sex, including "earthy" language described by the court as four-letter obscenities, including the use "of 'that four letter word' generally thought to be most offensive in polite company." The protagonist was a black male, described as a latter-day Holden Caulfield, the narrating central character in J. D. Salinger's *The Catcher in the Rye*. In *Schiff v. Williams* (1975),[166] the Fifth Circuit held that the President of Atlantic University violated the First Amendment by removing three editors of the student newspaper, allegedly because of the newspaper's poor quality—including bad grammar and poor literary value—faulting the students' editorial leadership. These rationales, the court held, were not the sort of problems that disrupted the educational mission of the university, and did not rise to a level sufficient to justify the abridgment of the students' First Amendment rights. In *Stanley v. Magrath* (1983),[167] the United States Court of Appeals for the

Eighth Circuit held that the University of Minnesota violated the First Amendment when its Board of Regents changed the method by which it funded the student newspaper, the *Minnesota Daily,* in the aftermath of its publication of a controversial humor issue. The court held that a "public university may not constitutionally take adverse action against a student newspaper, such as withdrawing or reducing the paper's funding, because it disapproves of the content of the paper." And in *Husain v. Springer* (2007),[168] the President of the College of Staten Island, part of the City University of New York system, nullified a student government election because of a student newspaper's endorsement of a particular slate of candidates. The United States Court of Appeals for the Second Circuit held that the actions of the President violated the First Amendment rights of the student paper, the *College Voice,* and its students, as the paper was a limited public forum and the President's actions were based on the viewpoints expressed in the paper.

Though this is how the story usually goes, it would be misleading to say that this is how it always goes. One of the most provocative explorations of the First Amendment position of campus newspapers arose from a case decided by the United States Court of Appeals for the Seventh Circuit, *Hosty v. Carter* (2005).[169] The majority opinion in the *Hosty* case, involving Governors State University in northern Illinois, decided "en banc" (meaning the court's full complement of eleven judges participated), was written by Judge Frank Easterbrook, himself a former university professor. Judge Easterbrook opened his opinion with wry flair: "Controversy began to swirl when Jeni Porche became editor in chief of the *Innovator,* the student newspaper at Governors State University. None of the articles concerned the apostrophe missing from the University's name. Instead the students tackled meatier fare, such as its decision not to renew the teaching contract of Geoffrey de Laforcade, the paper's faculty adviser."[170]

The *Innovator* was financed through the University's student activity fee program. The paper made accusations that the University administration deemed false and defamatory, refused to retract the statements, and even refused to print the administration's response.[171] The University then ordered the printer to stop printing the paper unless the content was submitted in advance to the administration for review. The student journalists would not accept this condition, and the printer would not print the paper without the green light from the administration, for fear that it would not be paid.[172]

The court held that the *Hazelwood* framework applied in the college and university context. To say that the *Hazelwood* "framework" applied, however, did not decide the outcome, for the critical question under *Hosty* was whether the *specific* student newspaper at Governors State University was an exercise in private student speech conducted as part of a public forum created by the University. On the side of the paper was the fact that the University had created an entity known as the Student Communications Media Board, consisting of seven members, all chosen by the Student Senate: four students, two faculty members, and one civil service or support unit employee. The Board distributed funds to student publications, and had as its established policy a rule stating that each funded publication would determine its own content and format "without censorship or advance approval."[173] On the side of the University, the court noted, was the fact that the Board was itself responsible to the University Director of Student Life, suggesting the possibility of University control, and that funded publications appeared to have faculty advisors, which also may have signaled University control. In this posture, the court sent the case back to the trial judge for additional clarification.[174]

The court in *Hosty* did not, in the end, resolve the question of whether University officials acted in violation of the First Amendment in taking its actions against the student newspaper. The suit was brought as a claim for money damages against the University officials for the alleged violations of the constitutional rights of the student journalists. Under the "qualified immunity" doctrine that applies to lawsuits for money damages against public officials for violations of constitutional rights, no money damages are allowed unless the law is clear, at the time the official undertakes the actions at issue, that those actions violate established constitutional principles. The Court in *Hosty* held that the First Amendment principles governing the university's actions were highly uncertain, given the lack of clarity as to whether the newspaper was properly deemed "independent." In this procedural posture, the court ordered the case against the officials dismissed under the doctrine of qualified immunity. What is most critical about *Hosty*, however, is the framework the court employed, a framework that did *not* treat student publications at the college level as automatically independent. Rather, under the *Hosty* approach the independence of the paper *in fact*, as determined by university policies and practices, will dictate whether, applying public forum doctrines, the paper is to be deemed independent *in law*.

Summing Up: The Campus as a Free and Ordered Space

In the end, the modern American university campus is best understood as a free and ordered space. As a marketplace of ideas, freedom reigns and no point of view is excluded. As a community of civility and learning, however, certain rules of order apply. The university is entitled to expect of its faculty and students the adherence to principles of academic integrity and rigor. The university is also entitled to carve out certain spaces and places on the campus in which the rough-and-tumble of the wide-open marketplace may be forced to yield to values of civility and respect for human dignity. The heart and soul of academic freedom is the elemental notion that ideas may not be censored. Yet while ideas ought never be censored, those who join a university community may rightly be expected to express their ideas, whatever they may be, in a manner consistent with the highest traditions of learned communities.

6

Competing Conceptions of Equality

A great deal of learning occurs informally. It occurs through interactions among students of both sexes; of different races, religions, and backgrounds; who come from cities and rural areas, from various states and countries; who have a wide variety of interests, talents, and perspectives; and who are able, directly or indirectly, to learn from their differences and to stimulate one another to reexamine even their most deeply held assumptions about themselves and their world. As a wise graduate of ours once observed in commenting on this aspect of the educational process, "People do not learn very much when they are surrounded only by the likes of themselves." . . . In the nature of things, it is hard to know how, and when, and even if, this informal learning through diversity actually occurs. It does not occur for everyone. For many, however, the unplanned, casual encounters with roommates, fellow sufferers in an organic chemistry class, student workers in the library, teammates on a basketball squad, or other participants in class affairs or student government can be subtle and yet powerful sources of improved understanding and personal growth.

—Justice Lewis F. Powell, writing in *Regents of the University of California v. Bakke* (1978), quoting the president of
Princeton University

Government cannot make us equal; it can only recognize, respect, and protect us as equal before the law. That these programs may have been motivated, in part, by good intentions cannot provide refuge from the principle that under our Constitution, the government may not make distinctions on the basis of race. As far as the Constitution is concerned, it is irrelevant whether a government's racial classifications are drawn by those who wish to oppress a race or by those who have a sincere desire to help those thought to be disadvantaged. There can be no doubt that the paternalism that appears to lie at the heart of this program is at war with the principle of inherent equality that underlies and infuses our Constitution.

These programs not only raise grave constitutional questions, they also undermine the moral basis of the equal protection principle. Purchased at the price of immeasurable human suffering, the equal protection principle reflects our Nation's understanding that such classifications ultimately have a destructive impact on the individual and our society. . . . There can be no doubt that racial paternalism and its unintended consequences can be as poisonous and pernicious as any other form of discrimination. So-called "benign" discrimination teaches many that because of chronic and apparently immutable handicaps, minorities cannot compete with them without their patronizing indulgence. Inevitably, such programs engender attitudes of superiority or, alternatively, provoke resentment among those who believe that they have been wronged by the government's use of race. These programs stamp minorities with a badge of inferiority and may cause them to develop dependencies or to adopt an attitude that they are "entitled" to preferences. . . .

In my mind, government-sponsored racial discrimination based on benign prejudice is just as noxious as discrimination inspired by malicious prejudice. In each instance, it is racial discrimination, plain and simple.

—Justice Clarence Thomas, writing in *Adarand
Constructors Inc. v. Peña* (1995)

Duke Lacrosse

When four members of the Duke University lacrosse team, all white students, were accused of raping an African American stripper hired by team members to perform at an off-campus party, Duke and the surrounding

[161]

community in Durham, North Carolina, were swept into the vortex of a perfect storm. For months, national discourse over the Duke lacrosse team allegations were filled with sound and fury over universities allegedly hijacked by runaway athletic programs, seething racial and class divisions, and privilege. With many members of its faculty urging it on, Duke suspended the students and canceled the lacrosse season. The allegations were ultimately exposed as a fabrication, driven by an unscrupulous prosecutor playing to racial divisions and class distinctions for political gain. The lacrosse players, cleared of wrongdoing, sued the University.[1]

What happened at Duke was connected in the constitutional unconscious to deeper, more primal American conflicts over race, and even more profoundly, over the meaning of our constitutional commitment to the "equal protection of the laws." With the election of President Barack Obama, the nation is being invited to enter a new "post-racial" period. But what will being "post-racial" mean for society at large, and for American higher education in particular?

Process and Outcome Equality

The nation continues to struggle between two competing conceptions of the meaning of "equality": "process equality" and "outcome equality."[2] Process equality is exemplified by the notion that our Constitution should be "colorblind." This approach appeals to American faith in the marketplace, to social Darwinism, the survival of the fittest, and the reward of merit. American society should be a meritocracy, and race should always be deemed irrelevant to merit. Colorblindness has the appeal of formal consistency with the "rule of law." Racial classifications are either always good or always bad, and it is logically inconsistent to say that discrimination is sometimes okay and sometimes not. Obviously, discrimination is not always good, so it must be always bad. As Yale's famous constitutional law theorist Alexander Bickel argued, any other view involves the unlearning of the lesson of equality, "and we are told that this is not a matter of fundamental principle but only a matter of whose ox is gored."[3]

To introduce distinctions among citizens based on color or identity is to convert the polity into a contest of racial spoils. Race-conscious activity carries with it the peril that society will degenerate into racial and ethnic factions, with government undertaking the odious business of umpiring amid a clamor of racial hate, suspicion, resentment, and recrimination. The philosophy professor Lisa H. Newton, for example, draws on the writings of Aristotle to posit that the rule of law is the embodiment of the ideal of political equality among citizens, arguing that it is undermined by any deviation from that ideal.[4] When distinctions are drawn on race and identity, citizens are converted from bearers of rights to petitioners for favors. Colorblindness also spares society from the unpalatable practice of deciding who qualifies as black or white or Hispanic or Indian. Langston Hughes once wrote of the power of the "one drop rule," through which even "one drop" of "black blood" was deemed to render someone African American.[5] The constitutional law scholar William Van Alstyne summarized the ethos of the colorblind position by arguing that "one gets beyond racism by getting beyond it now: by a complete, resolute, and credible commitment never to tolerate in one's own life—or in the life and practices of one's government—the differential treatment of other human beings by race." He continued, arguing, "That is the great lesson for government itself to teach: in all we do in life, to treat any person less well than another or to favor one any more than another for being black or white or brown or red, is wrong."[6]

Process equality and the colorblind position, however, have never managed to gain full ascendancy in modern American politics or law. The many federal, state, and local civil rights laws passed in the last fifty years have tended to combine elements of process equality with elements of "outcome equality," a conception of equality that focuses on the extent to which laws and policies produce genuinely integrated programs and institutions. Fourteen years after *Brown v. Board of Education* (1954),[7] for example, in *Green v. County School Board of New Kent County* (1968),[8] the Supreme Court held that a school district's belated adoption of a "freedom of choice" plan, permitting any child to transfer to the school of his or her choice, was not enough to comply with the district's obligation to remedy its past history of forced segregation. Under the freedom of choice plan, it turned out, no white children elected to attend the historically all-black school, while 85 percent of the black children chose not to transfer to the historically white school. The Supreme Court held that freedom of choice was a constitutionally inadequate remedy, arguing that the school board must come forward with a plan that realistically promises to work in the short term. In requiring a plan that would "work now," the Court obviously was demanding "results" that manifested actual racial mixing. Yet *Green* was not entirely an outcome equality case. When palpable outcomes are demanded as a remedy for past discrimination, one might still articulate the ultimate ethos as grounded in process equality thinking. When the school board had previously violated the norm of process equality, the Court would require that the remedy partake of outcome equality, so as to "undo" the warped outcomes that had become entrenched by years of tainted process.

Debates over the legality of affirmative action in higher education, and in society generally, turn on whether "process" or "outcome" conceptions of equality should govern American policy and law. The colorblind position in constitutional law is usually traced to one of the most famous dissenting opinions in Supreme Court history, Justice John Marshall Harlan's haunting dissent from the majority opinion in *Plessy v. Ferguson* (1896).[9] *Plessy* invented the "separate but equal" doctrine, upholding a Louisiana law requiring that blacks and whites ride in separate train cars. Justice Harlan's position suggested that for the government to even "know" the racial identity of citizens violated the Constitution: "In respect of civil rights, common to all citizens, the Constitution of the United States does not, I think, permit any public authority to know the race of those entitled to be protected in the enjoyment of such rights." Harlan wrote with reverence of the Thirteenth, Fourteenth, and Fifteenth Amendments, passed in the aftermath of the Civil War: "These notable additions to the fundamental law were welcomed by the friends of liberty throughout the world. They removed the race line from our governmental systems."[10] The majority in *Plessy* argued that the "separate but equal" law, which applied to both blacks and whites, did not stigmatize blacks, but this was simply disingenuous. "Every one knows" the purpose of the segregation laws, Harlan lectured, and that was to discriminate against blacks, and only persons "wanting in candor" would assert the contrary. And of course, Harlan was right. Everyone did know the racist motivation underlying the law, and those who denied it—including Harlan's seven colleagues in the Court's majority—were simply lacking in candor and anesthetized in conscience. In a vain but valiant effort to stir that conscience, Harlan wrote one of the most famous passages in the entire history of American law:

> The white race deems itself to be the dominant race in this country. And so it is, in prestige, in achievements, in education, in wealth and in power. So, I doubt not, it will continue to be for all time, if it remains true to its great heritage and holds fast to the principles of constitutional liberty. But in view of the Constitution, in the eye of the law, there is in this country no superior, dominant, ruling class of citizens. There is no caste here. Our Constitution is color-blind, and neither knows nor tolerates classes among citizens. In respect of civil rights, all citizens are equal before the law. The humblest is the peer of the most powerful. The law regards man as man, and takes no account of his surroundings or of his color when his civil rights as guaranteed by the supreme law of the land are involved. It is, therefore, to be regretted that this high tribunal, the final expositor of the fundamental law of the land, has reached the conclusion that it is competent for a State to regulate the enjoyment by citizens of their civil rights solely upon the basis of race.[11]

The meaning of these words has been much disputed. It is possible to argue that the words are themselves infected with racism, given the opening lines about the dominance of the white race. Even so, Harlan's opinion has endured as a powerful and courageous prophecy. Justice Harlan did not argue that we as a people do not know color. He argued only that the law does not know it. Harlan asserted that the destinies of blacks and whites in the United States are indissolubly linked together, and that laws sanctioning separation could only sow seeds of race hate:

> In my opinion, the judgment this day rendered will, in time, prove to be quite as pernicious as the decision made by this tribunal in the Dred Scott case. It was adjudged in that case that the descendants of Africans who were imported into this country and sold as slaves were not included nor intended to be included under the word "citizens" in the Constitution, and could not claim any of the rights and privileges which that instrument provided for and secured to citizens of the United States; that at the time of the

[165]

adoption of the Constitution they were "considered as a subordinate and inferior class of beings, who had been subjugated by the dominant race, and, whether emancipated or not, yet remained subject to their authority, and had no rights or privileges but such as those who held the power and the government might choose to grant them." The recent amendments of the Constitution, it was supposed, had eradicated these principles from our institutions. But it seems that we have yet, in some of the States, a dominant race—a superior class of citizens, which assumes to regulate the enjoyment of civil rights, common to all citizens, upon the basis of race. The present decision, it may well be apprehended, will not only stimulate aggressions, more or less brutal and irritating, upon the admitted rights of colored citizens, but will encourage the belief that it is possible, by means of state enactments, to defeat the beneficent purposes which the people of the United States had in view when they adopted the recent amendments of the Constitution, by one of which the blacks of this country were made citizens of the United States and of the States in which they respectively reside, and whose privileges and immunities, as citizens, the States are forbidden to abridge. Sixty millions of whites are in no danger from the presence here of eight millions of blacks. The destinies of the two races, in this country, are indissolubly linked together, and the interests of both require that the common government of all shall not permit the seeds of race hate to be planted under the sanction of law. What can more certainly arouse race hate, what more certainly create and perpetuate a feeling of distrust between these races, than state enactments, which, in fact, proceed on the ground that colored citizens are so inferior and degraded that they cannot be allowed to sit in public coaches occupied by white citizens? That, as all will admit, is the real meaning of such legislation as was enacted in Louisiana.[12]

If Justice Harlan was a prophet, what, precisely, was his prophecy? Above all else, the opinion is most cited and remembered for one sentence: "Our Constitution is color-blind, and neither knows nor tolerates classes among citizens."

The decline and demise of the *Plessy* "separate but equal" doctrine was uniquely linked to education. The cases that presaged the eventual overruling of *Plessy* in *Brown v. Board of Education* all involved higher education. The story began in 1938, with *Missouri ex rel. Gaines v. Canada* (1938).[13] The state of Missouri refused to allow African Americans to attend the University of Missouri Law School, instead offering to subsidize an African American applicant's attendance at a law school in another state. Chief Justice Hughes wrote the majority opinion, holding that Missouri's system did not meet the requirement that the benefit of legal education be available on an "equal" basis. Two Justices dissented, arguing that Missouri's actions were reasonable within the meaning of *Plessy*, but they lost.

Similarly, in *Sweatt v. Painter* (1950),[14] the Supreme Court rejected an effort by Texas to preserve the all-white status of the University of Texas Law School. Unlike Missouri, Texas tried to create a special state law school for African Americans, even using some of the same faculty members and law books available at the state's flagship university in Austin. The Supreme Court rejected the attempt, holding that the new law school could hardly be deemed the equal of the University of Texas Law School. The Court heavily focused on the intangible elements of a quality law school, such as "reputation of the faculty, experience of the administration, position and influence of the alumni, standing in the community, traditions and prestige."

In *McLaurin v. Oklahoma State Regents for Higher Education* (1950),[15] the Court held that the forced separation of graduate students into separate classroom seating areas, separate cafeteria seating areas, and separate library spaces violated the Fourteenth Amendment, even though African American students were admitted to the University's graduate program. In *McLaurin*, the African American students literally received the same education as white students, listening simultaneously to the same lectures and reading from the same books. The Court held, however, that interaction among students was an important part of the educational experience, and that the denial of this interaction was unconstitutional.

In 1954 the Supreme Court in *Brown v. Board of Education of Topeka* held that the concept of "separate but equal" had no place in American public education. In *Brown v. Board of Education II*, decided in 1955, the Court ordered the end of segregated school systems, "with all deliberate speed."[16] For higher education, showdowns at the University of Mississippi and University of Alabama were among the most dramatic conflicts in the struggle to dismantle segregation following *Brown*. In 1962, the University of Mississippi was plunged into turmoil when James Meredith, supported by federal authorities, broke the color barrier at Ole Miss. And in June of 1963, Governor George Wallace of Alabama stood in the entrance door of the University of Alabama to block the entry of two African American students, Vivian Malone and James A. Hood. President John F. Kennedy again used federal authority to secure the admission of the students, forcing Governor Wallace to yield.

For twenty years following *Brown I* and *Brown II*, Mississippi effectively continued its segregationist policies in higher education, operating five virtually all-white and three all-black state universities. And not until 1992, in *United States v. Fordice* (1992),[17] did the Supreme Court of the United States finally intervene directly to order the dismantling of Mississippi's dual system. The *Fordice* case begin in 1975 with a lawsuit filed by private parties and the United States government, challenging Mississippi's higher education system, claiming that the state had failed to satisfy its constitutional obligation to dismantle the dual "separate but equal" system that had existed prior to *Brown*. In the middle of the 1980s the student bodies of the universities were essentially unchanged in their racial compositions, with the traditionally white institutions still overwhelmingly white, and the traditionally black colleges still overwhelmingly black. The Supreme Court held that to the extent that Mississippi had perpetuated practices and policies traceable to its prior segregated system with no sound educational justifications, the state's failure to undertake measures to eliminate the vestiges of its dual system violated the Fourteenth Amendment. Even though none of the state's colleges any longer discriminated on the basis of race, a number of the state's policies effectively limited the choices available to applicants, and had the practical impact of perpetuating the racial identity of the various schools in the system.

It was against this backdrop that the Supreme Court in *Fordice* held that the Mississippi system, even in 1992, remained in constitutional violation. Among other things, the Court pointed to the unnecessary duplication of many of the state's educational programs, which appeared to represent a mere continuation of the separate but equal dual system. The Supreme Court ordered the case sent back to the federal district court in Mississippi for additional litigation, instructing the court to hear evidence on whether the retention and operation of all eight universities was educationally justified, and whether the maintenance of all eight institutions had the effect of perpetuating the dual system.

Justice Clarence Thomas in *Fordice* wrote a poignant concurring opinion, speaking to the role of historically black colleges. Justice Thomas clearly was torn between his strongly held view that admissions policies at universities should be race-neutral, and his affection and respect for the role of historically black colleges in the United States. Justice Thomas noted that "for many, historically black colleges have become a symbol of the highest attainments of black culture."[18] Yet he conceded that "a State cannot maintain such traditions by closing particular institutions, historically white or historically black, to particular racial groups."[19] This did not mean that all maintenance of the traditional identity of historically black colleges should be deemed constitutionally taboo. Instead, Justice Thomas argued that "it hardly follows that a State cannot operate a diverse assortment of institutions—including historically black institutions, open to all on a race-neutral basis, but with established traditions and programs that might disproportionately appeal to one race or another."[20]

Affirmative Action in Higher Education

The first affirmative action case to reach the Supreme Court was *DeFunis v. Odegaard* (1974).[21] DeFunis, a white male, challenged a minority-admissions program at the University of Washington School of Law when he was rejected as an applicant. The special admissions program reserved a portion of the law school class for blacks, Chicanos, American Indians, and Filipinos. By the time the case reached the Supreme Court, however, DeFunis was already in his third year at another law school, and the Court decided to duck the issue, holding the case moot. Justice William O. Douglas dissented, arguing that the case was not moot, and that Washington's program violated the Equal Protection Clause. Justice Douglas wrote that the law school must treat each applicant "*in a racially neutral way.*"[22] He argued that the Constitution should be deemed colorblind, rejecting the notion that affirmative action is justifiable if supported by "compelling" governmental objectives, stressing that if "discrimination based on race is constitutionally permissible when those who hold the reins can come up with 'compelling' reasons to justify it, then constitutional guarantees acquire an accordion-like quality."[23]

In *Regents of the University of California v. Bakke* (1978),[24] Alan Bakke, a rejected white applicant, challenged the validity of a special admissions program at the medical school of the University of California–Davis in which sixteen seats were set aside for minority students. Four Justices on the Supreme Court, Justices Stevens, Stewart, and Rehnquist, and Chief Justice Burger, voted to strike the program down on the ground that it violated a federal statute, Title VI of the Civil Rights Act of 1964, which they interpreted as adopting a "colorblind" rule that prohibited all use of race by institutions that receive federal aid. Because they interpreted the Civil Rights Act as imposing a colorblind standard, those four Justices did not choose to address the question of whether the Fourteenth Amendment imposed a colorblind rule as well.

Four other members of the Court, Justices Brennan, White, Marshall, and Blackmun, disagreed with the view that Title VI established a colorblind standard, instead holding that Title VI was merely intended by Congress to reinforce the Fourteenth Amendment by cutting off funds to universities that violated it. Substantively, they held, Title VI was identical to the Fourteenth Amendment. As to the Fourteenth Amendment, those four Justices voted to uphold the special admissions program, holding that the "benign" use of race to benefit historically disadvantaged groups did not merit even "strict scrutiny" review, instead holding that such programs were constitutional under a less demanding "intermediate scrutiny" standard. The government, they held, "may take race into account when it acts not to demean or insult any racial group, but to remedy disadvantages cast on minorities by past racial prejudice."[25]

Justice Powell cast the deciding vote, agreeing with the four liberals on the Court that Title VI did not create a colorblind standard and that the Constitution is not colorblind. Justice Powell parted with the liberals, however, in their claim that the benign use of race warranted a more permissive standard of judicial review than the invidious use of race. All racial classifications, Justice Powell held, must be subjected to strict scrutiny, requiring a compelling governmental interest to support the law, and also requiring that the law be narrowly tailored to effectuate that compelling interest.

Justice Powell rejected several of the interests proffered by University of California. California could not justify its law by saying that minorities were "underrepresented" in medical schools in relation to their proportions in California's general population, because this was outright racial balancing, the preferring of racial balance "for its own sake." Justice Powell thus rejected this pure "outcome equality" rationale. Justice Powell also rejected the claim that the program was justified to encourage better medical service for minority populations, reasoning that this indulged the impermissible racial assumption that minority doctors would choose to serve in minority neighborhoods or serve minority populations.

Justice Powell did, however, endorse as a "compelling interest" California's aim of attaining a diverse student body, building on Justice Frankfurter's articulation of the "four essential freedoms" that compose the academic freedom of a university. Relying on the words of the President of Princeton University, William G. Bowen, Justice Powell observed that the speculation, experiment, and creation so essential to higher education is promoted by a diverse student body.[26] Justice Powell concluded that "it is not too much to say that the nation's future depends upon leaders trained through wide exposure to the ideas and mores of students as diverse as this Nation of many peoples."[27] "Arguing that the pursuit of a diverse student body was of "paramount importance" to the fulfillment of the university's mission, Justice Powell stated that "even at the graduate level, our tradition and experience lend support to the view that the contribution of diversity is substantial." Invoking the Court's opinion in *Sweatt v. Painter*, Justice Powell noted the importance of the exchange of ideas among students of diverse backgrounds.

Notwithstanding his acceptance of the value of diversity, Justice Powell voted to strike down the set-aside quota system employed by the University of California–Davis Medical School, because it was not "narrowly tailored" enough to achieve the compelling interest in diversity. The program employed by the Medical School failed to give each student individualized consideration, and failed to encompass a broad definition of diversity, one that extended beyond race and ethnicity alone:

> It may be assumed that the reservation of a specified number of seats in each class for individuals from the preferred ethnic groups would contribute to

the attainment of considerable ethnic diversity in the student body. But petitioner's argument that this is the only effective means of serving the interest of diversity is seriously flawed. In a most fundamental sense the argument misconceives the nature of the state interest that would justify consideration of race or ethnic background. It is not an interest in simple ethnic diversity, in which a specified percentage of the student body is in effect guaranteed to be members of selected ethnic groups, with the remaining percentage an undifferentiated aggregation of students. The diversity that furthers a compelling state interest encompasses a far broader array of qualifications and characteristics of which racial or ethnic origin is but a single though important element. Petitioner's special admissions program, focused solely on ethnic diversity, would hinder rather than further attainment of genuine diversity.[28]

In contrast to the set-aside used by the University of California, Justice Powell commended as a preferable approach the admissions process at Harvard, in which "ethnic background may be deemed a 'plus' in a particular applicant's file, yet it does not insulate the individual from comparison with all other candidates for the available seats." The Harvard approach, in Justice Powell's view, treats individuals as individuals, and not fungible commodities of a racial or ethnic group.

In the aftermath of *Bakke*, the Supreme Court decided many affirmative action cases in the context of government employment contracts, but for twenty-five years it did not return to the question of affirmative action in education. The decisions in the government employment and government contract cases were not entirely consistent, largely because over the arch of those twenty-five years, neither the colorblind position nor the more deferential intermediate scrutiny position of Justice William Brennan and Justice Thurgood Marshall could ever command a clear five-Justice majority of the Court. The law instead settled on the strict scrutiny position advanced by Justice Powell in *Bakke*. As liberal members of the Court departed and were replaced by more conservative members, the voting pattern in *Bakke*, which was 4–1–4, was gradually displaced by a different voting pattern, in which the lax "intermediate scrutiny" position lost traction.

The battle that ensued was between those Justices who truly were in the colorblind camp, and would therefore abolish affirmative action altogether, and those who clung to strict scrutiny, and therefore held out the possibility that at least some affirmative action programs could satisfy constitutional standards. As this showdown emerged, the continued vitality of Justice Powell's diversity theory came under serious question. Several lower courts argued that the *only* governmental interest that could ever be "compelling" was the interest in remedying the lingering effects of past discrimination.[29] By the 1990s, this interest tended to be unavailable as a convincing argument for justifying affirmative action at most universities, namely because of the difficulty of proving that acts of discrimination in the 1950s or 1960s continued to bear some causal connection to contemporary admissions decisions.

During this period, Justices Antonin Scalia and Clarence Thomas were the intellectual leaders of the colorblind charge. In *Adarand Constructors Inc. v. Peña* (1995),[30] a case involving a challenge to the federal government's practice of providing financial incentives to hiring minority contractors for construction projects, Justice Scalia wrote, "Individuals who have been wronged by unlawful racial discrimination should be made whole; but under our Constitution there can be no such thing as either a creditor or a debtor race."[31] Justice Scalia argued that "government can never have a 'compelling interest' in discriminating on the basis of race in order to 'make up' for past racial discrimination in the opposite direction."[32] For Justice Scalia, to "pursue the concept of racial entitlement— even for the most admirable and benign of purposes—is to reinforce and preserve for future mischief the way of thinking that produced race slavery, race privilege and race hatred. In the eyes of government, we are just one race here. It is American."[33]

Justice Thomas expressed his opposition to affirmative action in even more passionate terms, arguing that the government "cannot make us equal; it can only recognize, respect, and protect us as equal before the law."[34] It did not matter to Justice Thomas that the programs may have been motivated by good intentions, for in his view, "under our Constitution, the government may not make distinctions on the basis of race." Justice Thomas concluded that "these programs stamp minorities with a badge of inferiority and may cause them to develop dependencies or to adopt an attitude that they are 'entitled' to preferences."

In *Grutter v. Bollinger* (2003),[35] and *Gratz v. Bollinger* (2003),[36] the Supreme Court heard and decided two cases simultaneously, each arising from the affirmative action admissions programs at the University of Michigan. *Grutter* dealt with the affirmative action admissions program adopted by the University of Michigan Law School, and *Gratz* with the affirmative action admissions policies used by the University of Michigan for its undergraduate admissions program. The Court upheld, by a 5–4 vote, the Michigan Law School program, and struck down, by a 6–3 vote, the undergraduate program.

The *Grutter* case was brought in 1996 by Barbara Grutter, a white applicant seeking admission to the University of Michigan Law School. Grutter had an LSAT score of 161 and an undergraduate grade point average of 3.8. She was first put on the waiting list, but eventually rejected. She sued the Law School, the University, and various officials, claiming that race was used as a predominant factor in admission decisions at the Law School, in violation of the Fourteenth Amendment. The record developed in the lawsuit indicated that Michigan, which is among the most elite and highly ranked law schools in the country, did indeed use race as a factor in admissions.[37] According to the Law School, in making admissions decisions its admissions committee focused on a blend of academic ability such as GPA, LSAT scores, the areas and difficulty of the applicant's undergraduate courses, other more flexible and subjective assessments of the applicant's talents, experiences, and potential, letters of recommendation, a personal statement, and an essay describing what the applicant could contribute to "life and diversity" at the Law School.[38] The Law School articulated its ultimate goal as arriving at an entering class who were "a mix of students with varying backgrounds and experiences who will respect and learn from one another."[39] The Law School faculty had drafted the admissions policy, which explained that it was designed to "achieve diversity which has the potential to enrich everyone's education and thus make a law school class stronger than the sum of its parts."[40] As used in the admissions policy, "diversity" was given a broad compass. Diversity included "many possible bases for diversity admissions," including an array of experiences and backgrounds. Still, the Law School openly acknowledged the aspiration to achieve enrollment of a "critical mass" of racial or ethnic minority students.[41]

Five members of the Supreme Court—Justices O'Connor, Stevens, Breyer, Souter, and Ginsburg—voted to uphold the Law School program.

The Court majority held that lawful affirmative action programs were not limited to those designed to remedy past discrimination. Michigan's goal of creating a critical mass of minority students to diversify its student body could also qualify as a "compelling governmental interest" sufficient to justify a race-conscious admissions program. The Court made it clear that recent affirmative action decisions did not preclude a finding that a diverse student body at public universities constitutes a compelling interest for the state's use of racial classifications. Drawing heavily on Justice Powell's opinion in *Bakke,* the Court deferred to the Law School's educational judgment that diverse classrooms were essential to its mission, a deference that the Court articulated as grounded in the Law School's academic freedom. The Court concluded, "That the Law School has a compelling interest in a diverse student body is informed by our view that attaining a diverse student body is at the heart of the Law School's proper institutional mission, and that 'good faith' on the part of a university is 'presumed' absent 'a showing to the contrary.'"[42]

Having decided that the interest in a diverse student body was sufficiently compelling to justify an affirmative action program, the Court turned to the specific design of the Law School's program, to determine if it met the constitutional requirement that such plans be "narrowly tailored" to effectuate the goal of diversity. In order to be narrowly tailored, a race-conscious admissions program must at a minimum not be a "quota system" employing some fixed percentage goal for minority admissions, in theory or in practice. For the program to be lawful, the Court held, it must be flexible, considering each applicant individually, with race or ethnicity being only a "plus factor" for the applicant. Racial or ethnic minority students cannot be separated into a distinct applicant pool or insulated from comparison to all candidates for available seats. Although there was evidence that the institution paid daily attention to the number of minorities admitted, the Court held that "the Law School engages in a highly individualized, holistic review of each applicant's file, giving serious consideration to all the ways an applicant might contribute to a diverse educational experience."[43] Critically, the Court found that the Law School gave genuine attention and weight to diversity factors other than race or ethnicity. An applicant's contribution to diversity could include knowing several languages, extensive travel, living abroad, family hardship, or community service, and the "Law School frequently accepts nonminority applicants with grades and test scores lower than underrepresented minority applicants (and other nonminority applicants) who are rejected."[44]

The use of race by the Law School in its admissions process was not an "undue burden," the Court ruled, on nonminority students. Given that the Law School considered and admitted many different types of diverse students, the Court reasoned, and given that race was only one "plus factor" in a holistic admissions judgment, no student—minority or nonminority—was foreclosed from consideration from any available seat in the incoming class.

Justice O'Connor's opinion ended with the warning that affirmative action should be regarded only as a temporary phase in American life, a necessary expedient in the near term employed to be phased out and replaced by a colorblind Constitution in the longer term. While the Michigan Law School program contained no explicit sunset date, the Court suggested that as soon as diversity could be achieved through race-neutral admissions policies, such policies should replace affirmative action plans. The Court even named its own number, stating that "we expect that 25 years from now, the use of racial preferences will no longer be necessary to further the interest approved today."[45]

Four Justices—Chief Justice Rehnquist, and Justices Scalia, Kennedy, and Thomas—dissented. Justice Thomas expressed the strongest views, echoing his stalwart position that all race-conscious measures are odious, and that programs such as those advanced by the Michigan Law School merely stigmatized minority applicants, sending the message that they cannot make it on their own.[46]

On the same day the Court decided *Grutter,* the Court in *Gratz v. Bollinger* held that the affirmative action program used by the University of Michigan's undergraduate College of Literature, Science, and the Arts violated the Constitution.[47] The undergraduate program was far more mechanical and "quota-like" in its operation than the admissions program at the Law School. Any applicant from an "underrepresented" racial or ethnic minority group was automatically awarded twenty of the one hundred points needed to guarantee admission.[48] This had the practical effect of making race decisive, all but guaranteeing admission for virtually every minimally qualified minority applicant. The Court in *Grutter* contrasted Michigan's program with the parameters set by Justice Powell in *Bakke*, which did not contemplate that any single characteristic could automatically ensure an applicant admission. The automatic twenty-point allocation was subject only to a factual verification that the applicant was indeed a member of the racial group he or she claimed. The Court rejected the argument advanced by Michigan that the sheer volume of applications made individualized consideration of students impractical. Whatever cost and energy such holistic consideration might entail, the Fourteenth Amendment did not permit the University to engage in shortcuts for convenience when racial classifications were at issue.[49]

While *Grutter* may have allowed affirmative action programs at state universities, provided they meet the "holistic" and "individualized" non-quota-like requirements articulated by the Court, it hardly put the affirmative action issue to rest. Indeed, Michigan, through its political process, joined other large states such as California and Texas in banning affirmative action as a matter of state constitutional law. In the wake of *Grutter* and *Gratz,* Michigan voters approved a state constitutional amendment, adopted by statewide ballot, known as "Proposal 2," which banned affirmative action programs. In *Coalition to Defend Affirmative Action v. Granholm* (2006),[50] the United States Court of Appeals for the Sixth Circuit rejected a challenge to the implementation of Proposal 2. Even if *Gutter* and *Gratz* established that race-conscious affirmative action preferences in higher education were in some instances constitutionally permissible, the court reasoned, that did not mean they were constitutionally required.

Granholm is one of the few judicial decisions to address the "institutional autonomy" academic freedom argument in the context of a state university challenging the state that created it. In contesting the validity of Proposal 2, those opposed to the law attempted to invoke Justice Powell's statement in *Bakke* that a university's academic freedom has "long has been viewed as a special concern of the First Amendment."

The court in *Granholm* did not find the invocation of Justice Powell's academic freedom theme persuasive, and was skeptical that a state university, as an organ of the state government itself, could even possess "rights" as a subordinate corporate institution, especially rights enforceable against the state government or the state's voters. As the court in

Granholm put it, "One does not generally think of the First Amendment as protecting the State from the people but the other way around—of the Amendment protecting individuals from the State."[51] Exploring the relationship between the First Amendment and the Fourteenth Amendment, the court noted that "while *Grutter* upheld the School of Law's use of racial classifications in making its admissions decisions, that was not because the First Amendment compelled it to do so."[52] Rather, the court observed, *Grutter* addressed academic freedom in the context of determining whether a law school's interest in achieving a diverse student body was a compelling interest for Fourteenth Amendment strict scrutiny analysis purposes.[53]

Observing that the Supreme Court in *Grutter* had taken note that some states had banned affirmative action programs at universities, the court in *Granholm* reasoned that it would not have made much sense for the Supreme Court to have cited these examples if it deemed them constitutionally impermissible. Moreover, the court noted that at the end of its opinion, the Supreme Court in *Grutter* suggested that twenty-five years from now the use of racial preferences might no longer be constitutionally permissible: "The First Amendment, by contrast, has no termination point, whether in 25, 50 or 250 years, making it improbable that the same Court that decided *Grutter* would hold that state universities have a First Amendment right to maintain racial preferences."[54]

In *Parents Involved in Community Schools v. Seattle School District No. 1* (2007),[55] the Supreme Court held that public elementary and high schools in Seattle, Washington, and Jefferson County, Kentucky (the Greater Louisville area), could not use race to assign students to schools for the purpose of maintaining racial balance among schools. Chief Justice Roberts delivered the principal opinion, writing for a four-Justice plurality that included Justices Scalia, Thomas, and Alito, holding that the very *goal* of the school districts—the maintenance of racial balance—was constitutionally impermissible. Although schools could assign students to schools on the basis of race in order to remedy the lingering effects of past discrimination, this rationale could not be used to justify the programs in Seattle and Jefferson County. The Seattle schools had never been guilty of past discrimination. The Jefferson County schools had been under a court-ordered desegregation decree from 1975 to 2000, at which point the order was lifted after the court found that all prior constitutional violations had been remedied. This meant that racial balancing could only be justified if the public schools could make use of a diversity rationale similar to that approved in *Grutter v. Bollinger*.

The four Justices, led by Chief Justice Roberts, rejected the comparison. Chief Justice Roberts noted that the pursuit of diversity by the University of Michigan Law School, approved by the Court in *Grutter,* had not been limited to race alone, but to a wider range of diversity factors, whereas the programs in the Seattle and Jefferson County were focused single-mindedly on race. Moreover, the student applicants in *Grutter* were considered as individuals, not as fungible commodities within a racial group. "The entire gist of the analysis in *Grutter,*" the Chief Justice observed, "was that the admissions program at issue there focused on each applicant as an individual, and not simply as a member of a particular racial group."[56] More significant, Chief Justice Roberts reasoned that the diversity rationale sustained in *Grutter* had been justified in that decision's invocation of the unique nature of higher education. "In upholding the admissions plan in *Grutter,*" the Chief Justice explained, "this Court relied upon considerations unique to institutions of higher education, noting that in light of 'the expansive freedoms of speech and thought associated with the university environment, universities occupy a special niche in our constitutional tradition.'"[57] He concluded that "before *Brown,* schoolchildren were told where they could and could not go to school based on the color of their skin," adding that "the way to stop discrimination on the basis of race is to stop discriminating on the basis of race."[58]

Justice Breyer, joined by Justices Souter, Ginsburg, and Stevens, filed a passionate dissent, arguing that the Court had broken faith with the promise of *Brown* and ignored the powerful interest that American public schools possessed in encouraging and facilitating environments in which students of different races may learn with, and from, one another.

The critical concurring opinion of Justice Kennedy joined the plurality in holding the plans unconstitutional, but suggested that the goal of achieving racial balance was not per se unconstitutional. School districts remained free, Justice Kennedy held, to pursue that goal through less draconian means, such as "strategic site selection of new schools; drawing attendance zones with general recognition of the demographics of neighborhoods; allocating resources for special programs; recruiting students and faculty in a targeted fashion; and tracking enrollments, performance, and other statistics by race."[59]

The decision in *Parents Involved* dealt with public secondary and elementary schools, not higher education. Even so, the dissonance between the outcome in *Parents Involved*, banning race-conscious measures to enhance racial balance, and the decision in *Grutter*, allowing race-conscious admissions at the University of Michigan Law School, is palpable. While Chief Justice Roberts in *Parents Involved* did not openly criticize *Grutter*, and while Justice Kennedy's opinion in *Parents Involved* modestly softened the impact of the ruling, the duality that now exists between lower and higher education is striking. The duality is rendered sharper in light of the fact that none of the students in *Parents Involved* were actually shut out of a seat in the school system—they merely were inconvenienced in not getting into the school of their choice, whereas the impact of affirmative action in higher education is arguably, at the margins, more biting, in that someone is denied a seat altogether. But the difference is only "arguably" more biting, in that one might argue that even in higher education, the more likely scenario is that the student passed over by a school such as the University of Michigan, one of the premier "top ten" law schools in the nation, is still quite likely to get into another law school, and almost certainly a very high-quality school. Yet however much we might wrestle with these fine distinctions, the fact remains that viewed from the perspective of constitutional philosophy, *Parents Involved* was far closer to a "colorblind" standard than the "diversity as a compelling interest" view adopted in *Grutter*, and the decision in *Parents Involved* certainly raises the distinct possibility that the twenty-five-year "deadline" suggested by Justice O'Connor in *Grutter* might well be shortened.

Gender

The Supreme Court was slow to take gender discrimination seriously. It was not until the 1970s, decades after *Brown*, that the Court began to strike down laws discriminating on the basis of gender.[60] The Court refused to equate gender discrimination with race discrimination, rejecting the invitation to apply "strict scrutiny" in gender cases. The Court instead adopted the "intermediate scrutiny" standard in gender cases. Even so, perhaps driven in some measure by influence of the Court's two women members, Justice O'Connor and Justice Ginsburg, the Court came increasingly to apply intermediate scrutiny in a manner virtually indistinguishable from the strict scrutiny standard it applied to race. Two higher education cases, one involving the exclusion of men from a nursing program, the other involving the exclusion of women from a state military academy, are illustrative.

In *Mississippi University for Women v. Hogan* (1982),[61] Joe Hogan, a registered nurse, sought admission to the School of Nursing at the Mississippi University for Women. At the time of his application, Hogan had been working for five years as a nursing supervisor in a medical center in Columbus, Mississippi, where the University is located. Hogan was admittedly qualified for admission, but he was rejected because he was a man. From its inception, the University had been for females only. In 1884, the Mississippi Legislature created the University, which was originally named the Mississippi Industrial Institute and College for the Education of White Girls of the State of Mississippi. The University's charter as described in state law, which had remained essentially unchanged since its founding, provided:

> The purpose and aim of the Mississippi State College for Women is the moral and intellectual advancement of the girls of the state by the maintenance of a first-class institution for their education in the arts and sciences, for their training in normal school methods and kindergarten, for their instruction in bookkeeping, photography, stenography, telegraphy, and typewriting, and in designing, drawing, engraving, and painting, and their industrial application, and for their instruction in fancy, general and practical needlework, and in such other industrial branches as experience, from time to time, shall suggest as necessary or proper to fit them for the practical affairs of life.[62]

The Supreme Court, in an opinion by Justice O'Connor, held the single-sex admissions policy of the University unconstitutional. The Court rejected the argument advanced by Mississippi that the restriction limiting enrollment to women could be justified on the theory that it compensated for discrimination against women. Instead of making up for discriminatory barriers faced by women, the Court held, the policy adopted by Mississippi actually perpetuated the sexual stereotype that nursing was a woman's job. Nor had Mississippi made a plausible case that the exclusion of men from the University benefited women students. Finally, the Court rejected an argument advanced by Mississippi that Congress, in passing Title IX of the Education Amendments of 1972,[63] had meant to endorse the continuation of single-sex colleges and universities. Title IX did indeed exempt from its general prohibition of gender discrimination the admissions polices of public institutions of higher education that had traditionally and continually admitted students of only one sex. The Court held that while Congress had the power to provide exemptions from its own antidiscrimination laws, Congress did not have the power to alter the meaning of the Constitution. The Equal Protection Clause of the Fourteenth Amendment, the Court held, barred Mississippi's female-only rule, and Congress had no power to abrogate or dilute that constitutional guarantee.[64]

In *United States v. Virginia* (1996),[65] the Supreme Court in a 7–1 decision, struck down the male-only admissions policy at the Virginia Military Institute (VMI). The Court rejected the alternative proffered by Virginia: the opening of a parallel program at a small private women's college about forty miles from VMI, Mary Baldwin College. VMI was founded in 1839 to produce "citizen-soldiers" fit for leadership in military service and civilian life.[66] By the end of the twentieth century, Virginia had fifteen higher education institutions.[67] Among them, VMI was the only single-gender school, offering an educational and character-building regimen involving what it called an "adversative method," modeled on English public schools and traditional military instruction.[68]

The core of the VMI experience is the "rat line."[69] For seven months first-year cadets, the rats, are treated like . . . rats. They are subjected to "rat training," an intense physical and mental ordeal designed to bond them to their fellow sufferers, specializing in training situations that are stressful and demanding physically and mentally, instilling self-confidence and demonstrating that they are capable of enduring much more than they had previously imagined. The school also used what was called the "dyke system," in which each rat was assigned a senior mentor.[70] VMI uses an honor system, with only one penalty—expulsion—for any violation. The system is grounded in the code that a cadet "does not lie, cheat, steal nor tolerate those who do."[71] Cadets live within a military framework; they wear military-style uniforms, live in barracks, eat in mess halls, and regularly engage in drills and parades. The barracks are, by design, the antithesis of the modern university seeking to attract students through modern dorms. At VMI the cadets live three to five to a room. The living spaces are intentionally stark, with poor ventilation, unattractive furniture, no locks on the doors, and no window coverings. Cadets are removed from their familiar social backgrounds and placed in an environment calculated to induce high stress.

As Justice Ginsburg acknowledged, VMI has succeeded in its mission to produce leaders; among its alumni are military generals, members of Congress, and business executives. The alumni of VMI are intensely loyal and supportive. VMI has the largest endowment, per student, of any public undergraduate university in the nation.[72]

Justice Ginsburg's opinion for the Court restated the constitutional test for gender discrimination in words that came very close to the test for race discrimination. Gender classifications, the Court held, must be justified by a rationale that is "exceedingly persuasive,"[73] and it is the government that bears the burden of proof. The government's justifications must be genuine, not something invented by lawyers during the litigation, and may not indulge in sexual stereotypes about the different talents, capacities, or preferences of males and females. Traditional arguments trotted out to defend sex-based classifications no longer wash for constitutional purposes. Loose claims about the "inherent differences" between men and women are not good enough, any more than loose claims about "inherent differences" between different races. While men and women plainly do have "inherent differences" in the physical and biological sense, the Court explained, those differences "remain cause for celebration, but not for denigration of the members of either sex or for artificial constraints on an individual's opportunity." Gender classifications, the Court warned sternly, may not be used "to create or perpetuate the legal, social, and economic inferiority of women."[74]

Applying this standard, the Court held that Virginia's categorical exclusion of women from VMI could not stand. Virginia had argued that the single-sex education at VMI yielded important educational benefits. But the Court was not persuaded, finding unconvincing VMI's claim that its rugged adversarial method of training could not be preserved if made available to women. While adding women would require some accommodation in housing and training regimens, the Court conceded, this did not mean that VMI would have to compromise its ultimate goal of producing citizen-soldiers. State officials who control gates to opportunity, the Court held, have no warrant to exclude qualified individuals based on "fixed notions concerning the roles and abilities of males and females." The Court also roundly rejected the attempt by Virginia to instead create an alternative program for women at Mary Baldwin College. There was simply no comparison between the two programs. Virginia had not offered a "separate but equal" solution, but a solution that was separate and woefully unequal.[75]

American campuses, like American society generally, are still working through the ongoing tensions between process and outcome conceptions of equality. While some exceptions undoubtedly exist, most American universities, large and small, public and private, embrace the educational benefits of diverse faculties and student bodies. We differ, however, on how to achieve this goal. Just as there are process-equality Justices on the Supreme Court who insist that that the nation's universities should be blind to the identities of faculty and students in making decisions as to whom to hire to teach and whom to admit to learn, there are process-equality educators who argue that universities should not know or care about the identities of faculty, staff, or students. Yet there are also Supreme Court Justices, and American higher education leaders, who believe that higher education will suffer, and society be the poorer, unless some attention to outcomes is allowed. The compromise charted by Justice Powell in *Bakke*, and endorsed by a slim majority of the Supreme Court in *Grutter*, appropriately starts with process equality as the dominate norm. Quotas are unconstitutional. Mechanical approaches to admissions in which minority students are awarded extra admission points across the board are not permitted. This process-equality baseline, however, is tempered by the equally appropriate recognition in *Bakke* and *Grutter* that universities ought not be so hamstrung in their efforts to achieve the laudable benefits of a diverse university community that they must be utterly indifferent to the identities and experiences of students, faculty, and staff in making decisions as to whom to invite to join the university community. The balance between process and outcome equality that currently reigns in American higher education may not be logically or ideologically pure. Yet the purest solutions are not always the best solutions, and our constitutional values often reflect a middle ground defined by the gravitational pulls of competing positive values. In *Grutter*, Justice O'Connor expressed the hope that there may come a time in the next twenty-five years in which American higher education could be forced to entirely abandon programs that deliberately aspire to diversify student bodies. Justice O'Connor's view in *Grutter* was that we are not there yet. I believe Justice O'Connor, like Justice Powell before her, has it right, and while I respect the dissenters, on the Supreme Court and within American university communities, I join the considered judgment of the majority of American educators, who continue to believe that while the pure ideal of a colorblind campus, like the pure ideal of a colorblind Constitution, is where we someday hope to be, we are not there yet.

7

Conclusion

There is a strong, if not universal or uniform, tradition of faculty participation in school governance, and there are numerous policy arguments to support such participation. . . . This Court has never recognized a constitutional right of faculty to participate in policymaking in academic institutions. . . . Faculty involvement in academic governance has much to recommend it as a matter of academic policy, but it finds no basis in the Constitution.

 —Justice Sandra Day O'Connor, for the Court in *Minnesota State Board for Community Colleges v. Knight* (1984)

First Amendment freedom to explore novel or controversial ideas in the classroom is closely linked to the freedom of faculty members to express their views to the administration concerning matters of academic governance.

 —Justice William Brennan, dissenting in *Minnesota State Board for Community Colleges v. Knight* (1984)

The *1940 Statement of Principles on Academic Freedom and Tenure*[1] provides an excellent vehicle for concluding this book's exploration of the influence constitutional ideas have had on the identity of public and private American colleges and universities. The *1940 Statement* was crafted by representatives of the American Association of University Professors, an organization dedicated to the interests of higher education faculty, and also by the Association of American Colleges, an association of universities and colleges led by college presidents and other senior administrators, representing the institutional interests of colleges and universities. The *1940 Statement*, which is a sort of labor-management pact, has over the years been "endorsed" by hundreds of other academic organizations representing a wide range of academic constituencies, and may thus make a solid claim to embodying a broad and enduring consensus that academic freedom is a core defining value of American higher education.

The *1940 Statement* begins with an elegant fusion of the ideals of Aristotle and John Stuart Mill, declaring that institutions of higher education "are conducted for the common good and not to further the interest of either the individual teacher or the institution as a whole." In turn, the "common good depends upon the free search for truth and its free exposition." Academic freedom, the *1940 Statement* proclaims, is essential to both teaching and research. Academic freedom is "fundamental to the advancement of truth," and "fundamental for the protection of the rights of the teacher in teaching and of the student to freedom in learning." Perhaps because the document was created both by professors and administrators, perhaps because the document recognized the natural link between "rights" and "duties," perhaps because the document accepted that a university is a *community* of teachers and learners, the *1940 Statement* acknowledges that academic freedom "carries with it duties correlative with rights."

These general statements of principle and purpose are followed in the *1940 Statement* by three aspects of academic freedom:

1. Teachers are entitled to full freedom in research and in the publication of the results, subject to the adequate performance of their other academic duties; but research for pecuniary return should be based upon an understanding with the authorities of the institution.

2. Teachers are entitled to freedom in the classroom in discussing their subject, but they should be careful not to introduce into their teaching controversial matter which has no relation to their subject. Limitations of academic freedom because of religious or other aims of the institution should be clearly stated in writing at the time of the appointment.

3. College and university teachers are citizens, members of a learned profession, and officers of an educational institution. When they speak or

write as citizens, they should be free from institutional censorship or discipline, but their special position in the community imposes special obligations. As scholars and educational officers, they should remember that the public may judge their profession and their institution by their utterances. Hence they should at all times be accurate, should exercise appropriate restraint, should show respect for the opinions of others, and should make every effort to indicate that they are not speaking for the institution.

The *1940 Statement* continues to exert a powerful and important influence on higher education in the United States, grounding American colleges and universities in a fundamental commitment to academic freedom. Yet, like many other broad proclamations of rights and freedoms—phrases such as "all men are created equal," or "due process of law," or "freedom of speech"—the litany of "shoulds" contained in the *1940 Statement* lacks the concrete bite of hard law, which would have required many more "shalls" and "shall nots" to effectively resolve campus conflicts. Perhaps this is why the *1940 Statement* is not principally enforced by courts, but instead by the political pressure applied by the AAUP through its committees, investigations, and published reports. As Professor William Van Alstyne has explained, the *1940 Statement* is at best "soft law," in that it is typically not "policed by courts."[2]

The *1940 Statement* acknowledges, as it should, that there is a necessary tension between academic freedom and academic responsibility, but it does little to provide guidance as to how the balance among these competing values should be struck. And finally, the *1940 Statement* is clearly a professor-centric document, phrased almost entirely in terms of the rights of teachers, with the rights of students included almost as an afterthought. It does not comprehensively address the complexity of the modern campus world, and the dynamic interactions of university trustees, alumni, donors, presidents, senior administrators, tenured faculty, nontenured faculty, nontenure-track faculty, students, and support staff. Nor does the *1940 Statement* contain much more than a faint hint, in the cryptic phrase dealing with "religious or other aims of the institution," that colleges or universities *as institutions* may possess certain rights of academic freedom.

For all its limits, however, the *1940 Statement* is an elegant and resonant summary of American custom regarding our widely shared commitment to academic freedom and shared university governance. As emphasized throughout this book, it is not sound constitutional law to presume that the ideals of academic freedom and shared university governance are constitutionally compelled. In *Minnesota State Board for Community Colleges v. Knight* (1984),[3] for example, a labor law decision, the Supreme Court rejected the claim that there is a constitutional right, derived from academic freedom principles, entitling university faculty members to participate in policy-making at academic institutions.[4] Even if the values of the *1940 Statement* are not constitutionally compelled, however, those values, as explained throughout this book, are certainly constitutionally influenced.

Harking back to Daniel Webster's argument in the *Dartmouth College* case,[5] universities have long held a special place in both our corporate and constitutional law. Universities are curious legal creatures. Private universities are typically nonprofit corporations, while public universities are agencies of government, often part of larger state systems of higher education. Yet the private university is not just any nonprofit, and the public university is not just any government agency. Setting aside for the moment the distinctions between the publics and the privates, virtually *all* modern American universities partake of a peculiar blend of corporate and political organizational structure; they have qualities that resemble both companies and political democracies.

On the corporate side of the ledger, universities are legally controlled by governing boards—boards of trustees, boards of regents, boards of rectors, boards of visitors. Whatever they are called, these boards are usually vested with powers similar to for-profit corporate boards directors. University boards normally choose the university president, just as corporate boards choose the corporate CEO. University boards oversee fundamental financial decisions, and establish or endorse major institutional priorities and policies.

And at the higher executive level, the organizational structure of a complex modern university does indeed resemble that of a complex modern company. There will be a president and multiple vice presidents: chief financial officers, chief academic officers, chief administrative and operating officers, and so on. "Senior management" will also typically include deans, athletic directors, directors of human resources, campus security, and facilities management. These are the "corporate faces" of the university, and many of those who occupy positions within this corporate hierarchy get hired and fired, promoted and demoted, much like their counterparts in the for-profit corporate sector. Authority originates at the top, first through a board, then through a president, and spreading outward and downward across the expanding hierarchical pyramid.

As suggested throughout this book, however, universities are also "constitutional creatures" of sorts, entities that resemble political and governmental organizations. Aside from civil rights and civil liberties, there are many striking parallels between the *structural* elements of the American constitutional scheme and the typical arrangements of university organization and governance. The framers of the Constitution were not concerned only with constitutional rights *as rights*, they were also acutely attuned to issues of process and structure. Before the Bill of Rights was drafted and adopted, the framers set out to establish processes and structures of government grounded in our famous systems of "checks and balances" and "federalism," dividing power between the national government and the states. James Madison stated the challenge elegantly: "In framing a government which is to be administered by men over men, the great difficulty lies in this: You must first enable the government to control the governed; and in the next place, oblige it to control itself."[6]

The parallels between the procedural and structural elements of our Constitution and a modern university are perhaps more metaphorical than literal, but the analogy is deep nonetheless. Our constitutional notions of checks and divided power is mimicked in higher education through our tradition of shared governance. While universities are certainly corporations, they are thus not just any corporations. They are a fascinating blend of the corporate and the political. A university is part corporation and part federal republic.

In the United States, our political institutions differ in several critical respects from our corporate institutions. Sovereignty rests with the people, who elect legislatures and executives through popular vote. Unlike the corporate sector, where money literally and lawfully buys voting power through the accumulation of corporate shares, in the political system every voter has one vote, and buying votes is a crime. Unlike the corporation, where ultimate power is concentrated, power in government is divided through a system of checks and balances, with power distributed among the executive, legislative, and judicial branches.

Universities partake of many of the values and governing principles of constitutional democracies. University faculties exercise authority in faculty meetings or through elected representative bodies (such as faculty senates), where they are granted substantial authority and autonomy over many of the mainstay elements of the academic mission. Students elect student body presidents and student government associations, which at some universities exercise significant legal authority, including the dispensing of funds to various student organizations and publications, and control of certain student disciplinary functions, such as honor counsels that adjudicate charges of plagiarism, cheating, and other forms of academic dishonesty. Most significant, faculty and students alike hold tenaciously to certain legally enforceable "academic freedom" rights that correspond to the rights of freedom of speech, freedom of religion, and due process of law enjoyed by citizens under the Constitution.

To extend the simile, if universities are in part democracies, they are also democracies in the model of "federal republics." Universities typically have many constituent units, often operating with some measure of independence and sovereignty, not unlike states and localities within the complex American federal system. Larger universities have multiple schools or colleges—in arts and sciences, business, engineering, medicine, law, architecture, or journalism—each with their own deans, faculties, staff, students, directors, chairs, advisory boards, budgets, or endowments, many of which are in turn broken down into numerous departments, institutes, and centers.

American political life is characterized by a perpetual competition over the allocation of scarce resources, and fights for influence, power, and autonomy among different states, localities, and agencies of the government. Anyone who has ever spent time working on an American campus knows that competition for scarce resources among different campus units is a staple of university governance as well. So too, a large part of university decision-making involves difficult judgments over the distribution of resources, and the working out of complex cultural, legal, and economic relationships among different academic disciplines and units, and between each unit and the larger central campus authority.

The exercise of adapting and translating constitutional norms to the world of higher education, public and private, does not yield any mechanistic or formulaic set of answers that push inexorably toward any specific balance among the competing norms of freedom, morality, and order. What the exercise does do is provide us with a vocabulary, with a set of tools for analysis, analogy, comparison, judgment, and introspection, that help us to marry the "idea of the university" with the "idea of America."

NOTES

Notes to Chapter 1

The epigraphs for this chapter are drawn from Sweezy v. New Hampshire, 354 U.S. 234 (1957); and Adler v. Board of Education of the City of New York, 342 U.S. 485, 510 (1952) (Douglas, J., dissenting).

1. ALEXIS DE TOCQUEVILLE, DEMOCRACY IN AMERICA 110 (University of Chicago Press 2002).

2. WALTER ISAACSON, EINSTEIN: HIS LIFE AND UNIVERSE 241 (Simon and Schuster 2007).

3. WALTER ISAACSON, EINSTEIN: HIS LIFE AND UNIVERSE 241, 242 (Simon and Schuster 2007).

4. D. H. LAWRENCE, STUDIES IN CLASSIC AMERICAN LITERATURE (Penguin Classics 1990).

5. NEIL W. HAMILTON, ACADEMIC ETHICS: PROBLEMS AND MATERIALS ON PROFESSIONAL CONDUCT AND SHARED GOVERNANCE 65 (Greenwood Publishing 2002); WILLIAM G. TIERNEY, PROMOTION AND TENURE: COMMUNITY AND SOCIALIZATION IN ACADEME 22 (State University of New York Press 1996).

6. Lochner v. New York, 198 U.S. 48, 76 (1905) (Holmes, J., dissenting).

7. Civil Rights Act of 1964, Pub.L. No. 88-352, 78 Stat. 241. See also Heart of Atlanta Motel Inc. v. United States, 379 U.S. 241 (1964) (upholding application of the Civil Rights Act to motels); and Katzenbach v. McClung, 379 U.S. 294 (1964) (upholding application of the Civil Rights Act to restaurants).

8. Title IX of the Education Amendments of 1972, Pub.L. 92-318, 86 Stat. 373, as amended, 20 U.S.C.A. §§ 1681 et seq. See also Grove City College v. Bell, 465 U.S. 555, 575–76 (1984) (upholding application of Title IX to private college).

9. Thus, in the conception of philosophers such as John Locke, rights are liberties enjoyed by man in his natural condition, or "state of nature," before the creation of government. See JOHN LOCKE, TWO TREATISES ON GOVERNMENT (Cambridge University Press 1988).

10. JAMES MADISON, THE FEDERALIST PAPERS, No. 51, at 349 (1788) (J. Cooke, ed., Wesleyan University Press 1961) ("In framing a government which is to be administered by men over men, the great difficulty lies in this: You must first enable the government to control the governed; and in the next place, oblige it to control itself.").

11. The Declaration of Independence (1776) was nominally the work of the drafting committee of the Second Continental Congress, but Jefferson wrote it virtually in full.

12. See, for example, Connecticut Bd. of Pardons v. Dumschat, 452 U.S. 458, 463 (1981) (discussing parole as not implicating any "underlying right"); Leis v. Flynt, 439 U.S. 438, 442–43 (1979) (characterizing pro hac vice practice as a "privilege of appearing upon motion" but "not a right granted either by statute or the Constitution"); William W. Van Alstyne, "The Demise of the Right-Privilege Distinction in Constitutional Law," 81 Harv. L. Rev. 1439 (1968); and Rodney A. Smolla, "The Reemergence of the Right-Privilege Distinction in Constitutional Law: The Price of Protesting Too Much," 35 Stan. L. Rev. 69 (1982).

13. See, for example, Kathleen M. Sullivan, "Unconstitutional Conditions," 102 Harv. L. Rev. 1415 (1989); Richard A. Epstein, "The Supreme Court 1987 Term: Unconstitutional Conditions, State Power, and the Limits of Consent," 102 Harv. L. Rev. 5 (1988); and Robert L. Hale, "Unconstitutional Conditions and Constitutional Rights," 35 Colum. L. Rev. 321, 322 (1935).

14. Cass Sunstein, "Why the Unconstitutional Conditions Doctrine Is an Anachronism," 70 B.U. L. Rev. 593, 620 (1990) (doctrine is "too crude and too general to provide help in contested cases"); Kathleen Sullivan, "Unconstitutional Conditions," 102 Harv. L. Rev. 1415, 1416 (1989) (doctrine is "riven with inconsistencies"); Robert L. Hale, "Unconstitutional Conditions and Constitutional Rights," 35 Colum. L. Rev. 321, 322 (1935) ("The Supreme Court has sustained many such exertions of power even after announcing the broad doctrine that would invalidate them."); Rodney A. Smolla, "The Reemergence of the Right-Privilege Distinction in Constitutional Law: The Price of Protesting Too Much," 35 Stan. L. Rev. 69 (1982) (arguing that the right-privilege distinction, while diminished by the doctrine of unconstitutional conditions, was not destroyed by it).

15. Abraham Lincoln, "Special Message to Congress," in SPEECHES AND WRITINGS, 1859–1865 253 (Library of America, 1989).

16. A. Bartlett Giamatti, A FREE AND ORDERED SPACE: THE REAL WORLD OF THE UNIVERSITY (Norton 1990).

17. JONATHAN D. CASPER, THE POLITICS OF CIVIL LIBERTIES 148–49 (Harper & Row 1972); Rodney A. Smolla, "In Pursuit of Racial Utopias: Fair Housing, Quotas, and Goals in the 1980s," 58 S. Cal. L. Rev. 947 (1985).

18. Mark G. Yudof, "Equal Opportunity and the Courts," 51 Tex. L. Rev. 411, 457 (1973).

19. MARK G. YUDOF ET AL., EDUCATIONAL POLICY AND THE LAW 383 (Wadsworth Publishing 2001).

20. *Plessy v. Ferguson*, 163 U.S. 537 (1896).

21. *Missouri ex rel. Gaines v. Canada*, 305 U.S. 337 (1938).

22. *Sweatt v. Painter*, 339 U.S. 629 (1950).

23. *McLaurin v. Oklahoma State Regents for Higher Education* et al., 339 U.S. 637 (1950).

24. *Brown v. Board of Education* of Topeka, 349 U.S. 294, 301 (1955).

25. *United States v. Fordice*, 505 U.S. 717 (1992).

26. *Regents of the University of California v. Bakke*, 438 U.S. 265 (1978).

27. *Grutter v. Bollinger*, 539 U.S. 306 (2003).

28. *Gratz v. Bollinger*, 539 U.S. 244 (2003).

Notes to Chapter 2

The epigraphs for this chapter are drawn from Regents of the University of California v. Bakke, 438 U.S. 265 (1978) (Opinion of Powell, J.); and University of Pennsylvania v. Equal Employment Opportunity Commission, 493 U.S. 182 (1990).

1. Griswold v. Connecticut, 381 U.S. 479 (1965).

2. Griswold v. Connecticut, 381 U.S. 479, 484 (1965) (Douglas, J., for the Court).

3. Griswold v. Connecticut, 381 U.S. 479, 492 (1965) (Goldberg, J., concurring).

4. Griswold v. Connecticut, 381 U.S. 479, 492 (1965) (Goldberg, J., concurring).

5. Griswold v. Connecticut, 381 U.S. 479, 400 (1965) (Harlan, J., concurring) quoting Palko v. Connecticut, 302 U.S. 318, 325 (1937).

6. Eisenstadt v. Baird, 405 U.S. 438 (1972).

7. Lawrence v. Texas, 539 U.S. 558 (2003).

8. Roe v. Wade, 410 U.S. 113 (1973).

9. Marbury v. Madison, 5 U.S. (1 Cranch) 137 (1803).

10. Marbury v. Madison, 5 U.S. (1 Cranch) 137, 177 (1803).

11. Branzburg v. Hayes, 408 U.S. 665, 697 (1972).

12. Branzburg v. Hayes, 408 U.S. 665 (1972).

13. University of Pennsylvania v. Equal Employment Opportunity Commission, 493 U.S. 182 (1990).

14. MARCIA MOBILIA BOUMIL ET AL., WOMEN AND THE LAW 531 (William S. Hein Publishing 1992).

15. University of Pennsylvania v. Equal Employment Opportunity Commission, 493 U.S. 182, 197 (1990). Justice Blackmun described the Supreme Court's prior decisions in *Sweezy* and *Keyishian*, discussed later in this chapter, as situations in which the "government was attempting to control or direct the content of the speech engaged in by the university or those affiliated with it." Justice Blackmun explained that *Sweezy* and *Keyishian* were applications of standard free-speech principles. "When, in those cases, the Court spoke of 'academic freedom' and the right to determine on 'academic grounds who may teach,'" Justice Blackmun thus explained, "the Court was speaking in reaction to content-based regulation."

16. University of Pennsylvania v. Equal Employment Opportunity Commission, 493 U.S. 182, 197, 199 (1990).

17. Adler v. Board of Education of the City of New York, 342 U.S. 485 (1952).

18. Adler v. Board of Education of the City of New York, 342 U.S. 485n3 (1952).

19. Adler v. Board of Education of the City of New York, 342 U.S. 485, 510 (1952).

20. Sweezy v. New Hampshire, 354 U.S. 234 (1957).

21. Sweezy v. New Hampshire, 354 U.S. 234, 243 (1957).

22. Sweezy v. New Hampshire, 354 U.S. 234, 260 (1957).

23. Sweezy v. New Hampshire, 354 U.S. 234, 250 (1957).

24. Watkins v. United States, 354 U.S. 178 (1957).

25. Sweezy v. New Hampshire, 354 U.S. 234, 255 (1957).

26. Sweezy v. New Hampshire, 354 U.S. 234, 255 (1957).

27. Sweezy v. New Hampshire, 354 U.S. 234, 255 (1957) (Frankfurter, J., concurring).

28. Sweezy v. United States, 354 U.S. 178, 263 (1957) (Frankfurter, J., concurring).

29. Sweezy v. United States, 354 U.S. 178, 261 (1957) (Frankfurter, J., concurring).

30. Sweezy v. United States, 354 U.S. 178, 261 (1957) (Frankfurter, J., concurring).

31. Sweezy v. United States, 354 U.S. 178, 261 (1957) (Frankfurter, J., concurring).

32. Sweezy v. United States, 354 U.S. 178, 261 (1957) (Frankfurter, J., concurring).

33. Sweezy v. United States, 354 U.S. 178, 261 (1957) (Frankfurter, J., concurring).

34. Keyishian v. Board of Regents of the University of New York, 385 U.S. 589 (1967).

35. Keyishian v. Board of Regents of the University of New York, 385 U.S. 589, 603 (1967).

36. Rumsfeld v. Forum for Academic and Institutional Rights Inc., 547 U.S. 47 (2006).

37. Grove City College v. Bell, 465 U.S. 555 (1984).

38. Regents of the University of California Regents v. Bakke, 438 U.S. 265 (1978).

39. Gratz v. Bollinger, 539 U.S. 244 (2003).

40. Grutter v. Bollinger, 539 U.S. 306 (2003).

41. Central State University v. American Association of University Professors, Central State University Chapter, 526 U.S. 124 (1999).

42. Minnesota State Board for Community Colleges v. Knight, 465 U.S. 271 (1984).

43. National Labor Relations Board v. Yeshiva University, 444 U.S. 672 (1980).

44. Garcetti v. Ceballos, 547 U.S. 410 (2006).

45. STUART TAYLOR JR. AND K. C. JOHNSON, UNTIL PROVEN INNOCENT (Macmillan 2007).

46. Emergency Coalition to Defend Educational Travel v. United States Department of the Treasury, 545 F.3d 4, 238 Ed. Law Rep. 45 (D.C. Cir. 2008).

47. Emergency Coalition to Defend Educational Travel v. United States Department of the Treasury, 545 F.3d 4, 15, 238 Ed. Law Rep. 45 (D.C. Cir. 2008) (Edwards, J., concurring) ("The disposition of the First Amendment issue in this case on grounds other than academic freedom is relatively straightforward and uncomplicated. Therefore, it is unnecessary for us to parse the many difficult issues relating

to the concept and scope of 'academic freedom,' including, inter alia: whether academic freedom is a constitutional right at all; the breadth of academic freedom; whether academic freedom implicates additional constitutional interests that are not fully accounted for by the Supreme Court's customary employee-speech jurisprudence; whether a professor may assert an individual constitutional right of academic freedom against a university employer; how academic freedom should be enforced in public versus private universities; whether and how we distinguish between the university-as-a-speaker and the university-as-an-employer in assessing the contours of academic freedom; and the extent to which professors have rights of academic freedom in university governance.") Citing Judith Areen, "Government as Educator: A New Understanding of the First Amendment Protection of Academic Freedom and Governance," 97 Geo. L. Rev. 945 (2009).

48. Emergency Coalition to Defend Educational Travel v. United States Department of the Treasury, 545 F.3d 4, 18, 238 Ed. Law Rep. 45 (D.C. Cir. 2008) (Silberman, J., concurring).

49. University of Pennsylvania v. Equal Employment Opportunity Commission, 493 U.S. 182 (1990).

50. Emergency Coalition to Defend Educational Travel v. United States Department of the Treasury, 545 F.3d 4, 18, 238 Ed. Law Rep. 45 (D.C. Cir. 2008) (Silberman, J., concurring).

51. Emergency Coalition to Defend Educational Travel v. United States Department of the Treasury, 545 F.3d 4, 18, 238 Ed. Law Rep. 45 (D.C. Cir. 2008) (Silberman, J., concurring).

52. Emergency Coalition to Defend Educational Travel v. United States Department of the Treasury, 545 F.3d 4, 18, 238 Ed. Law Rep. 45 (D.C. Cir. 2008) (Silberman, J., concurring).

53. Emergency Coalition to Defend Educational Travel v. United States Department of the Treasury, 545 F.3d 4, 20, 238 Ed. Law Rep. 45 (D.C. Cir. 2008) (Silberman, J., concurring).

54. David M. Rabban, "Functional Analysis of 'Individual' and 'Institutional' Academic Freedom Under the First Amendment," 53 L. & Contemp. Prob. 272 (1990).

55. David M. Rabban, "Functional Analysis of 'Individual' and 'Institutional' Academic Freedom Under the First Amendment," 53 L. & Contemp. Prob. 272, 300 (1990).

Notes to Chapter 3

The epigraphs for this chapter are drawn from the Civil Rights Cases, 109 U.S. 3, 17–18 (1883); and Rosenberger v. Rector and Visitors of the University of Virginia, 515 U.S. 819, 835–36 (1995).

1. Trustees of Dartmouth College v. Woodward, 17 U.S. 518 (1819).

2. The First Amendment was not formally recognized as binding against state governments until the 1926 decision in *Gitlow v. New York*, 268 U.S. 652 (1925).

3. Daniel Webster, "Peroration, the Dartmouth College Case, March 10, 1818," available at http://www.dartmouth.edu/~dwebster/speeches/dartmouth-peroration.html.

4. Daniel Webster, "Peroration, the Dartmouth College Case, March 10, 1818," available at http://www.dartmouth.edu/~dwebster/speeches/dartmouth-peroration.html.

5. Daniel Webster, "Peroration, the Dartmouth College Case, March 10, 1818," available at http://www.dartmouth.edu/~dwebster/speeches/dartmouth-peroration.html.

6. Trustees of Dartmouth College v. Woodward, 17 U.S. 518, 636 (1819).

7. Trustees of Dartmouth College v. Woodward, 17 U.S. 518, 636 (1819).

8. Trustees of Dartmouth College v. Woodward, 17 U.S. 518, 634 (1819).

9. Trustees of Dartmouth College v. Woodward, 17 U.S. 518, 634 (1819).

10. Civil Rights Cases, 109 U.S. 3 (1883).

11. Princeton University and New Jersey v. Schmid, 455 U.S. 100 (1982).

12. Civil Rights Act of 1964, Pub.L. 88-352, 78 Stat. 241.

13. Civil Rights Act of 1968, Title VIII, 42 U.S.C. § 3601 et seq.

14. Civil Rights Act of 1964, Pub.L. 88-352, 78 Stat. 241.

15. Civil Rights Act of 1964, Pub.L. 88-352, 78 Stat. 241.

16. Brown v. Board of Education of Topeka, 347 U.S. 483 (1954).

17. Mississippi University for Women v. Hogan, 458 U.S. 718 (1982).

18. United States v. Virginia, 518 U.S. 515 (1996).

19. Bob Jones University v. United States, 461 U.S. 574 (1983).

20. There is virtually unanimous agreement in the United States on at least this much: government may not persecute any one religion, banning that religion or enacting laws deliberately penalizing that religion and its adherents. In *Church of the Lukumi Babalu Aye v. Hialeah* (1993), for example, the city of Hialeah, Florida, made it a crime to engage in the ritual sacrifice of animals, but did not prohibit a vast number of other forms of animal slaughter, including slaughter for food production. It was plain that the motivation for the law was to suppress ritualistic animal sacrifices of the Santeria religion. The Supreme Court unanimously struck the Hialeah ordinance down, invoking the fundamental notion that government may not enact laws targeting a specific religion. Beyond this bedrock principle, however, variants emerge among the high, middle, and low positions. High separationists tend to claim that the antidiscrimination principle goes beyond the mere rule that government may not discriminate *against* any *particular* religion. High separationists also tend to insist that government not discriminate in *favor* of any particular religion, and more broadly, *in favor of religion in general.* The door swings both ways. For high separationists it thus violates the nondiscrimination principle to favor religion in general, even if no specific religion is deliberately treated better

or worse than any other. Middle separationists, in contrast, will tend to argue that while government may never discriminate *against* religion, government has greater latitude to discriminate in *favor* of religion in general. As long as no one religion is singled out for especially favorable treatment, some modest favoring of religion in general is fine, and indeed promotes religious freedom. Low separationists tend to argue that governmental favoring of religion in general is entirely appropriate, and need not be modest or restrained. Some low separationists go even further, arguing that government is actually allowed to play favorites among religions, so long as no religion is actually banned or persecuted. Policies that favor a majority religion, for example, are permitted so long as no minority religion is shunned, banned, persecuted, or oppressed.

21. See, generally, Elk Grove Unified School District v. Newdow, 542 U.S. 1 (2004) (dealing with recitation of Pledge of Allegiance in public schools); Lynch v. Donnelly, 465 U.S. 668 (1984) (in which the Court allowed a display of a crèche that included other holiday symbols in close proximity); and County of Allegheny v. Greater Pittsburgh ACLU, 492 U.S. 573 (1989) (in which the Court held that a crèche display was unconstitutional because there were no surrounding secular holiday symbols, yet allowed a display of a menorah because it was deemed to have both secular and religious meanings).

22. As the issue of coercion of religious profession or belief assumes an increasingly critical role in assessing the appropriate distance between church and state, greater pressure is correspondingly placed on the meaning of "coercion." At the very least it means that individuals may not be compelled, under penalty of law, into professing or denouncing any religious belief. High separationists will sweep much more within the definition of "coercion." The "anti-coercion meter" is set to very high sensitivity; almost everything is coercive. The anti-coercion rule applies to actions by government that penalize certain activity, such as criminal prosecutions or civil fines, and actions by government that harm citizens by denying them benefits for which they would otherwise qualify, such as welfare awards or educational scholarships.

A number of decisions at the high school level have turned on the meaning of coercion. In Lee v. Weisman, 505 U.S. 577 (1992), the Court struck down the practice of delivering a prayer at high school graduation ceremonies. While graduation was "voluntary," and no student was required to actively participate in the prayer, the Court held that the importance of graduation in the life of a high school student and the inability of the student to shut out the prayer while sitting in the ceremony rendered the practice unconstitutional. In a sequel, Santa Fe Independent School District v. Doe, 530 U.S. 290 (2000), the Supreme Court dealt with a challenge to a practice at a high school under which a student who occupied the school's elective office of "student council chaplain" delivered a prayer over the public address system before each varsity football game. At the threshold, the Court rejected the defense that the speech at issue was merely the private speech of students, and thus outside the purview of the Establishment Clause. The Court noted that the speech was authorized by a government body and took place on government property at events sponsored by the government. The Court in *Santa Fe* held that the football prayer was not saved by the fact that the student delivering the prayer was elected by the student body. The student election did nothing to protect minority views, the Court reasoned, but instead simply placed the students who hold such views at the mercy of the majority. Fundamental rights may not be submitted to vote, the Court held; they depend on the outcome of no elections. Expanding the concept of coercion, the Court rejected the view that the practice was saved because football games were completely voluntary, holding that the mere fact that a school-sponsored event is voluntary does not by itself insulate the practice from being an Establishment Clause violation. Applying a commonsense appreciation of the important role of time-honored American rituals like high school football games in the lives of high school–aged children, the Court held that high schoolers should not be forced by a school district to choose between attendance at such an event and surrender of their religious scruples. Echoing the theme that decisions involving alleged religious establishment at the college and university level tend to be more lax than at the lower public school grade levels, however, some lower courts have refused to strike down the use of nonsectarian prayers or moments of silence at state university ceremonies. In Chaudhuri v. Tennessee, 130 F.3d 232 (6th Cir. 1997), for example, the United States Court of Appeals for the Sixth Circuit rejected a challenge to such practices, brought by a Hindu professor in protest against prayers at ceremonies of Tennessee State University. Similarly, in Tanford v. Brand, 104 F.3d 982 (7th Cir. 1997), the United States Court of Appeals for the Seventh Circuit rejected a challenge brought by an Indiana University law professor and a group of law students against the University President and Vice President challenging the ritual of prayer at the University commencement exercises. The decisions, however, are by no means uniform. In Mellen v. Bunting, 327 F.3d 355 (4th Cir. 2003), the United States Court of Appeals for the Fourth Circuit struck down the practice at the Virginia Military Academy of "supper prayer" at the beginning of meals at the academy, finding the practice coercive and a violation of the *Lemon* test (see note 30, below).

23. Slouching toward laxity, low or middle separationists may invoke a doctrinal approach that may be described awkwardly but aptly as the "historical de minimis" exception. If a more down-to-earth label is desired, it might be called the "it's been around a long time and it's no big deal" exception. This approach excuses from the rigors of *Lemon* relatively low-grade and nondenominational invocations of religion and God that have long been part of our civic and political

culture. Nominees for such an exception would include the practice of opening legislative sessions with a prayer, upheld by the Supreme Court in Marsh v.
Chambers, 463 U.S. 783 (1983); the use of the phrase "God Save the United States
and This Honorable Court" at the ceremonial opening of federal court sessions,
including the Supreme Court; the motto "In God We Trust" on our currency;
the fourth verse to "The Star-Spangled Banner" (which, unlike the other three
verses, has many religious references); or the phrase "One nation, under God"
in the Pledge of Allegiance. In *Marsh*, which involved a long-standing practice
by the Nebraska legislature of opening its unicameral legislative sessions with a
prayer from a chaplain (who was consistently a Presbyterian), the Supreme Court
openly acknowledged that a straightforward application of Lemon v. Kurtzman,
403 U.S. 602 (1971), would result in striking down the ceremony. It is difficult to
find a "secular purpose" in praying, unless one is willing to strip the prayer of all
spirituality, and it certainly seems to advance religion and entangle government
with it. In dismissing the practice as relatively trivial in its impact and as grounded
in long-standing tradition, including the practices of the framers of the Constitution at the Constitutional Convention in Philadelphia and the practices of the
very first American Congress, the Court simply refused to apply *Lemon*, crafting
the historical de minimis exception.

The state of California would invoke this historical argument in Elk Grove
Unified School District v. Newdow, 542 U.S. 1 (2004), to defend California's practice
of beginning public school sessions with the Pledge of Allegiance. The opponents
of the phrase "under God" argued that the historical "it's no big deal" argument
was itself unprincipled, but even if one grudgingly accepts the legitimacy of the
exception, the phrase "under God" in the Pledge ought not qualify, since those
words were not part of the Pledge when it was originally created but were added by
Congress in 1954. In a somewhat anticlimactic ruling, the Court held that Michael
Newdow, the father of the child who purportedly did not want to recite the Pledge,
did not have standing to litigate the claim on behalf of his child, because he was not
the child's custodial parent.

24. Rosenberger v. Rector and Visitors of the University of Virginia, 515 U.S. 819
(1995).

25. Rosenberger v. Rector and Visitors of the University of Virginia, 515 U.S. 819,
865 (1995).

26. Rosenberger v. Rector and Visitors of the University of Virginia, 515 U.S. 819,
898 (1995).

27. Susan Kinzie, "William and Mary President Resigns," *Washington Post*, February 13, 2008.

28. McCreary County v. ACLU of Kentucky, 545 U.S. 844 (2005).

29. Van Orden v. Perry, 545 U.S. 677 (2005).

30. Modern Establishment Clause doctrine begins with the three-pronged "*Lemon* test," a standard articulated in *Lemon v. Kurtzman*, 403 U.S. 602 (1971). The *Lemon* test is demanding and highly separationist. Under it, for a law to be constitutional it must (1) have a "secular purpose"; (2) its "principal or primary effect must be one that neither advances nor inhibits religion"; and (3) it must not foster "an excessive government entanglement with religion." Precisely because the test, if conscientiously applied, will often result in laws being struck down, it tends to not be applied conscientiously. *Lemon* is most likely to be invoked by justices and judges in the service of holding some governmental program or display unconstitutional, and most likely to be ignored or applied laxly when upholding a law. To soften the impact of *Lemon* and allow for less separation between government and religion, several less stringent alternative doctrines have emerged.

31. Stone v. Graham, 449 U.S. 39 (1980).

32. McCreary County v. ACLU of Kentucky, 545 U.S. 844, 847 (2005)

33. Unlike Justice Souter's high separationist perspective in *McCreary*, which openly embraced and applied *Lemon v. Kurtzman*, the Chief Justice in *Van Orden* distanced his opinion from *Lemon*, arguing that *Lemon* is not useful in dealing with the sort of "passive monument" that Texas had erected on its capitol grounds.

34. Lee v. Weisman, 505 U.S. 577 (1992).

35. Healy v. James, 408 U.S. 169 (1972).

36. Civil Rights Act of 1964, Pub.L. No. 88-352, 78 Stat. 241.

37. Civil Rights Act of 1968, Title VIII, 42 U.S.C. § 3601 et seq.

38. Title IX, Education Amendments of 1972, 20 U.S.C. §§ 1681–88.

39. Katzenbach v. McClung, 379 U.S. 294 (1964).

40. Heart of Atlanta Motel v. United States, 379 U.S. 241 (1964).

41. McDaniel v. Paty, 435 U.S. 618 (1978).

42. Smith v. Allwright, 321 U.S. 649 (1944).

43. Terry v. Adams, 345 U.S. 461 (1953).

44. Board of Directors of Rotary International v. Rotary Club of Duarte, 481 U.S. 537 (1987).

45. Roberts v. United States Jaycees, 468 U.S. 609 (1984).

46. Hurley v. Irish-American Gay, Lesbian, and Bisexual Group of Boston, 515 U.S. 557 (1995).

47. Boy Scouts of America v. Dale, 530 U.S. 640 (2000).

48. Christian Legal Society Chapter of the University of California–Hastings v. Martinez, 2010 WL 2555187 (June 28, 2010).

49. Christian Legal Society Chapter of the University of California–Hastings v. Martinez, 2010 WL 2555187 (June 28, 2010).

50. Christian Legal Society Chapter of the University of California–Hastings v. Martinez, 2010 WL 2555187 (June 28, 2010).

Notes to Chapter 4

The epigraphs for this chapter are drawn from McAuliffe v. Mayor of New Bedford, 155 Mass. 216, 220 (1892); and Perry v. Sindermann, 408 U.S. 593, 597 (1972).

1. McAuliffe v. Mayor of New Bedford, 155 Mass. 216 (1892).
2. Commonwealth v. Davis, 162 Mass. 510 (1895).
3. Hamilton v. Regents of the University of California, 293 U.S. 245 (1934).
4. Urofsky v. Gilmore, 216 F.3d 401 (4th Cir. 2000).
5. Goldberg v. Kelly, 397 U.S. 254 (1970).
6. CHARLES REICH, THE GREENING OF AMERICA (Three Rivers Press 1995).
7. Charles Reich, "The New Property," 73 Yale L. J. 733 (1964).
8. Charles Reich, "The New Property," 73 Yale L. J. 733 (1964).
9. Board of Regents v. Roth, 408 U.S. 564 (1972).
10. Perry v. Sindermann, 408 U.S. 593 (1972).
11. Perry v. Sindermann, 408 U.S. 593, 599 (1972).
12. Perry v. Sindermann, 408 U.S. 593 (1972) (emphasis added by author).
13. Arnett v. Kennedy, 416 U.S. 134 (1974).
14. Arnett v. Kennedy, 416 U.S. 134, 228 (1974).
15. Grove City College v. Bell, 465 U.S. 555 (1984).
16. Grove City College v. Bell, 465 U.S. 555, 559 (1984).
17. Grove City College v. Bell, 465 U.S. 555, 575 (1984).
18. Grove City College v. Bell, 465 U.S. 555, 575 (1984).
19. Grove City College v. Bell, 465 U.S. 555, 575 (1984).
20. Rumsfeld v. Forum for Academic and Institutional Rights Inc., 547 U.S. 47 (2006).
21. 10 U.S.C. § 983.
22. West Virginia State Board of Education v. Barnette, 319 U.S. 624 (1943).
23. Wooley v. Maynard, 430 U.S. 705 (1977).
24. Pruneyard Shopping Center v. Robins, 447 U.S. 74 (1980).
25. Boy Scouts of America v. Dale, 530 U.S. 640 (2000).
26. Rumsfeld v. Forum for Academic and Institutional Rights Inc., 547 U.S. 47, 69 (2006).
27. Burt v. Gates, 502 F.3d 183 (2d Cir. 2007).
28. Rosenberger v. Rector of the University of Virginia, 515 U.S. 819 (1995).
29. As discussed in chapter 3, the case that is most strongly identified with the high level of separation of church and state at the lower grade level is Lemon v. Kurtzman 403 U.S. 602 (1971). See also Aguilar v. Felton, 473 U.S. 402 (1985); and Grand Rapids School District v. Ball, 473 U.S. 373 (1985); Meek v. Pittenger, 421 U.S. 349 (1975). But the Supreme Court has allowed aid to parochial schools in some circumstances, in which the aid flows to students as part of general educational assistance programs. See Zobrest v. Catalina Foothills School District, 509 U.S. 1 (1993)

(permitting a school district to provide an interpreter to a deaf student attending a Catholic high school).

30. Zelman v. Simmons-Harris, 536 U.S. 639 (2002).
31. Mueller v. Allen, 463 U.S. 388 (1983).
32. Tilton v. Richardson, 403 U.S. 672 (1971).
33. Hunt v. McNair. 413 U.S. 734 (1973).
34. Roemer v. Board of Public Works of Maryland, 426 U.S. 736 (1976).
35. Locke v. Davey, 540 U.S. 712 (2004).

Notes to Chapter 5

The epigraphs for this chapter are drawn from Palko v. Connecticut, 302 U.S. 319, 324–25 (1937) (internal case citations omitted from the quotation); and Papish v. Board of Curators of the University of Missouri, 410 U.S. 667, 676–77 (1973) (Rehnquist, J., dissenting).

1. THOMAS L. FRIEDMAN, THE WORLD IS FLAT (Farrar, Straus & Giroux 2005).

2. WALTER ISAACSON, EINSTEIN: HIS LIFE AND UNIVERSE 241 (Simon and Schuster 2007).

3. PLATO, THE APOLOGY. In SIX GREAT DIALOGUES: APOLOGY, CRITO, PHAEDO, PHAEDRUS, SYMPOSIUM, THE REPUBLIC, 11 (Benjamin Jowett, trans., Dover 2007).

4. ARISTOTLE, THE POLITICS, BOOK I, CHAPTER 1. In ARISTOTLE'S POLITICS AND POETICS, 5 (Benjamin Jowett, trans., Viking 1962).

5. JOHN STUART MILL, ON LIBERTY (1869).

6. See Abrams v. United States, 250 U.S. 616, 630 (1919) (Holmes, J., dissenting); and Whitney v. People of the State of California, 274 U.S. 357, 375–77 (1927) (Brandeis, J., concurring). See also RODNEY A. SMOLLA, FREE SPEECH IN AN OPEN SOCIETY 95–108 (Knopf 1992); Vincent Blasi, "Reading Holmes Through the Lens of Schauer: The *Abrams* Dissent," 72 Notre Dame L. Rev. 1343 (1997); William Mayton, "Seditious Libel and the Lost Guarantee of Freedom of Expression," 84 Colum. L. Rev. 91 (1984); and David Rabban, "The Ahistorical Historian: Leonard Levy on Freedom of Expression in Early American History," 37 Stan. L. Rev. 795 (1985).

7. JOHN MILTON, AREOPAGITICA: A SPEECH OF MR. JOHN MILTON FOR THE LIBERTY OF UNLICENSED PRINTING TO THE PARLIAMENT OF ENGLAND (1644).

8. Abrams v. United States, 250 U.S. 616, 630 (1919) (Holmes, J., dissenting).

9. Abrams v. United States, 250 U.S. 616, 630 (1919) (Holmes, J., dissenting).

10. Chaplinsky v. New Hampshire, 315 U.S. 568 (1942).

11. Chaplinsky v. New Hampshire, 315 U.S. 568, 571–72 (1942). See also RODNEY A. SMOLLA AND MELVILLE B. NIMMER, SMOLLA AND NIMMER ON FREEDOM OF SPEECH § 2:70 (Thomson Reuters West 2009) (updated biannually).

12. In *Cohen v. California*, 403 U.S. 15 (1971), the Supreme Court held that the First Amendment protected Paul Cohen from prosecution for wearing a jacket with the words "Fuck the Draft" while in the public corridors of a Los Angeles courthouse. Justice Hugo Black dissented, arguing that Cohen's actions were "conduct," not "speech," and thus outside the ambit of First Amendment protection.

13. See National Social Party of America v. Village of Skokie, 432 U.S. 43 (1977).

14. See Brandenburg v. Ohio, 396 U.S. 444 (1969); and Virginia v. Black, 538 U.S. 343 (2003) (author's disclosure: the author, Rodney A. Smolla, was lead counsel and presented the oral argument in this case).

15. See Texas v. Johnson, 491 U.S. 397 (1989); and United States v. Eichman, 496 U.S. 310 (1990).

16. See Olmer v. Austin, 192 F.3d 1176 (8th Cir. 1999).

17. See Miller v. California, 413 U.S. 15 (1973); and Paris Adult Theatre I v. Slaton, 413 U.S. 49 (1973).

18. Cohen v. California, 403 U.S. 15 (1971).

19. Erznoznik v. City of Jacksonville, 422 U.S. 205 (1975).

20. Erznoznik v. City of Jacksonville, 422 U.S. 205, 210–11 (1975).

21. United States v. Playboy Entertainment Group Inc., 529 U.S. 80–83 (2000).

22. United States v. On Lee, 193 F.2d 306, 315–16 (2d Cir. 1951) (Frank, J., dissenting).

23. Poe v. Ullman, 367 U.S. 497, 551 (1961) (Harlan, J., dissenting).

24. Federal Communications Commission v. Pacifica Foundation, 438 U.S. 726 (1978).

25. Federal Communications Commission v. Pacifica Foundation, 438 U.S. 726, 729 (1978).

26. CBS Corporation v. Federal Communications Commission, 535 F.3d 167 (3d Cir. 2008).

27. Public Utilities Commission v. Pollak, 341 U.S. 451 (1952).

28. Public Utilities Commission v. Pollak, 341 U.S. 451, 468–69 (1952) (Douglas, J., dissenting).

29. Lehman v. City of Shaker Heights, 418 U.S. 298 (1974).

30. Lehman v. City of Shaker Heights, 418 U.S. 298, 304 (1974).

31. The Supreme Court has created a relatively stylized, multitiered body of doctrine governing public forum law. While some scholars have criticized the highly mechanical nature of this body of doctrine, this approach to public forum problems is now well entrenched. The Court has recognized several classes of forums and non-forums: (1) "traditional" public forums; (2) "designated" public forums; (3) "limited" public forums; and (4) "non-forums." The "traditional" or "quintessential"

public forum consists of places, such as streets or parks, that "have immemorially been held in trust for the use of the public and, time out of mind, have been used for purposes of assembly, communicating thoughts between citizens, and discussing public questions." Perry Educational Association v. Perry Local Educators' Association, 460 U.S. 37, 45 (1983), quoting Hague v. Committee for Industrial Organization, 307 U.S. 496, 515 (1939). In United States v. Grace, 461 U.S. 171, 179 (1983), the Court declared sidewalks traditional public forums: "Sidewalks, of course, are among those areas of public property that traditionally have been held open to the public for expressive activities and are clearly within those areas of public property that may be considered, generally without further inquiry, to be public forum property."

Content-based regulation of speech in a traditional public forum is governed by principles of heightened scrutiny, such as the strict scrutiny test. Under these heightened scrutiny standards, attempts to regulate speech will usually be struck down. When the strict scrutiny test is applied, for example, the regulation must therefore serve a compelling state interest and be narrowly drawn to achieve that end. Content-neutral regulation in a traditional public forum, such as regulation of the time, place, and manner of speech, is judged under the less rigorous intermediate scrutiny test (see discussion of time, place, and manner regulations below).

32. The "designated" public forum consists of public property not falling within the category of "traditional" public forums that has nonetheless been opened by the state for use as a place for expressive activity, either for the public generally or for a particular class of speakers. If the government treats a piece of public property as if it were a traditional public forum, intentionally opening it up to the public at large for assembly and speech, then it will be bound by the same standards applicable to a traditional public forum. Alternatively, if the government opens up a facility as a place for expression for a particular class of speakers, the government will not be permitted to discriminate among speakers *within* that class. This form of designated public forum restricted to a defined class of speakers is sometimes referred to as a "limited public forum." The Supreme Court explained the distinction between "general access" and "selective access" in Arkansas Educational Television Commission v. Forbes, 523 U.S. 666 (1998):

> A designated public forum is not created when the government
> allows selective access for individual speakers rather than general
> access for a class of speakers. These cases illustrate the distinc-
> tion between "general access," which indicates the property is a
> designated public forum, and "selective access," which indicates
> the property is a nonpublic forum. On one hand, the government
> creates a designated public forum when it makes its property gener-
> ally available to a certain class of speakers, as the university made
> its facilities generally available to student groups in *Widmar*. On
> the other hand, the government does not create a designated public

forum when it does no more than reserve eligibility for access to the
forum to a particular class of speakers, whose members must then,
as individuals, "obtain permission" to use it.

"Non-forums" consist of publicly owned facilities that have been dedicated
to use for either communicative or noncommunicative purposes but that never
have been designated for indiscriminate expressive activity by the general public.
The "First Amendment does not guarantee access to property simply because it
is owned or controlled by the government." United States Postal Service v. Council of Greenburgh Civic Associations, 453 U.S. 114, 129, (1981). In United States v.
Kokinda, 497 U.S. 720 (1990), for example, volunteers for a political organization
who set up a table on the sidewalk in front of a post office were convicted of violating a Postal Service regulation that prohibited "soliciting alms and contributions . . .
on postal premises." In upholding the conviction, Justice O'Connor's plurality
opinion stated that a sidewalk in front of a post office, unlike ordinary sidewalks, is
not a public forum because "[t]he purpose of the forum in this case is to accomplish
the most efficient and effective postal delivery system." In addition, "the fact that
the sidewalk resembles the municipal sidewalk across the parking lot from the Post
Office was irrelevant to forum analysis." "Time, place, or manner" regulations do
not regulate *what* is said, but merely such matters as *when, where,* and *how loudly*
it is said. The First Amendment allows reasonable time, place, or manner regulations. To determine whether time, place, or manner regulations are reasonable, the
Supreme Court employs a three-part test. The Supreme Court has held that "the
government may impose reasonable restrictions on the time, place, or manner of
protected speech, provided the restrictions 'are justified without reference to the
content of the regulated speech, that they are narrowly tailored to serve a significant governmental interest, and that they leave open ample alternative channels for
communication of the information." Ward v. Rock Against Racism, 491 U.S. 781, 791
(1989). Genuine time, place, or manner regulations are *by definition* content-neutral.
If the regulation at issue is not content-neutral, then it is not appropriate for a court
to apply the standard of review applicable to content-neutral regulations. Thus the
Supreme Court has admonished that "while a municipality may constitutionally
impose reasonable time, place, and manner regulations on the use of its streets and
sidewalks for First Amendment purposes . . . and may even forbid altogether such
use of some of its facilities . . . what a municipality may *not* do under the First and
Fourteenth Amendments is to discriminate in the regulation of expression on the
basis of the content of that expression." Hudgens v. National Labor Relations Board,
424 U.S. 507, 520 (1976). See also Heffron v. International Society for Krishna Consciousness, 452 U.S. 640 (1981). In Clark v. Community for Creative Non-Violence,
468 U.S. 288, 293 (1984), a group sought a permit from the National Park Service to
hold a demonstration in Lafayette Park and the National Mall in Washington DC to

illustrate the plight of the homeless. The group's desire to sleep overnight in tents on the first day of winter was prohibited by a Park Service regulation banning camping in Lafayette Park and the Mall. The Court conceded that "overnight sleeping in connection with the demonstration is expressive conduct protected to some extent by the First Amendment." It then found that the regulation passed constitutional muster under the time, place, and manner test.

33. Widmar v. Vincent, 454 U.S. 263 (1981).

34. Widmar v. Vincent, 454 U.S. 263, 265n3 (1981).

35. Widmar v. Vincent, 454 U.S. 263, 273 (1981).

36. Commonwealth v. Davis, 162 Mass. 510 (1895).

37. American Civil Liberties Union v. Mote, 423 F.3d 438 (4th Cir. 2005).

38. American Civil Liberties Union v. Mote, 423 F.3d 438, 441 (4th Cir. 2005).

39. American Civil Liberties Union v. Mote, 423 F.3d 438, 441 (4th Cir. 2005).

40. American Civil Liberties Union v. Mote, 423 F.3d 438, 442 (4th Cir. 2005).

41. American Civil Liberties Union v. Mote, 423 F.3d 438, 442 (4th Cir. 2005).

42. American Civil Liberties Union v. Mote, 423 F.3d 438, 442 (4th Cir. 2005).

43. American Civil Liberties Union v. Mote, 423 F.3d 438, 442 (4th Cir. 2005).

44. American Civil Liberties Union v. Mote, 423 F.3d 438, 444 (4th Cir. 2005).

45. American Civil Liberties Union v. Mote, 423 F.3d 438, 442 (4th Cir. 2005).

46. See Shaila Dewan, Stephanie Saul, and Katie Zezimia, "For Professor, Fury Just Beneath the Surface," *New York Times*, February 20, 2010.

47. See MASS SHOOTINGS AT VIRGINIA TECH, APRIL 16, 2007: REPORT OF THE REVIEW PANEL, PRESENTED TO TIMOTHY M. KAINE, GOVERNOR, COMMONWEALTH OF VIRGINIA (August 2007).

48. "Report of the February 14, 2008, Shootings at Northern Illinois University," published by Northern Illinois University, available at http://www.niu.edu/feb14report/.

49. GARY LAVERGNE, A SNIPER IN THE TOWER: THE CHARLES WHITMAN MURDERS (University of North Texas Press 1997); DAVID CULLEN, COLUMBINE (Twelve/Hachette Book Group 2009); "Remembering November 1: A University Tragedy 10 Years Later," *FYI*, October 19, 2001, available at http://www.uiowa.edu/~fyi/issues/issues2001_v39/10192001/november.html; "30 Years Ago Seven Were Slain in Cal State Fullerton Shooting," *North County Times*, April 17, 2007, available at http://www.nctimes.com/news/state-and-regional/article_f264d4c4-b2df-58d9-a57c-b79dd6e200eb.html; National Public Radio, "Timeline: Shootings at U.S. College Campuses," April 16, 2007, available at http://www.npr.org/templates/story/story.php?storyId=9603275.

50. Abrams v. United States, 250 U.S. 616, 630 (1919) (Holmes, J., dissenting).

51. Brandenburg v. Ohio, 395 U.S. 444 (1969).

52. Brandenburg v. Ohio, 395 U.S. 444, 446–47 (1969).

53. Brandenburg v. Ohio, 395 U.S. 444, 444–45 (1969).

54. Brandenburg v. Ohio, 395 U.S. 444, 447 (1969).

55. Hess v. Indiana, 414 U.S. 105 (1973).

56. Cohen v. California, 403 U.S. 15 (1971).

57. See Kammy Au, "Freedom from Fear," 15 Lincoln L. Rev. 45 (1984); Richard Delgado, "Words That Wound: A Tort Action for Racial Insults, Epithets, and Name-Calling," 17 Harv. CR-CL L. Rev. 133 (1982); Kent Greenawalt, "Insults and Epithets: Are They Protected Speech?" 42 Rutgers L. Rev. 287 (1990); David Kretzmer, "Freedom of Speech and Racism," 8 Cardozo L. Rev. 445 (1987); Kenneth Lasson, "Group Libel Versus Free Speech: When Big Brother Should Butt In," 23 Duquesne L. Rev. 77 (1984); Charles R. Lawrence III, "If He Hollers Let Him Go: Regulating Racist Speech on Campus," 1990 Duke L. J. 431; Jean C. Love, "Discriminatory Speech and the Tort of Intentional Infliction of Emotional Distress," 47 Wash. & Lee L. Rev. 123 (1990); Toni M. Massaro, "Equality and Freedom of Expression: The Hate Speech Dilemma," 32 Wm. & Mary L. Rev. 211 (1991); Mari J. Matsuda, "Public Response to Racist Speech: Considering the Victim's Story," 87 Mich. L. Rev. 2320 (1989); Robert C. Post, "Racist Speech, Democracy, and the First Amendment," 32 Wm. & Mary L. Rev. 267 (1991); Dean M. Richardson, "Racism: A Tort of Outrage," 61 Oregon L. Rev. 267 (1982); Rodney A. Smolla, "Rethinking First Amendment Assumptions about Racist and Sexist Speech," 47 Wash. & Lee L. Rev. 171 (1990); Nadine Strossen, "Regulating Racist Speech on Campus: A Modest Proposal?" 1990 Duke L. J. 484; R. George Wright, "Racist Speech and the First Amendment," 9 Miss. Col. L. Rev. 1 (1988); and Note, "A Communitarian Defense of Group Libel Laws," 101 Harv. L. Rev. 682 (1988).

58. See, generally, Steve France, "Hate Goes to College," ABA J. 44 (July 1990); Connie Leslie, "Lessons from Bigotry 101: Racism on Campus," *Newsweek*, September 25, 1989, 48–49; Cheryl M. Fields, "Colleges Advised to Develop Strong Procedures to Deal with Incidents of Racial Harassment," *Chronicle of Higher Education*, July 20, 1988; and Robin Wilson, "Colleges' Anti-harassment Policies Bring Controversy Over Free-Speech Issues," *Chronicle of Higher Education*, October 4, 1989. It has also received abundant attention in editorial pages. See, for example, Nat Hentoff, "The Colleges: Fear, Loathing, and Suppression," *Village Voice*, May 8, 1990; Nat Hentoff, "Campus Follies: From Free Speech . . . ," *Washington Post*, November 4, 1989; George Will, "Liberal Censorship," *Washington Post*, November 5, 1989; Debra Everson, "On Outlawing Hate Speech," *Guild Notes*, November–December 1989; Charles Lawrence, "The Debates Over Placing Limits on Racist Speech Must Not Ignore the Damage It Does to Its Victims," *Chronicle of Higher Education*, October 25, 1989; James T. Laney, "Why Tolerate Campus Bigots?" *New York Times*, April 6, 1990; and Paul Verkuil, "Free to Speak, but Willing to Listen and Learn," *New York Times*, April 25, 1990.

59. See Rodney A. Smolla, "Academic Freedom, Hate Speech, and the Idea of a University," 53 L. & Contemp. Prob. 195 (1990).

60. See Harris v. Forklift Systems Inc., 510 U.S. 17 (1993); and Meritor Savings Bank, FSB v. Vinson, 477 U.S. 57, 66 (1986).

61. Watts v. United States, 394 U.S. 705 (1969).

62. Watts v. United States, 394 U.S. 705, 706 (1969).

63. Watts v. United States, 394 U.S. 705, 708 (1969).

64. Beauharnais v. Illinois, 343 U.S. 250 (1952).

65. Beauharnais v. Illinois, 343 U.S. 250, 252 (1952).

66. Beauharnais v. Illinois, 343 U.S. 250, 252 (1952).

67. Beauharnais v. Illinois, 343 U.S. 250, 258n9 (1952).

68. Beauharnais v. Illinois, 343 U.S. 250, 259 (1952).

69. Beauharnais v. Illinois, 343 U.S. 250, 259 (1952).

70. Beauharnais v. Illinois, 343 U.S. 250, 259 (1952).

71. Beauharnais v. Illinois, 343 U.S. 250, 261 (1952)

72. Beauharnais v. Illinois, 343 U.S. 250, 263 (1952).

73. R.A.V. v. City of St. Paul, 505 U.S. 377 (1992).

74. St. Paul Bias-Motivated Crime Ordinance, St. Paul, Minn., Legis. Code § 292.02 (1990). The case involved a challenge to a St. Paul, Minnesota, ordinance that provided, "Whoever places on public or private property a symbol, object, appellation, characterization or graffiti, including, but not limited to, a burning cross or Nazi swastika, which one knows or has reasonable grounds to know arouses anger, alarm or resentment in others on the basis of race, color, creed, religion or gender commits disorderly conduct and shall be guilty of a misdemeanor."

75. R.A.V. v. City of St. Paul, 505 U.S. 377, 391 (1992).

76. R.A.V. v. City of St. Paul, 505 U.S. 377, 391 (1992).

77. R.A.V. v. City of St. Paul, 506 U.S. 377, 391–92 (1992). ("Displays containing some words—odious racial epithets, for example—would be prohibited to proponents of all views. But 'fighting words' that do not themselves invoke race, color, creed, religion, or gender—aspersions upon a person's mother, for example—would seemingly be usable *ad libitum* in the placards of those arguing in *favor* of racial, color, etc. tolerance and equality, but could not be used by that speaker's opponents. One could hold up a sign saying, for example, that all 'anti-Catholic bigots' are misbegotten; but not that all 'papists' are, for that would insult and provoke violence 'on the basis of religion.' St. Paul has no such authority to license one side of a debate to fight freestyle, while requiring the other to follow Marquis of Queensberry Rules.").

78. Virginia v. Black, 538 U.S. 343 (2003).

79. Virginia Code § 18.2–423 (1996).

80. Virginia v. Black, 538 U.S. 343, 359 (2003).

81. Virginia Code § 18.2–423 (1996).

82. Virginia v. Black, 528 U.S. 343, 364 (2003).

83. Virginia v. Black, 528 U.S. 343, 365–66 (2003).

84. Virginia v. Black, 528 U.S. 343, 367 (2003).

85. Virginia v. Black, 528 U.S. 343, 380–87 (2003). (Souter, J., concurring in the judgment in part and dissenting in part).

86. Justices Scalia and Thomas, apparently defecting from their positions in *R.A.V.*, would have gone well beyond the plurality. It seems that Justice Thomas would have been willing to allow a state to attack all cross burnings, employing a prima facie evidence provision. Justice Scalia wrote primarily to express the view that the prima facie evidence provision is probably a mere permissible inference of the sort that in his view would not violate the First Amendment. Virginia v. Black, 528 U.S. 343, 368 (2003) (Scalia, J., concurring in the judgment in part and dissenting in part); Virginia v. Black, 528 U.S. 343, 388 (2003) (Thomas, J., dissenting).

87. Virginia v. Black, 528 U.S. 343, 388 (2003) (Thomas, J., dissenting).

88. Virginia v. Black, 528 U.S. 343, 388 (2003) (Thomas, J., dissenting).

89. Doe v. University of Michigan, 721 F.Supp. 852 (E.D. Mich. 1989).

90. Doe v. University of Michigan, 721 F.Supp. 852, 855–57 (E.D. Mich. 1989).

91. Doe v. University of Michigan, 721 F.Supp. 852, 855–57 (E.D. Mich. 1989).

92. Doe v. University of Michigan, 721 F.Supp. 852, 855–57 (E.D. Mich. 1989).

93. Doe v. University of Michigan, 721 F.Supp. 852, 857 (E.D. Mich. 1989). In these areas, persons were subject to discipline for:

> 1. Any behavior, verbal or physical, that stigmatizes or victimizes an individual on the basis of race, ethnicity, religion, sex, sexual orientation, creed, national origin, ancestry, age, marital status, handicap or Vietnam-era veteran status, and that
>   a. Involves an express or implied threat to an individual's academic efforts, employment, participation in University sponsored extra-curricular activities or personal safety; or
>   b. Has the purpose or reasonably foreseeable effect of interfering with an individual's academic efforts, employment, participation in University sponsored extra-curricular activities or personal safety; or
>   c. Creates an intimidating, hostile, or demeaning environment for educational pursuits, employment or participation in University sponsored extra-curricular activities.
> 2. Sexual advances, requests for sexual favors, and verbal or physical conduct that stigmatizes or victimizes an individual on the basis of sex or sexual orientation where such behavior:

a. Involves an express or implied threat to an individual's academic efforts, employment, participation in University sponsored extra-curricular activities or personal safety; or

b. Has the purpose or reasonably foreseeable effect of interfering with an individual's academic efforts, employment, participation in University sponsored extra-curricular activities or personal safety; or

c. Creates an intimidating, hostile, or demeaning environment for educational pursuits, employment or participation in University sponsored extra-curricular activities.

94. Doe v. University of Michigan, 721 F.Supp. 852, 857–58 (E.D. Mich. 1989). In reaching its decision the court drew heavily from an interpretive guide to the Michigan policy, published by the University of Michigan's Office of Affirmative Action. The guide, written to help students understand what the University's policy meant, in concrete practical terms, included the following examples of impermissible conduct:

- A flyer containing racist threats distributed in a residence hall.
- Racist graffiti written on the door of an Asian student's study carrel.
- A male student makes remarks in class like "Women just aren't as good in this field as men," thus creating a hostile learning atmosphere for female classmates.
- Students in a residence hall have a floor party and invite everyone on their floor except one person because they think she might be a lesbian.
- A black student is confronted and racially insulted by two white students in a cafeteria.
- Male students leave pornographic pictures and jokes on the desk of a female graduate student.
- Two men demand that their roommate in the residence hall move out and be tested for AIDS.

95. Doe v. University of Michigan, 721 F.Supp. 852, 858 (E.D. Mich. 1989). In addition, the guide contained a separate section titled "You are a harasser when . . . ," which included the following examples of discriminatory conduct:

- You exclude someone from a study group because that person is of a different race, sex, or ethnic origin than you are.
- You tell jokes about gay men and lesbians.
- Your student organization sponsors entertainment that includes a comedian who slurs Hispanics.
- You display a confederate flag on the door of your room in the residence hall.

- You laugh at a joke about someone in your class who stutters.
- You make obscene telephone calls or send racist notes or computer messages.
- You comment in a derogatory way about a particular person or group's physical appearance or sexual orientation, or their cultural origins, or religious beliefs.

96. UWM Post v. Board of Regents of the University of Wisconsin, 774 F.Supp. 1163 (E.D. Wis. 1991).

97. UWM Post v. Board of Regents of the University of Wisconsin, 774 F.Supp. 1163, 1177–78 (E.D. Wis. 1991).

98. UWM Post v. Board of Regents of the University of Wisconsin, 774 F.Supp. 1163, 1177–78 (E.D. Wis. 1991).

99. See Harris v. Forklift Systems Inc., 510 U.S. 17 (1993); and Meritor Savings Bank, FSB v. Vinson, 477 U.S. 57, 66 (1986).

100. Connick v. Myers, 461 U.S. 138 (1983).

101. Pickering v. Board of Education, 391 U.S. 563 (1968).

102. Pickering v. Board of Education, 391 U.S. 563, 568 (1968).

103. Pickering v. Board of Education, 391 U.S. 563, 568 (1968).

104. Garcetti v. Ceballos, 547 U.S. 410 (2006).

105. See Gorum v. Sessoms, 561 F.3d 179 (3d Cir. 2009) (holding that a professor's speech at Delaware State University involving speaking out on behalf of a student at a disciplinary hearing and withdrawing from the University President's invitation to speak at a fraternity prayer breakfast constituted speech within the professor's official job duties and was not speech on a matter of public concern).

106. See Weinstein v. University of Illinois, 811 F.2d 1091 (7th Cir. 1987).

107. Cohen v. San Bernardino Valley College, 883 F.Supp. 1407 (C.D Cal. 1995) (district court opinion siding with the College); reversed by Cohen v. San Bernardino Valley College, 92 F.3d 968 (9th Cir. 1996); cert. denied, 520 U.S. 1140 (1997) (Supreme Court declining to review the court of appeals decision).

108. Cohen v. San Bernardino Valley College, 883 F.Supp. 1407 (C.D Cal. 1995).

109. Cohen v. San Bernardino Valley College, 92 F.3d 968 (9th Cir. 1996).

110. Bonnell v. Lorenzo, 241 F.3d 800 (6th Cir. 2001).

111. Levin v. Harleston, 770 F.Supp. 895 (S.D.N.Y. 1991); affirmed in part and reversed in part, Levin v. Harleston, 966 F.2d 85 (2nd Cir. 1992).

112. See Dan Frosch, "Fired Colorado Professor is Cross-Examined in Lawsuit," *New York Times*, March 24, 2009. A jury awarded Professor Churchill one dollar in damages, and as this book was going to press, an appeal was pending.

113. In 2009 Professor Yoo took a leave from the Berkeley law faculty to teach as a visitor at the Chapman University Law School, in Orange, California. See Susannah

Rosenblatt, "Bush Policymaker Escapes Berkeley's Wrath," *Los Angeles Times*, February 11, 2009.

114. Legal Services Corporation v. Velazquez, 531 U.S. 533 (2001).

115. Brown v. Li, 308 F.3d 939 (9th Cir. 2002).

116. Brown v. Li, 308 F.3d 939, 943 (9th Cir. 2002).

117. Brown v. Li, 308 F.3d 939, 943 (9th Cir. 2002).

118. Brown v. Li, 308 F.3d 939, 950 (9th Cir. 2002).

119. Arkansas Educational Television Commission v. Forbes, 523 U.S. 666 (1998).

120. Arkansas Educational Television Commission v. Forbes, 523 U.S. 666, 673–74 (1998).

121. Brown v. Li, 308 F.3d 939, 950–53 (9th Cir. 2002).

122. Brown v. Li, 308 F.3d 939, 953 (9th Cir. 2002).

123. Brown v. Li, 308 F.3d 939, 953 (9th Cir. 2002).

124. Brown v. Li, 308 F.3d 939, 952 (9th Cir. 2002).

125. Tinker v. Des Moines Independent Community School District, 393 U.S. 503 (1969).

126. Tinker v. Des Moines Independent Community School District, 393 U.S. 503, 510–11 (1969).

127. Tinker v. Des Moines Independent Community School District, 393 U.S. 503, 513 (1969).

128. Tinker v. Des Moines Independent Community School District, 393 U.S. 503, 506 (1969).

129. Bethel School District No. 403 v. Fraser, 478 U.S. 675 (1986).

130. Bethel School District No. 403 v. Fraser, 478 U.S. 675, 678 (1986).

131. Bethel School District No. 403 v. Fraser, 478 U.S. 675, 687 (1986) (Brennan, J., concurring).

132. Bethel School District No. 403 v. Fraser, 478 U.S. 675, 682 (1986).

133. Bethel School District No. 403 v. Fraser, 478 U.S. 675, 685 (1986).

134. Hazelwood School District v. Kuhlmeier, 484 U.S. 260 (1988).

135. Hazelwood School District v. Kuhlmeier, 484 U.S. 260, 271 (1988).

136. Hazelwood School District v. Kuhlmeier, 484 U.S. 260, 271 (1988).

137. Morse v. Frederick, 551 U.S. 393 (2007).

138. Morse v. Frederick, 551 U.S. 393, 404 (2007).

139. Settle v. Dickson County School Board, 53 F.3d 152 (6th Cir. 1995).

140. Settle v. Dickson County School Board, 53 F.3d 152, 158 (6th Cir. 1995).

141. Settle v. Dickson County School Board, 53 F.3d 152, 155–56 (6th Cir. 1995).

142. Axson-Flynn v. Johnson, 356 F.3d 1277 (10th Cir. 2004).

143. Axson-Flynn v. Johnson, 356 F.3d 1277, 1286 (10th Cir. 2004).

144. Axson-Flynn v. Johnson, 356 F.3d 1277, 1289 (10th Cir. 2004).

145. Axson-Flynn v. Johnson, 356 F.3d 1277, 1293 (10th Cir. 2004).

146. Axson-Flynn v. Johnson, 356 F.3d 1277, 1293 (10th Cir. 2004).

147. Regents of the University of Michigan v. Ewing, 474 U.S. 214 (1985).

148. Regents of the University of Michigan v. Ewing, 474 U.S. 214, 226 (1985).

149. Regents of the University of Michigan v. Ewing, 474 U.S. 214, 226 (1985).

150. Regents of the University of Michigan v. Ewing, 474 U.S. 214, 226 (1985).

151. Axson-Flynn v. Johnson, 356 F.3d 1277, 1292–93 (10th Cir. 2004).

152. Papish v. Board of Curators of the University of Missouri, 410 U.S. 667 (1973) (per curiam).

153. Papish v. Board of Curators of the University of Missouri, 410 U.S. 667, 668 (1973) (per curiam).

154. Papish v. Board of Curators of the University of Missouri, 410 U.S. 667, 670 (1973) (per curiam).

155. Papish v. Board of Curators of the University of Missouri, 410 U.S. 667, 671 (1973) (per curiam).

156. Papish v. Board of Curators of the University of Missouri, 410 U.S. 667, 672 (1973) (Burger, C.J., dissenting).

157. Papish v. Board of Curators of the University of Missouri, 410 U.S. 667, 672 (1973) (Burger, C.J., dissenting).

158. Papish v. Board of Curators of the University of Missouri, 410 U.S. 667, 677 (1973) (Rehnquist, J., dissenting).

159. Chaplinsky v. New Hampshire, 315 U.S. 568 (1942).

160. Chaplinsky v. New Hampshire, 315 U.S. 568, 571–72 (1942).

161. Papish v. Board of Curators of the University of Missouri 410 U.S. 667, 677–78 (1973) (Rehnquist, J., dissenting).

162. Papish v. Board of Curators of the University of Missouri 410 U.S. 667, 677–78 (1973) (Rehnquist, J., dissenting).

163. Mazart v. State, 109 Misc.2d 1092, 441 N.Y.S.2d 600 (N.Y. Ct. Cl. 1981).

164. Joyner v. Whiting, 477 F.2d 456 (4th Cir. 1973).

165. Bazaar v. Fortune, 476 F.2d 570 (5th Cir. 1973); affirmed as modified, Bazaar v. Fortune, 489 F.2d 225 (5th Cir. 1973) (en banc).

166. Schiff v. Williams, 519 F.2d 257 (5th Cir. 1975).

167. Stanley v. Magrath, 719 F.2d 279 (8th Cir. 1983).

168. Husain v. Springer, 494 F.3d 108 (2nd Cir. 2007).

169. Hosty v. Carter, 412 F.3d 731 (7th Cir. 2005).

170. Hosty v. Carter, 412 F.3d 731, 732 (7th Cir. 2005).

171. Hosty v. Carter, 412 F.3d 731, 732 (7th Cir. 2005).

172. Hosty v. Carter, 412 F.3d 731, 732 (7th Cir. 2005).

173. Hosty v. Carter, 412 F.3d 731, 732, 737 (7th Cir. 2005).

174. Hosty v. Carter, 412 F.3d 731, 732 (7th Cir. 2005).

Notes to Chapter 6

The epigraphs for this chapter are drawn from Regents of University of California v. Bakke, 438 U.S. 265, 313 (1978); and Adarand Constructors Inc. v. Peña, 515 U.S. 200, 240 (1995).

1. STUART TAYLOR JR. AND K. C. JOHNSON, UNTIL PROVEN INNOCENT (Macmillan 2007).

2. Jonathan D. CASPER, THE POLITICS OF CIVIL LIBERTIES 148–49 (Harper & Row 1972); Rodney A. Smolla, "In Pursuit of Racial Utopias: Fair Housing, Quotas, and Goals in the 1980s," 58 S. Cal. L. Rev. 947 (1985).

3. Regents of University of California v. Bakke, 438 U.S. 265, 295 (1978).

4. Lisa H. Newton, "Reverse Discrimination as Unjustified," in REVERSE DISCRIMINATION 373, 373–76 (B. Gross, ed., Prometheus 1977).

5. LANGSTON HUGHES, THE BIG SEA: AN AUTOBIOGRAPHY (Knopf 1940).

6. PAUL BURSTEIN, EQUAL EMPLOYMENT OPPORTUNITY 415 (Transaction Publishers 1994).

7. Brown v. Board of Education of Topeka, 347 U.S. 483 (1954).

8. Green v. County School Board of New Kent County, 391 U.S. 430 (1968).

9. Plessy v. Ferguson, 163 U.S. 537 (1896).

10. Plessy v. Ferguson, 163 U.S. 537, 555 (1896).

11. Plessy v. Ferguson, 163 U.S. 537, 559 (1896) (Harlan, J., dissenting).

12. Plessy v. Ferguson, 163 U.S. 537, 559 (1896) (Harlan, J., dissenting).

13. Missouri ex rel. Gaines v. Canada, 305 U.S. 337 (1938).

14. Sweatt v. Painter, 339 U.S. 629 (1950).

15. McLaurin v. Oklahoma State Regents for Higher Education et al., Citations, 339 U.S. 637 (1950).

16. Brown v. Board of Education of Topeka, 349 U.S. 294, 301 (1955).

17. United States v. Fordice, 505 U.S. 717 (1992).

18. United States v. Fordice, 505 U.S. 717, 748 (1992) (Thomas, J., concurring), citing JEAN L. PREER, LAWYERS V. EDUCATORS: BLACK COLLEGES AND DESEGREGATION IN PUBLIC HIGHER EDUCATION 2 (Greenwood Press 1982).

19. United States v. Fordice, 505 U.S. 717, 748 (1992) (Thomas, J., concurring).

20. United States v. Fordice, 505 U.S. 717, 748 (1992) (Thomas, J., concurring).

21. DeFunis v. Odegaard, 416 U.S. 312 (1974) (Douglas, J., dissenting).

22. DeFunis v. Odegaard, 416 U.S. 312, 334 (1974) (Douglas, J., dissenting).

23. DeFunis v. Odegaard, 416 U.S. 312, 343 (1974) (Douglas, J., dissenting).

24. Regents of the University of California v. Bakke, 438 U.S. 265 (1978).

25. Regents of the University of California v. Bakke, 438 U.S. 265, 325 (1978).

26. Regents of the University of California v. Bakke, 438 U.S. 265, 312 (1978).

27. Regents of the University of California v. Bakke, 438 U.S. 265, 314 (1978).

28. Regents of the University of California v. Bakke, 438 U.S. 265, 315 (1978).

29. The most well-known lower court decision rejecting the pursuit of a diverse student body as a compelling governmental interest, as well as limiting the justifications for affirmative action toward the remedying of past discrimination, was Hopwood v. Texas, 78 F.3d 932, 944 (5th Cir. 1996), which struck down affirmative action initiatives at the University of Texas Law School. See also Podberesky v. Kirwan, 38 F.3d 147 (4th Cr. 1994) (The court struck down a scholarship program at the University of Maryland that targeted African American students, holding the program unconstitutional because it could not be justified as a remedy to cure the lingering effects of past discrimination by the University of Maryland. The court reasoned that too much time had passed between the discriminatory actions once practiced by the University and the modern conditions at the University, which were purged of all discrimination against African Americans.)

30. Adarand Constructors Inc. v. Peña, 515 U.S. 200 (1995).

31. Adarand Constructors Inc. v. Peña, 515 U.S. 200, 239 (1995) (Scalia, J., concurring in part and concurring in the judgment).

32. Adarand Constructors Inc. v. Peña, 515 U.S. 200, 239 (1995) (Scalia, J., concurring in part and concurring in the judgment).

33. Adarand Constructors Inc. v. Peña, 515 U.S. 200, 239 (1995) (Scalia, J., concurring in part and concurring in the judgment).

34. Adarand Constructors Inc. v. Peña, 515 U.S. 200, 240 (1995).

35. Grutter v. Bollinger, 539 U.S. 306 (2003).

36. Gratz v. Bollinger, 539 U.S. 244 (2003).

37. Grutter v. Bollinger, 539 U.S. 306, 312–16 (2003).

38. Grutter v. Bollinger, 539 U.S. 306, 312–16 (2003).

39. Grutter v. Bollinger, 539 U.S. 306, 314 (2003).

40. Grutter v. Bollinger, 539 U.S. 306, 315 (2003).

41. Grutter v. Bollinger, 539 U.S. 306, 314 (2003).

42. Grutter v. Bollinger, 539 U.S. 306, 308 (2003).

43. Grutter v. Bollinger, 539 U.S. 306, 337 (2003).

44. Grutter v. Bollinger, 539 U.S. 306, 338 (2003).

45. Grutter v. Bollinger, 539 U.S. 306, 343 (2003).

46. Grutter v. Bollinger, 539 U.S. 306, 349–51 (2003) (Thomas, J., concurring in part and dissenting in part).

47. Gratz v. Bollinger, 539 U.S. 244 (2003).

48. Gratz v. Bollinger, 539 U.S. 244, 274–76 (2003).

49. Gratz v. Bollinger, 539 U.S. 244, 274–76 (2003).

50. Coalition to Defend Affirmative Action v. Granholm, 473 F.3d 237 (6th Cir. 2006).

51. Coalition to Defend Affirmative Action v. Granholm, 473 F.3d 237, 247 (6th Cir. 2006).

52. Coalition to Defend Affirmative Action v. Granholm, 473 F.3d 237, 248 (6th Cir. 2006).

53. Coalition to Defend Affirmative Action v. Granholm, 473 F.3d 237, 248 (6th Cir. 2006).

54. Coalition to Defend Affirmative Action v. Granholm, 473 F.3d 237, 248 (6th Cir. 2006).

55. Parents Involved in Community Schools v. Seattle School District No. 1, 551 U.S. 701 (2007).

56. Parents Involved in Community Schools v. Seattle School District No. 1, 551 U.S. 701, 722 (2007).

57. Parents Involved in Community Schools v. Seattle School District No. 1, 551 U.S. 701, 724 (2007).

58. Parents Involved in Community Schools v. Seattle School District No. 1, 551 U.S. 701, 748 (2007).

59. Parents Involved in Community Schools v. Seattle School District No. 1, 551 U.S. 701, 789 (2007). (Kennedy, J., concurring).

60. See Frontiero v. Richardson, 411 U.S. 677 (1973); and Craig v. Boren, 429 U.S. 190 (1976).

61. Mississippi University for Women v. Hogan, 458 U.S. 718 (1982).

62. Mississippi Code Ann. § 37-117-3 (1972).

63. Title IX, Education Amendments of 1972, 20 U.S.C. §§ 1681–88.

64. Mississippi Code Ann. § 37-117-3 (1972).

65. United States v. Virginia, 518 U.S. 515 (1996).

66. United States v. Virginia, 518 U.S. 515, 520 (1996).

67. United States v. Virginia, 518 U.S. 515, 520 (1996).

68. United States v. Virginia, 518 U.S. 515, 520 (1996).

69. United States v. Virginia, 518 U.S. 515, 522 (1996).

70. United States v. Virginia, 518 U.S. 515, 522 (1996).

71. United States v. Virginia, 518 U.S. 515, 522 (1996).

72. United States v. Virginia, 518 U.S. 515, 517 (1996).

73. United States v. Virginia, 518 U.S. 515, 524 (1996).

74. United States v. Virginia, 518 U.S. 515, 534 (1996).

75. United States v. Virginia, 518 U.S. 515, 543–58 (1996).

Notes to the Conclusion

The epigraphs for this chapter are drawn from Minnesota State Board for Community Colleges v. Knight, 465 U.S. 271 (1984); and Minnesota State Board for Community Colleges v. Knight, 465 U.S. 271 (1984) (Brennan, J., dissenting).

1. AAUP 1940 STATEMENT OF PRINCIPLES ON ACADEMIC FREEDOM AND TENURE, available at http://www.aaup.org/AAUP/pubsres/policydocs/contents/1940statement.htm.

2. William W. Van Alstyne, "Academic Freedom and the First Amendment in the Supreme Court of the United States," L. & Contemp. Prob. 79 (Summer 1990).

3. Minnesota State Board for Community Colleges v. Knight, 465 U.S. 271 (1984).

4. In National Labor Relations Board v. Yeshiva University, 444 U.S. 672 (1980), the Supreme Court held that faculty members at Yeshiva University were not entitled to organize as union members under the National Labor Relations Act, because the NLRA exempts "managerial employees" from its coverage. In an opinion written by Justice Lewis Powell, the Supreme Court held that the professors at Yeshiva were managerial employees, given their substantial rights to participate in university governance on a wide range of issues.

5. Trustees of Dartmouth College v. Woodward, 17 U.S. 518 (1819).

6. JAMES MADISON, THE FEDERALIST PAPERS, No. 51, at 160 (1788) (J. Cooke, ed., Wesleyan University Press 1961).

INDEX

ABOUT THE AUTHOR

RODNEY SMOLLA is the President of Furman University, and the author of several books, including *Free Speech in an Open Society*; *Suing the Press: Libel, the Media, and Power*; *Jerry Falwell v. Larry Flynt: The First Amendment on Trial*; *Deliberate Intent*; and *The First Amendment: Freedom of Expression, Regulation of Mass Media, Freedom of Religion*.